NATIONAL GEOGRAPHIC
TRAVELER
Vietnam

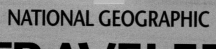

NATIONAL GEOGRAPHIC

TRAVELER
Vietnam

By James Sullivan
Photography by Kris LeBoutillier

National Geographic
Washington, D.C.

Contents

How to use this guide 6–7 About the author & photographer 8
The regions 59–234 Travelwise 235–266
Index 265–270 Credits 270–271

Page 1: **A Vietnamese woman in a traditional
conical hat**
Pages 2–3: **Ha Long Bay**
Page 4: **Paper lanterns for sale in Hoi An**

How to use this guide

See back flap for keys to text and map symbols.

The *National Geographic Traveler* brings you the best of Vietnam, in text, pictures, and maps. Divided into three main sections, the guide begins with an overview of Vietnam today, its history and culture.

Following are eight area chapters with featured sites selected by the author for their particular interest. Each chapter opens with its own contents list for easy reference. A map introduces the parameters covered in the chapter, highlighting the featured sites and locating other places of interest. Walks and drives are plotted on

their own maps and suggest routes for discovering the most about an area. Features and sidebars offer intriguing detail on the area.

The final section, Travelwise, lists essential information for the traveler—pre-trip planning, special events, getting around, practical advice, and emergency contacts—plus provides a selection of hotels and restaurants arranged by area, shops, activities and entertainment.

To the best of our knowledge, information is accurate as of press time. However, it's always advisable to call ahead when possible.

Color coding

158

Each region is color coded for easy reference. Find the region you want on the map on the front flap, and look for the color flash at the top of the pages of the relevant chapter. Information in **Travelwise** is also color coded to each region.

Visitor information

Hanoi Citadel

- 61 B2–B3
- (04) 734-2862
- Closed Mon.
- Ky Dai tower: $ (pay to Army Museum).
  Doan Mon: $

Practical information for most sites is given in the side column (see key to symbols on back flap). The map reference gives the page number of the map and grid reference. Other details are address, telephone number, days closed, entrance charge in a range from $ (under $5) to $$$$$ (over $20). Other sites have information in italics and parentheses in the text.

City spellings

In general, the city names in the text and on the maps in this guide follow native Vietnamese spellings. However, in some cases, conventional spellings have been used, reflecting more common usage among travelers. These exceptions include Hanoi, Haiphong, Danang, Dalat, and Saigon.

Tourism information

Consult p. 242 in the Travelwise to understand the differences between tourism offices, which tend to not be very helpful to visitors, and local travel agents.

TRAVELWISE

HO CHI MINH CITY — Color-coded region name

CARAVELLE HOTEL — Hotel name & price range
$$$$$

19 LAM SON SQUARE
TEL 08/823-4999 — Address, telephone & fax numbers, website
FAX 08/824-3999
www.caravellehotel.com

Opened in 1959, the Caravelle is a Saigon classic and landmark unto itself. — Brief description of hotel

335 — Hotel facilities & credit card details
All major cards

L'OLIVIER — Restaurant name, price range
$$$$$

17 LE DUAN, DISTRICT 1 — Address, telephone & fax numbers
TEL 08/824-1555
FAX 08/824-1666

The Sofitel Plaza's French restaurant, overlooking the old embassy row. — Brief description of restaurant

80 — All major cards — Restaurant facilities & details

Hotel & restaurant prices

An explanation of the price bands used in entries is given in the Hotels & Restaurants section (beginning on p. 245).

AREA MAPS

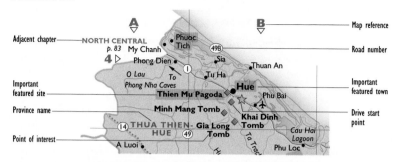

Adjacent chapter

Important featured site

Province name

Point of interest

Map reference

Road number

Important featured town

Drive start point

- A locator map accompanies each area map and shows the location of that area in the country.

WALKING TOURS

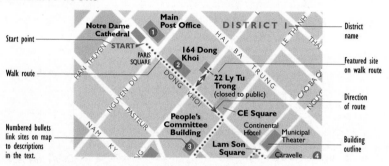

Start point

Walk route

Numbered bullets link sites on map to descriptions in the text.

District name

Featured site on walk route

Direction of route

Building outline

- An information box gives the starting and ending points, time and length of walk, and places not to be missed along the route.

DRIVING TOURS

Drive start point

Drive route

Numbered bullets link sites on map to descriptions in the text.

Province name

Road number

Important featured site

Province boundary

- An information box provides details including starting and finishing points, time and length of drive, and places not to be missed along the route.

NATIONAL GEOGRAPHIC

TRAVELER

Vietnam

About the author & photographer

After graduating from the Iowa Writer's Workshop in 1992, James Sullivan bicycled solo from Saigon to Hanoi up Vietnam's Highway 1. This trip led to the publication of *Over the Moat,* a memoir of courtship in Vietnam. He has written travel features for *National Geographic Traveler, The New York Times,* and other leading publications. He lives with his wife and two children in Hue, where he is working on a novel about Vietnam.

Kris LeBoutillier has photographed assignments for *National Geographic Traveler,* including stories about Tasmania, Singapore, Rajasthan, and Vietnam. He is the author and photographer of *Journey Through Phnom Penh* and *Journey Through Ho Chi Minh City,* both published by Marshall Cavendish. Represented by Getty Images, LeBoutillier has worked for such diverse clients as *Forbes Asia, Smithsonian, Spa Magazine,* and the Discovery Channel.

History & culture

Soldiers at drill in Hanoi

Vietnam today

VIETNAM. SAY THE WORD TODAY AND IT CALLS TO MIND MUCH MORE THAN a country—still. In the popular imagination, the name of the place has swelled with so many passions that, in a random lineup of nations, Vietnam is the one that's always throbbing, that always draws the eye. But the exclamation point that has dogged the country since the turmoil of the 1950s is withering, thanks largely to the passage of time, to a reorientation of economic policies, and to the normalization of relations with the United States.

Today, Vietnam is a nation on the rise. The capital, Hanoi, was born under the name Thang Long, which means "dragon ascending," an image now befitting the country as a whole. The ascent began in 1986 when the government abandoned command economics and launched *doi moi,* a market-driven policy of fiscal reform. Doi moi rescued Vietnam from a decade of postwar privation and groomed it for emergence as one of Southeast Asia's so-called Little Tiger economies.

Now the economy is booming at 8 percent annually, one of the fastest rates worldwide. Vietnam is the second largest coffee exporter in the world, after Brazil, and the largest exporter of pepper. Trade with the United States jumped fivefold in the early 2000s, and Nike is the country's largest private employer.

Following a severe hiccup during the Asian economic flu of the 1990s, invest-ment dollars are pouring in by the bil-lions. On his visit to the United States in 2005—the first by a leader of commu-nist Vietnam—Prime Minister Phan Van Khai rang the opening bell of the New York Stock Exchange, as symbolic a break from command economics as you're likely to get.

Call it capitalist communism, or com-munist capitalism. That bugaboo is hardly relevant anymore and seems almost quaint in the age of al Qaeda. While terrorism has tarnished other places in Southeast Asia, like Bali and even Thailand, Vietnam's star is rising as a peaceful haven. In 2005, the world's second largest insurance broker dubbed Vietnam one of the six safest travel destinations in the world.

GOOD MORNING NO MORE

Headlines started blaring GOOD MORNING, VIETNAM in the early 1990s, though breakfast may be over, brunch has only just begun. Traveling through Vietnam now, you'll feel like you've been made privy to a secret the rest of world has yet to hear. Backpackers blazed many of the popular routes and still represent a huge contingent of foreign travelers. But the days of encoun-tering rats in the country's best lodgings are over. Luxury hotels command the highest occupancy rates in Ho Chi Minh City and Hanoi. And Vietnam Airlines flies one of the world's newest fleets.

Word is getting out—about Ha Long Bay's incomparable seascape, the cloud-wreathed highland peaks, Mekong Delta vistas, and world-class limestone grottoes. UNESCO has chosen five locations in Vietnam for inscription on its World Heritage List, posi-tioning the country as a rival to Thailand and second only to Indonesia as a cultural destination in Southeast Asia.

Its imperial vestiges evoke the dreamy world of the Orient. Its sublime pagodas and venerable temples form eddies in the rushing currents of modern life, inspiring slowness and contemplation. Its cuisine is winning raves for its lightness, commingled textures, and presentational panache. Vietnam, at last, is ready for prime time. It's not quite high noon yet, but morning has indeed broken.

OPEN ARMS

Although Vietnam suffered an estimated five million dead in its war with the United States (more than one million combatants and four million civilians), there's no visible

Hanoi youth indulge in the sweet treats of life, thanks to Vietnam's booming economy.

animosity toward Americans. The Vietnamese tend not to hold grudges.

This "let bygones be bygones" attitude can puzzle Americans especially, many of whom show up with hat in hand. But no act of contrition is called for or expected. *We're glad you're here* is the gist of the reception. *We're glad you're back* is how it feels in the south.

As a population, the 84 million inhabitants of Vietnam are young, with a median age of 25. (In the United States, the median age is 36; in Thailand, it's 30.) The 93 percent literacy rate is far higher than the rate in neighboring Cambodia and Laos, and on a par with China and Thailand, where personal incomes are much higher.

They're studiously book smart as a people, but street smart, too. "They know how to do things. They know how things work," said one American lawyer who's been practicing in Ho Chi Minh City for more than a decade.

Horse sense is an unwitting perk in a relatively undeveloped economy. That will change as the economy demands specialists. Much will change, from the colorfully exotic costumes of the northern highlanders to the dearth of Western chains (McDonald's has yet to sell a Big Mac in Vietnam). As a traveler, you're likely to rue what you know is coming as Vietnam steps up its engagement with the rest of the world.

In the meantime, revel in what already feel like anachronisms: the teenage schoolgirls pedaling to school three and four abreast, in their immaculate silk *ao dai* dresses, like a mobile tableau on its way to yet another exhibit, or the bubbly grade-school pupils, heeding the summons from a drum, not a bell, in their blue slacks, white shirts, and red kerchiefs. Stop among them, and they'll mob you like a rock star, lobbing the same suite of questions in just-learned, imperfect English: "What your name?" "Where you from?" "What the time?" They don't care much about the answers; the

Ho Chi Minh City is the country's most bustling municipality, though still far from a modern metropolis.

chance to elicit a response from a *tay* (Westerner) is enough.

Many will ask whether you're married, how old you are, and even how much money you earn in a month. The point is not mere nosiness, but a matter of relativism. In Vietnam, getting a fix on a new acquaintance is necessary to determine the proper form of address.

The Vietnamese make scant use of the personal pronoun "I" *(toi)*. Instead, they defer to the pronoun that defines their relation to another person. For example,

"I" wouldn't tell an older person about my recent trip to Nha Trang; instead, "younger brother" would tell the story. Likewise, the generic form of "you" is much less common than the relational pronoun. A young woman in need of directions to a nearby pagoda would not address an older man on the street as "you"; she would refer to him as "uncle." Everybody is related to everybody else in Vietnam. That's the way the language works.

Understanding this dynamic is crucial to understanding the Vietnamese. They do not extol individualism. The laconic loner is not one of their heroes. Nguyen is by far the dominant surname, with as much as 60 percent of the population bearing the name. That's not a problem. The Vietnamese don't value distance between each other the way Westerners do. They don't need "space." They truly believe it takes a village.

In fact, this social cohesion was forged in the village, where the cultivation of wet rice historically required a collective effort. The bonds to the village and the home are more like cables than ties. Every year during

the Tet lunar new year, Vietnamese migrate from all over the country, and increasingly from all over the world, for the beacon of home (see p. 33).

PRECEDENTS & DECEDENTS

Today, Vietnam remains communist, though the hallmarks of communism—collectivization of agriculture, a planned central economy—have been dismantled in favor of a free market. Other old laws are falling by the wayside as Vietnam gussies up for accession to the World Trade Organization.

Hanoi still won't broach political opposition. The ruling clique controls the courts, the state-run press is a dutiful mouthpiece for government leaders, and contrary letters to the editor rarely see the light of day. But those issues aren't ideological flaws. They're the prerogatives of fearful rulers who can't quite fathom the benefits of a participatory democracy

and who have the mandates of Confucianism hardwired into their genes. The reforms of doi moi, like the former Soviet Union's perestroika, have not been complemented by an equivalent of glasnost (openness). The door is open here, but not all the way.

Historically, Vietnamese scholars aspired to know what had already been discovered and avoided exploration of the unknown. Similarly, as the Vietnamese chart their way

Terraced rice fields corrugate the flanks of big-shouldered mountains around Sa Pa.

both individually and socially, they often look over their shoulders to precedents set by their fathers and ancestors in general. The dead never really die in Vietnam and only fade away, traditionally, after nine generations have passed. The Vietnamese believe their ancestors return annually at

Tet, for communion with and sustenance from their living descendants.

Ask a Vietnamese his religion, and he's likely to say Buddhism. That may be true, but it's probably just as true that he's devoted to the cult of his ancestors, as well as to the hierarchies of Confucianism, and to the mystical world view of Taoism. Names, dogma and ideologies only go so far with the Vietnamese. During the war, that was a problem for the U.S. military,

which was culturally at odds with a people whose politics were marked more by expedience than principle.

REGIONAL DISTINCTIONS

Together with China, Japan, and Korea, Vietnam belongs to the classical world of East Asia. These countries, bound by Confucianism, Buddhism, and Taoism, are more like each other than any are like the world of the Khmer, the Thai, or the

three distinct regions of their country—four if you allow for the rugged highlands and the four million members of ethnic minority groups that inhabit them. The south, with Ho Chi Minh City as its hub, is aggressively commercial and socially progressive. The lion's share of foreign investment orbits Saigon, as the heart of the onetime capital of South Vietnam is still known. The north holds the keys to Vietnam's ancient past. Vietnamese civilization emerged along the Red River Delta, and northerners tend to cling more tightly to precedent and protocol. Similarly, Hue, the third region, seat of the last imperial dynasty in the central part of the country, is culturally conservative, the people more genteel and poetically inclined.

Of course, similarities abound. Throughout Vietnam, the men drink high-test coffee and smoke cigarettes. Women do neither. The ao dai silk dress hangs in the regular wardrobe, not the closet where traditional costumes await special occasions. Women also seem to do more than their fair share of physical labor, from farming the rice paddies to roadwork. Most Vietnamese love the moon and treacly sentimental pop songs. Kitsch is not derided but exalted—in sculpted topiary, candy-colored lights that illuminate sober French railroad trestles, and the coronas of disco lights that halo Buddhist statuary in otherwise venerable pagodas.

After years of having virtually nothing, tens of thousands of Vietnamese are suddenly nouveau riche. They're building rococo villas that don't really reflect any one architectural aesthetic but as many as possible—from Slavic Europe to classical Greece and Rome and the Middle East and Disneyland, sometimes all in the same building.

In short, they're having fun, and the humor—all across Vietnam—is infectious. Thailand is known as the "Land of Smiles," but that sentiment is as relevant from the Red River to the Mekong Delta. The Viet-

Malays. The Vietnamese, like their East Asian neighbors, adhere to social hierarchies of deference—the son to the father, the student to the teacher, the young to the old. Education is king. In Vietnam, a teacher is more highly esteemed than a medical doctor, though that pecking order is now changing as prosperity and higher salaries impel admiration for the trappings of wealth.

Domestically, the Vietnamese recognize

namese laugh at everything, from bawdy jokes to misfortune to questions they'd rather not answer, and themselves as well.

THE VIETNAM WAR

There's no escaping the war in Vietnam. The cyclo driver who ferries you across a southern city may launch his taxi banter with a reference to "before 1975" and his work as a soldier in the army of South Vietnam. In Saigon, the old American embassy was demolished in the 1990s, but the streets and shops retain haunting reminders of U.S. involvement in the country—traffic-switching devices manufactured in Cedar Rapids in the 1960s, MacGregor golf clubs in the antique shops. And you'll find Zippo lighters and dog tags for sale outside the hotels.

More affecting than these nostalgic reminders are the rank and file who still suffer the war's repercussions. The country-

side remains littered with some 300,000 tons (270,000 metric tons) of ordnance that failed to detonate during the conflict but blows up all too often today. Since the end of the war in 1975, an average of four people per day have been killed by land mines and bombs. Agent Orange, an herbicide used to defoliate the countryside during the war, has been linked to myriad health problems, including cancer and genetic deformities, in untold numbers

Water gypsies subsist in several "floating villages" along the Perfume River in Hue.

of civilians and former soldiers.

Nevertheless, the war is now far from center stage, and there are more compelling reasons to visit Vietnam. After more than a century of instability, the Vietnamese are starting to make the kind of hay the country always believed it might have if not for all that fighting—and

Food & drink

LONG OVERSHADOWED BY THE CUISINES OF CHINA AND THAILAND, Vietnamese food is rapidly developing a following all its own. Foodies worldwide are bellying up to the country's tables in droves and filing scrumptious reports to the West, praising the lightness of the typical Vietnamese dish, the simplicity of technique, the freshness of ingredients, the deftness of presentation, and the artful mingling of flavors, textures, and temperatures.

As with many aspects of Vietnam, foreign tastes have done much to elaborate on the native palate and board. The ever influential Chinese stimulated the use of chopsticks and desire for noodles. The Cham added spice and curry. The Mongols spurred an appetite for beef. Or maybe it was the French, harbingers of bread, coffee, yogurt, and cheese, who truly turned on the taste buds to beef. No matter—it's all been absorbed and made new as Vietnamese.

A typical meal—a selection of different dishes—is delivered as it's prepared. Expect a multitude of tastes in a single dish and, often, in a single bite. Yin and yang are necessary companions in many dishes. If there's hot, there's got to be cold. If sweet, then sour. If soft, then crunchy.

You'll find little butter in Vietnamese cuisine, little salt, no reduction sauces, no salad oil, no gooey red bastings—hence the Vietnamese reputation for lightness. A lot happens at the table itself. Wrapping, rolling, dipping, simmering, grilling— they're all part of a typical Vietnamese meal. Not to say there's not a lot of prep work. The chopping, slicing, and dicing of meats, seafood, and vegetables, the concoction of dipping sauces, and the intricacies of presentation are labor intensive and time consuming.

THE STAPLES

The ingredient that is most indispensable to Vietnamese cuisine is *nuoc mam* (fish sauce), a pungent condiment that takes some getting used to. To make a batch, the fishermen of Phu Quoc, Phan Thiet, and other fishing villages fill vats with alternating layers of *ca com* (anchovies) and salt, wait some months, drain off the liquid, pour it back over the fermenting catch, and wait

some more. Each batch is drained for a premium and lesser grades of sauce, as the Vietnamese are as finicky about nuoc mam as the Italians are about olive oil.

Rice, of course, is the preeminent staple. So fundamental is this grain to the Vietnamese diet that the term for it is virtually synonymous with consumption. When you sit down to a meal in Vietnam, you *an com* (eat cooked rice), whether your meal includes rice or not. It usually does. Most noodles are rice based, the wraps in which you roll up finger food are rice based, the ubiquitous hard liquor drunk nationwide is distilled from rice. No wonder the grain is known as white gold.

Unlike anywhere else in Southeast Asia, people here consume aromatic herbs like vegetables. A bounty of herbs accompanies many dishes, usually uncooked to retain flavor and each on a dish of its own. Asian basil, coriander, and mint top the list of favorites, joined by spring onion, chives, and watercress. Warranting special mention is lemongrass, which seems to sprout everywhere in the Vietnamese kitchen.

WHERE TO EAT

Vietnamese eateries break down into four broad categories—restaurants, bistros, rice-and-noodle shops, and street stalls. Except at high-end venues, the ambience at most places includes fluorescent lighting, pink tablecloths, and too many chairs around smallish tables.

Typically found in hotels and larger cities, the *nha hang* (restaurant) is especially popular with foreigners. But while the best restaurants in Hanoi and Ho Chi Minh City

Hanoi's popular Green Tangerine offers a fusion of Occidental and Oriental tastes.

certainly serve exquisite meals, the nha hang in general doesn't necessarily offer the best food. The kitchens are fixed, and menus typically include English translations.

The *quan* (bistro) stirs up traditional Vietnamese fare, often in a garage-like setting on the ground floor of a building or in an outdoor food court shaded by a metal roof. Stools and folding chairs are the norm. Menus are occasionally in English.

Barbecue prawns with chili and pasta provide a twist on the traditional noodle dish.

The ubiquitous *com/pho* (rice-and-noodle shop) doesn't bother with a menu; you simply pick what you want from a glass case near the front of the shop. Expect simple rice and noodle dishes. However sterile the setting, these meals can be fabulous. If the sign reads COM, they only do rice; if just PHO, only noodle soup.

At street stalls, marked by a canopy to ward off the elements, you'll sit down to a tiny stool to a bowl of something—perhaps fish noodle soup, *banh xeo* (Vietnamese crepes), or *bun cha* (noodles with barbecue pork).

In the Vietnamese home, meals are traditionally served at a straw mat unfurled on the floor or on a multipurpose platform bed.

Each diner eats from his or her own rice bowl, solicitously filled and refilled by mother. Otherwise, diners serve themselves and others from communal bowls.

WHAT TO EAT

Given Vietnam's 2,135-mile (3,444 km) coastline and countless rivers, lagoons, canals, and waterways, seafood is plentiful, fresh, and wonderfully prepared. The Vietnamese have a particular yen for squid and cuttlefish. Shrimp are cultivated up and down the seaboard. The coastal fishing villages net tuna, sea bass, and an array of succulent white fish. Crabs, clams, and oysters are perched on the high end of menus.

Unless you're dining at a fine place with the resources to import, the lamb and beef are likely to be inferior—in fact, the beef is as likely to be water buffalo as cow. Pork is a safe bet everywhere. Chicken is tougher and leaner than its plump Western counterpart, while duck is almost as popular as chicken. Thanks to Buddhist influences, vegetarian food is widely available and a beneficiary of long culinary cultivation.

Traditionally, fruit in Vietnam is served at dessert. Options include the usual tropical suspects such as bananas and papayas and a variety of lesser known succulents. The fibrous white pulp of the dragon fruit is peppered with edible black seeds and grows in bulbs from a Medusa-like coif of fronds. The pomelo is a sweet grapefruit. Egg-shaped sapodilla has a sweet brown pulp. Stay alert, too, for ripe longans, star fruit, and milk fruit.

Given Vietnam's size, there are regional differences to the cuisines. Southern cuisine is longer on herbs, sweet-and-sour dishes, and curries. In the north, where the Chinese influence has been heavier, congees are popular, as are stir-fry and charcoal-grilled meats and fish. In the central region, chili spices much of the seafood. Hue has long been a culinary hub, thanks to persnickety emperors who demanded a wide variety of small, visually enticing dishes. But that was then. You'll eat better in Hanoi and Ho Chi Minh City these days.

While each region boasts its own specialties, the following dishes are typically available in urban centers nationwide. Be sure to try:

Banh chung. This square cake of sticky rice, bean curd, and pork meat is wrapped in banana leaves and cooked all night. It is as integral to Tet celebrations as turkey is to Thanksgiving.

Banh xeo. A Saigon sidewalk specialty, known in Hue as *banh khoai,* this crispy crepe is folded over thin strips of pork, shelled shrimp, mushrooms, and other vegetables.

Bun bo hue. This spicy rice-noodle stew combines spaghetti-thick rice noodles, pork, beef, lots of chili, and lemongrass. A Hue specialty, it is usually eaten at breakfast.

Bun cha. This snack of skewered, grilled pork and noodles is eaten with fish sauce, vinegar, and the *lang* herb, grown near Hanoi. It's a Hanoi specialty, as is **cha ca,** a grilled white fish.

Pho. Steeped in aromatic herbs, including coriander and mint, this rice-noodle broth features thin-sliced morsels of parboiled beef and as many as two dozen other ingredients. It's the most widely known Vietnamese dish in the West and a great source of national pride. Hanoi is the traditional home of pho and the reputed source of the best bowls.

Spring rolls. The most popular spring roll (aka imperial roll) is *cha gio,* or *nem Saigon.* These fried rice-paper wraps are filled with minced pork, bean sprouts, mushrooms, glass noodles, mint, and egg yolk. The *banh uot cuon,* often referred to as a fresh spring roll, is a spongy, pork-based rice wrap dipped in a thick peanut sauce.

WHAT TO DRINK

Tea is the de facto national drink, served whenever people sit down together. Families keep a thermos of boiling water at the ready and fill tiny ceramic teapots with green tea leaves as visitors arrive. The Vietnamese are not as refined about their consumption as the Japanese, nor do they cultivate as many varieties as China, but green tea, jasmine, artichoke, and other varieties are popular.

Coffee has been booming here for years, and Vietnam now ranks as the world's second largest exporter. Most common is the lesser grade Robusta bean, though Arabica is

The marketplace in Bac Ha is a great venue for adventurous dining.

gaining popularity as growers tune into the world's bean of choice. Men throng the cafés each morning, patiently waiting for brews to drip from tin filters into small glasses. Most Vietnamese drink potent, espresso-size portions black or on ice, or perhaps mixed with sweetened condensed milk.

According to a popular Vietnamese proverb, "A man who does not drink alcohol is like a flag without wind." Rice wine is the traditional festive beverage, often consumed at holidays and ceremonies. No ethnic minority celebration is complete unless the men swarm a communal jar of rice wine with a bouquet of bamboo straws.

Over the last several decades, beer has trumped wine as the most widely consumed alcoholic beverage. Vietnam brews several decent lagers, including Saigon Lager, Festival, and 333. Beer lovers often gather at streetside *bia hoi* (fresh beer) joints for cheap draft. ■

The land

A MAP OF VIETNAM DESCRIBES AN ELONGATED S, SWERVING SYMMETRICALLY along its southern sweep, tapering neatly through the midsection, but foreshortened and bulging in the north. Mountains form the spine of this 1,025-mile-long (1,650 km) country, roughly paralleling its borders with Cambodia and Laos. But rivers and the sea provide greater definition, both visually and culturally, along the 2,135-mile (3,444 km) seaboard and the two great waterways of the Mekong and Red Rivers.

Though Vietnam is slightly larger than New Mexico, it has more than 50 times as many inhabitants. Its 84 million people inhabit just 20 percent of its land area, on the two deltas of the Red and Mekong Rivers, in the valleys, and along the littoral. It is the world's 13th most populous country, with three-quarters of its people living in rural areas. Its ethnic minority population of four million, grouped in 50 distinct tribes, dwells amid the less fertile mountains.

During the Vietnam War, U.S. planes bombed and defoliated enemy strongholds in the North and South, as well as throughout the highlands, where the Ho Chi Minh Trail carried supplies and ammunition. The bombing campaigns transformed the lush jungle and verdant farmland into denuded moonscapes. But travelers won't find much evidence of the destruction today. After 1975, the fecundity of this tropical country renewed the land with vigor. Around Khe Sanh, one of the most heavily bombed areas in the history of war, the landscape today is as picturesque as a nature reserve.

THE DELTAS

Historically, Vietnam's defining topographical feature has been the Red River. Originating in China's Yunnan Province, the Red flows southeast for 730 miles (1,170 km), exhausting itself in a delta east of Hanoi. The river's nutrient-rich alluvium buoyed Vietnamese civilization more than 2,000 years ago, though its floodwaters remain a grave threat. Despite a 1,864-mile (3,000 km) network of dikes, an engineering feat one historian likened to the Great Wall of China, the river still on occasion rises 30 to 45 feet (10–14 m), washing away houses, people, and livestock.

Thanks to a link with Cambodia's Tonle Sap Lake and its stabilizing influence as an absorbent reservoir, the Mekong presents a lesser threat to people of the southern delta. The Mekong's waters annually flood the region's paddies with an additional 3 to 6 feet (1–2 m) of water, spreading alluvial deposits that support three rice crops annually and sowing far less destruction. The 2,700-mile (4,320 km) river drains through nine mouths in the country's southeasternmost provinces. These branches are interlaced by a web of interconnecting channels and canals, which explains why the Vietnamese term for country is *dat nuoc* (land water).

THE HIGHLANDS

North of the Mekong Delta, the Truong Son (Long Mountains) rear up in the provinces just north of Ho Chi Minh City. In a bygone era, these highlands were a big-game paradise, harboring Indochinese tigers, Asian elephants, and Javan rhinos, though these have since been driven to near extinction by poaching and habitat destruction. The southern and central highlands now offer less lethal attractions, including a burgeoning suite of nature reserves and national parks, as well as several ethnic minority villages. In Kontum and Dak Lak, soaring thatched communal halls and longhouses are anachronistic marvels. To meet growing worldwide demand, coffee plantations have sprung up across the region in recent years.

From Danang to Vinh, the country's slender waist cinches to a width of 25 to 50 miles (40–80 km) between the sea and the Laotian border. The mountains here march to the sea,

Nearly 2,000 karst islands rise from the jade-green waters of Ha Long Bay. Myths credit the thrashing tail of a dragon for this seascape, while geologists point to 300 million years of erosion and subduction.

plunging into the waters from great prom-ontories at the Ngang and Hai Van Passes. Remarkably, a spate of new, large mammals, including the saola and giant muntjac (see pp. 186–187), has been discovered in the hinterlands of these highlands since the 1990s.

North of Nghe An and Thanh Hoa, home territory to Vietnam's greatest leaders, the country bulges again and the mountains run northwest, paralleling the Red River to the east. Vietnam's tallest peak, Fan Si Pan, summits at 10,312 feet (3,143 m) near Sa Pa, whose vibrantly costumed denizens are one of the country's chief tourists attractions. To the north and northeast, the mountains aren't as lofty, but wind and water have sculpted their karst flanks into the country's most fantastic mountainscapes.

SEABOARD

On the northern coast, similar geological forces have carved one of the wonders of the world at Ha Long Bay, a 580-square-mile (1,500 sq km) seascape of karst towers and clustered conical peaks. Undercut by the rise and fall of the tides, many towers seem to hover magically over the jade green waters.

South of the Red River Delta, the South China Sea breaks against a long, fairly regular coastline that's well endowed with sandy beaches. Few beaches north of Hue attract much attention from foreign visitors, but south of Hue, the sandy spit of Lang Co heralds a tantalizing string of sandy crescents that bight the coast as far south as the Mekong Delta. The Bay of Danang has lately come into its own as one of the most beautiful bays of the world. The bays and island waters of Khanh Hoa Province (Nha Trang) host marvelous beds of coral.

Farther south, from Danang to Vung Tau, the South China Sea breaks on the coconut- and casuarina-fringed beaches of the central and south-central coast. As seafarers, the Vietnamese seldom ventured far from their shores. But the clogged harbors in places like Nha Trang and Phan Thiet speak to the nation's age-old ties to the ocean and affinity for seafood. Vietnam's best-known island, Phu Quoc, hangs like a pendant off the southern coast of Cambodia, featuring placid waters and gleaming white sand.

CLIMATE

Vietnam lies in the tropics and subtropics, but its varied latitudes and altitudes, and the fact that it lies in the East Asian monsoon zone, means that the country experiences diverse conditions.

Hanoi and the north in January and February can feel downright cold. Snow can fall in Sa Pa. The region experiences its greatest rainfall during the May-to-October monsoon season. Average daily highs range

from 66°F (19°C) in January to 91°F (33°C) in June.

The south and central regions are dependably tropical. From May to October, southwesterly monsoon winds blow through Ho Chi Minh City and the south, dumping 90 percent of the region's rain during this six-month stretch. Temperatures remain fairly stable year-round. November is the "coolest" month, with average daily highs of 88°F (31°C), while the temperature

Once the realm of fishermen, beaches along the south-central coast are fast becoming popular international tourist destinations.

peaks at 94°F (34°C) in March and April.

In central Vietnam, the rains begin in September and continue through January, with the greatest concentration in October and November. Daily highs in Hue range from 74°F (23°C) in December to 94°F (34°C) in June, July, and August. ■

The smaller dragon

In Vietnam today, you're apt to see ball caps on the heads of the middle-aged and berets on the heads of old-timers, but make no mistake: Twenty years of American sway and one hundred years of the French are nothing next to the influence spawned by a thousand years of Chinese rule and cultural osmosis.

Just as the United States and modern Europe have mined the glories of ancient Greece and Rome to enrich their own cultures, so the Vietnamese have absorbed the politics, religion, sociology, and arts of China to refine their own. The impact is no mere accident of proximity. From 111 B.C. to A.D. 939, China controlled Vietnam as a vassal state, setting the stage for a cultural reorientation that goes right to the marrow of what it means to be Vietnamese.

The most obvious inheritance was Confucianism, a system of ethics so thoroughly woven into the fabric of Chinese and Vietnamese society that other political overlays (e.g. Marxism) are, by comparison, mere window dressing. Confucianism was especially dominant as a state religion in the imperial courts. In the 19th century, the Nguyen kings, like their counterparts in Beijing, anointed themselves as Sons of Heaven, a term that combines the mandate of a king with that of a pope.

Shortly after Vietnam cast off its Chinese overlords in the tenth century, the fledgling nation found the wherewithal to run the state in a bureaucracy staffed by mandarins. Like China, which founded its mandarinate in the first century B.C., the Ly kings established nine ranks of mandarins. They borrowed the Chinese exam system and held literary competitions to distinguish between lesser and greater officials.

Though the Vietnamese retained their language through the thousand-year occupation, a third of its lexicon derives from Chinese. The native ideographic script, *chu nom*, evolved as a vernacular alternative to the Chinese Han script. Still, even after popularization of the nom script in the 14th century, Chinese persisted as the script of preference for scholars and official business until the dawn of the 20th.

The greatest of all Vietnamese poems, "The Tale of Kieu," stems from a novel penned in the 16th century by a Ming dynasty writer. Though the story is set in China, its essence is Vietnamese. Similarly, stories at the heart of Vietnamese theater, be it folk opera *(cheo)* or classical theater *(tuong)*, often hark back to age-old tales with origins along the Yangtze and Yellow Rivers.

The Vietnamese holiday of Tet is better known in the West as Chinese New Year (see p. 33). Tet begins with a tale that revolves around three star-crossed lovers, which is a reinterpretation of a Chinese story.

China also influenced Vietnamese architecture, notably in Hue. The Nguyen kings built their imperial capital with one eye fixed on the local landscape and the other on Beijing, modeling walls, gates, moats, bridges, and audience halls after landmarks in the Chinese capital. This cultural mimicry even extends to nomenclature; both Beijing and Hue boast a Zenith Gate, a Forbidden City, and a Hall of Supreme Harmony. As the Nguyen

kings prepared for death, they ordered construction of vast temple complexes anchored by mausoleums, modeled after the tombs of China's Ming dynasty.

There are, of course, cultural differences. But after more than 2,000 years of shared history, the similarities, especially to the traveler, remain obvious. ■

Hue's Imperial City (above) was modeled, in part, on Beijing's imperial capital. Burning joss sticks, mandarin orange trees, and blossoms decorate temples and pagodas such as Hanoi's Tran Quac Pagoda (below) at Tet, the Vietnamese version of Chinese new year.

Beliefs

VIETNAMESE BELIEFS ARE AN IRREDUCIBLE TANGLE OF CONFUCIANISM, Buddhism, and Taoism, all coiled about an ancient core of native dependency on spirits and goddesses. Ancestor altars anchor most homes to a spiritual realm where the dead are not inert but vital and prone to interaction with the living. Each year, the living and the dead commune in a celebratory feast during the Tet lunar new year.

Though most Vietnamese identify themselves as Buddhist, the term is shorthand for a range of beliefs, which often seem like anything and everything. There's a great tradition of syncretism in Vietnam. The Chinese brought Confucianism south in the second century B.C., Buddhism arrived from India and China in the second and third centuries A.D., and Taoism seeped in as both a preoccupation of the elite and a receptacle for all those indigenous genii.

These traditions aren't mutually exclusive but pliable and absorbent. In fact, it's often said in Vietnam that you need all three— Confucianism, Buddhism, and Taoism, a trinity known collectively as Tam Giao. The Cao Dai, a homegrown sect founded in the 1920s, formally synthesized the Tam Giao as the foundation of their religion, then grafted on shoots of Catholicism and other Western religions to boot.

There's no dogma in these faiths, no over-arching scripture, no clerical hierarchy. No one "attends pagoda" on a set schedule. Apart from monks, you're unlikely to see anyone meditating. "Religion," a term fraught with Western doctrine and distinctions, has little relevance in the ethos of most Vietnamese.

The cult of Confucius keeps house at temples of literature *(van mieu)* and smaller temples in villages *(van tu* and *van chi)*. Tutelary spirits are worshipped in communal houses *(dinh)*. Various genii and deities are worshipped at temples *(den* and *mieu)*. Taoist gods are commonly met in temples *(quan)*. But no place of worship is as ubiquitous as the Buddhist pagoda *(chua)*.

CONFUCIANISM

As China consolidated its hold on Vietnam in the second century B.C., it insisted vassals renounce their liberal matriarchal ways and adhere to the more rigid cult of Confucius. Seeking societal harmony, Confucian ethics prescribe a hierarchy of obeisance: The son obeys the father, the subject obeys the king, the wife obeys the husband, and the disciple the master. Such patriarchal arrangements served the prerogatives of the ruling Chinese.

After Vietnam liberated itself in the tenth century, Buddhism flourished under the Ly and Tran dynasties. The country's oldest extant pagodas date from this period. Later, the Le and Nguyen dynasties hewed strongly to Confucianism, though they also built and repaired Buddhist pagodas.

The trappings of Confucianism persist today. Men dominate women. A son trumps a daughter. Education is more important than wealth. The cult of the ancestors is a form of a filial piety and jibes neatly with native beliefs in omnipresence of spirits.

In nearly every home, the family altar occupies the most hallowed place in the living room. Continually refreshed with flowers, fruit, wine, and, on anniversaries, prepared foods, this altar tethers one's departed ancestors to the living family. It's the responsibility of the family to nourish the dead, as if through a supernatural umbilical cord, with rituals and oblations.

BUDDHISM

As Confucianism governs societal relations, Buddhism serves the Vietnamese desire for personal salvation. If Confucianism plays to the head, Buddhism plays to heart.

Most Vietnamese Buddhists subscribe to the Mahayana branch of Buddhism, also known as the greater vehicle, and its three branches of Zen, Pure Land, and Tantra. The Pure Land school especially is preoccupied with bodhisattvas—those who've already achieved enlightenment and could go on to Nirvana but prefer instead to help devotees.

Costumed devotees of the Cao Dai worship at their cathedral near Tay Ninh.

Thai sculptors carved this recumbent Buddha at Nha Trang's Long Son Pagoda.

In its purest form, there's no divinity in Buddhism. But you wouldn't know that from visiting a Vietnamese pagoda, where a pantheon of deities—warriors, kings, guardians, and other bodhisattvas—reigns from altars throughout the main sanctuary. A trinity of three Buddhas *(tam the),* representing the Buddha of the past, present, and future, perches on the uppermost tier. The terrace below is occupied by the Amitabha Buddha, while other manifestations of Buddha and bodhisattvas occupy still lower terraces.

TAOISM

Taoism is the least visible and most mystical element of Tam Giao. With the jade emperor as supreme divinity, this philosophy dwells on nothingness, on the absence of personal ambition, desire, and sensual pleasure, on simplicity, and on a belief in the world as an illusion. The yin and the yang symbolize the harmony of contradictions.

Outside the temples, Taoism is subtle and rarified. It's in the laughter you get after asking someone a question he'd rather not answer and in a pervasive lack of conviction. The populist part of Taoism trades on magic and melds nicely with native Vietnamese beliefs.

SPIRITS & GENII

In the supernatural world, the celestial sovereign Ong Troi (Mister Sky) lords over the universe. The Vietnamese invoke this deity—*Troi oi!*—as often as Westerners exclaim,

"Oh, my God." Closer to home, spirits dwell in stones and the bowers of trees. If a boat wrecks on a stone, the spirit within is malevolent. If a tree is lush with fruit, the spirit is good.

These genii can be cajoled. The faithful, hoping for better days or a reprieve from misfortune, will burn paper oblations depicting money, motorbikes, and other proxies for the spirit's sustenance. Fortune-tellers, known as *thay,* often direct such rituals, which are held in the home, at temples, or at the site of a particular misfortune.

The Vietnamese have grafted a number of Chinese gods and bodhisattvas into their native tradition. Quan Am, the goddess of mercy, springs as much from the ancient cult of the mother saints (Tho Mau) as from the pantheon of bodhisattvas. The Taoist jade emperor reigns over the immortals and plays a crucial role at Tet.

CHRISTIANITY

With the exception of the Philippines and Indonesia, Catholic missionaries were more successful in Vietnam than any other country in Southeast Asia, partly because Vietnamese spiritual beliefs were scattered among so many traditions. Though the 19th-century Nguyen emperors executed a small number of missionaries, the reasons had more to do with a foreign threat to their reign and less to do with ideological opposition. Today, Vietnam harbors some six million Catholics (8 percent of the population). ■

Tet

This weeklong celebration of the lunar new year, falling sometime at the end of January or the beginning of February, dwarfs all other holidays in Vietnam. For an apt Western comparison, you'd have to combine Christmas, for the way the year revolves around it; Easter, for its spirit of renewal; and Thanksgiving, for the feast. It's also a nationwide birthday party: The Vietnamese don't mark their ages by the day they were born; instead, a baby turns one at Tet no matter when he or she was born that year.

Above: *Banh chung* **for sale during Tet. Below: Unicorn dances, symbolizing wealth and prosperity, take place during Tet.**

Tet comes from the word *tiet,* which is the belted knot between segments of a bamboo stalk and describes the notion of transition. In preparation, Vietnamese take to the railways, highways, and airways, streaming home to clean the graves of ancestors, scrub the family altar, settle old debts, and cook. Pink and peach blossoms are brought into the house and temples to ward off evil spirits. And *banh chung,* a sticky rice cake, is available everywhere.

At midnight on new year's eve, the family marks the transition with prayers in the Gia Thua ceremony. They invite deceased ancestors home through the ritual of Gia Tien. The kitchen god that dwells in each house reports to the jade emperor, the supreme lord of Taoism, and the family prays that the report is favorable.

On the first morning, the first visitor to any house—the so-called first footer—heralds the family's luck for the coming year. Older relatives present children with *ly sy* (money) stuffed in small red envelopes. Immediate family members spend the day visiting each other. On the second day, they widen the circle to more distant relatives, and on the third day, friends come together.

Tet rarely ends precisely after the third day, when the ancestors return to their spiritual realm sated with burnt offerings. The festivities often drift into a fourth, fifth, or sixth day, eventually petering out as people return to work. ■

History

THE VIETNAMESE TRACE THEIR ORIGINS TO A LEGENDARY UNION BETWEEN a dragon, Lac Long Quan, who came from the sea, and a fairy, Au Co, who dwelled in the mountains. Their union spawned a hundred sons, including one who became the first of the country's Hung kings. The 18 kings of this dynasty ruled over an era grounded in fact but largely embellished by myths.

The actual rise of the Hung kings was probably coincidental with the unification of different cultures in the Red River Valley in the seventh century B.C. These people were a commingling of the Austro-Indonesians who'd claimed the land and the Thai and Viets who came later, migrating south from China's Lower Yangtze River Valley. Their Dong Son culture persevered from the seventh century B.C. to the first century A.D. and forged abiding fame with bronze drums that have been unearthed by archaeologists throughout the region.

Archaeology aside, the Vietnamese as a people did not register their first appearance in the annals of history until the emergence of King An Duong late in the third century B.C. An Duong yanked the crown away from the last of the Hung kings and established the Au Lac Kingdom at Co Loa ("snail city"). An Duong lost his throne in a supernatural power play by his son-in-law's father, a Chinese general named Trieu Da, who first identified the fledgling country as a nation of the Viets.

The Viets didn't enjoy autonomy for long. China, even in antiquity, had too many people and too little fertile land. Thus, in 111 B.C. Han dynasty soldiers surged south and wrested control of the Red River Delta from the Viets, expanding an empire that would ultimately stretch as far as Turkistan and Korea. Experts in dike building and irrigation, the Chinese taught the Vietnamese how to keep rivers at bay, brought the plow to farmers, and opened schools to teach the art of writing.

Over the next millennium, Vietnam gradually absorbed the trappings of Chinese culture. Although the people continued to cultivate their own language, they adopted Chinese characters for written communication and replaced the more liberal tenets of their own social structure with the stricter hierarchies of Confucianism, a philosophy of social organization that persists in Vietnam to this day.

Still, the Vietnamese never stopped trying to oust their foreign masters. The first great rebellion under Chinese rule was led by Trung Trac, a fearless woman who drove the Chinese from power in A.D. 40 and took to the throne as queen with her sister as a constant companion. For two years, these two Trung heroines ruled a flimsy union that collapsed shortly after the Chinese dispatched an able general to pacify the south. But Chinese dominion could not expunge the glories of Au Lac and the Hung kings, whose legendary reigns would help sustain the Vietnamese struggle for independence for the next 900 years.

In the tenth century, China's Tang dynasty deteriorated, and a Vietnamese leader seized the day. In a decisive battle at the Bach Dang River, Gen. Ngo Quyen (898–944) implanted iron-tipped wooden stakes into a riverbed and lured the Chinese fleet upriver at high tide. When the tide turned, the stakes impaled and sank the fleet, clinching the Vietnamese victory. The victorious general founded the Ngo dynasty at Co Loa, the ancient capital of the Au Lac Kingdom, strategically affirming Vietnam's sense of itself as an independent nation.

In 1010, the first of the great Vietnamese imperial dynasties, the Ly, came to power. Ly Thai To moved his seat of power from Hoa Lu, where Ngo Quyen's successor had established his dynasty, to Dai La, the site of present-day Hanoi. According to legend, he renamed the city Thang Long ("dragon tled the kingdom of Champa to the south and tangled with the Mongols in a series of 13th-century invasions. Unlike the Koreans, however, who were subdued by the Mongols, 200,000 Vietnamese soldiers under the command of Tran Hung Dao repelled the great imperialists of the 13th century.

Above: The Vietnamese still celebrate the Trung sisters, who led the first great rebellion against Chinese occupation in A.D. 40. Left: Archaeologists have unearthed dozens of bronze drums dating from the Dong Son culture, which thrived more than two millennia ago.

ascending") after sighting a soaring dragon en route along the Red River.

The Ly founded a bureaucracy run by mandarins and, in 1070, dedicated the renowned Temple of Literature to the cult of Confucius. The Ly and the succeeding dynasty, the Tran, also ushered Vietnam into prosperity, building roads, a postal system, fleets, pagodas, and parks. But the warring continued unabated.

The Khmer (modern-day Cambodians) launched a series of attacks against the new Vietnamese state. The Vietnamese also bat-

After the Mongol repulsion, the Vietnamese resumed their wars with the Cham, impoverishing and weakening the Tran until the Chinese seized a chance and swept back to power in Vietnam.

THE LE

The Vietnamese paid a harsh price under the new Chinese regime. The Ming invaders forced the peasantry to labor in the mines for gold and ores, the forests for elephant tusks and rhinoceros horns, and the fields for the cultivation of spices—all for export

to China. Now the Vietnamese were riled, and to the hour came a man who ranks with Ho Chi Minh as the greatest of all Vietnamese heroes. Le Loi (1385–1433), a wealthy landowner from Thanh Hoa, resorted to the guerrilla tactics that worked so well for Tran Hung Dao, badgering the Chinese in ambush after ambush and finally winning a decisive victory at the Chi Lang defile in 1427.

Although Le Loi is remembered as the greatest Le hero, one of his successors, Le Thanh Tong (1442–1497), ushered in Vietnam's golden age during his reign from 1460 to 1497. Le Thanh Tong was a progressive and a scholar. He drew up a remarkably liberal legal code, granting rights to women and civil rights for citizens. He promoted journals for the advancement of math and science. He dispatched troops to help rebuild flood-damaged dikes. With the population burgeoning, Le Thanh Tong set his sights on the Cham lands to the south. In 1471, his troops razed the capital of their southern Cham neighbors at Indrapura, killing 40,000 inhabitants and opening the door to land-hungry pioneers, a movement known as the March to the South.

Though the Le persevered through 1788, their golden age was short-lived. In the early 16th century, a Vietnamese general usurped power from the reigning Le king, and the country divided into two camps of rival lords, each of which continued to recognize the Le as overlords. But these Le kings were feckless rulers. The Trinh held true sway in the north, while the Nguyen consolidated their power below the 17th parallel.

ARRIVAL OF THE EUROPEANS
The fractious relationship between the Trinh and the Nguyen opened the door to intervention by European powers. In 1545, the seafaring Portuguese established the first European settlement in Vietnam, a land they dubbed Cochinchina after an approximation of a Chinese name. The Dutch bested the Portuguese as masters of the Asia trade in

the 17th century, opening factories in the north and south. Not to be left out, the English showed up in 1672, and the French opened shop in Hanoi in 1680. By 1700, both the English and the Dutch had decamped, frustrated by an inability to turn a profit.

As profits declined, the missionaries took center stage. Alexandre de Rhodes (1591–1660), a French Jesuit from Avignon, reinvigorated the linguistic work of earlier missionaries and created a Romanized alphabet as an alternative to the unwieldy native *chu nom* script and Chinese ideographs favored by the educated elite. At the same time, he baptized thousands of new Christians every year, unsettling the royalty in Vietnam. As long as the Trinh and Nguyen needed the upper hand of European technology, the missionaries were allowed a fairly liberal hand in the north and south. But once the rival camps achieved a rapprochement, the opponents of Christianity won the day: Rhodes and his Catholic colleagues were thrown out of the country.

Rhodes lobbied the governments of France and the Vatican to help reopen the door to missionary work in Vietnam, touting it as a land of incalculable riches, but he died before either got serious about the country again. While others picked up the cause Rhodes had championed, none would advance the mission as hard or as far as the French bishop Pigneau de Behaine (1741–1799).

FRENCH COLONIZATION
In the latter half of the 18th century, the discontent that had rendered Vietnam into fertile ground for missionaries gave rise to an insurrection that united northern and southern Vietnam. In 1765, three brothers from a merchant family in Tay Son, a village on the south-central coast, rebelled against accusations of fraud. Their movement swelled with peasants bristling under a harsh mandarin system. The Tay Son wiped out most of the Nguyen lords in the south and by 1786 had wrested control of the capital in Hanoi. Mandarins from the old regime called for help from China, but the youngest Tay Son brother was able to repel the most significant Chinese incursion in several hundred years.

In Hanoi's Temple of Literature *(van mieu)*, the 200-year-old Constellation of Literature *(khue van cac)* typifies the elegance of Vietnam's architecture.

Meanwhile, de Behaine threw his support behind Nguyen Anh, a surviving member of the vanquished southern lords. He lobbied the cause of his protégé in the salons of Paris, persuading most of the government that Vietnam was the future of France in Asia. Though de Behaine would die of dysentery in 1799, his efforts bore fruit. In 1802, Nguyen Anh assumed the throne as Gia Long, the first king in the last imperial dynasty of Vietnam. He moved the capital from Hanoi to Hue, the centuries-old seat of the Nguyen lords, and began construction of an imperial city, using the Chinese capital as a model.

Gia Long was a Confucian king, somewhat conservative and unenlightened. His successor, Minh Mang (1791–1841), was bold and dogmatic, but, unlike his father, he would come to power during a resurgence of interest in Vietnam by European powers. Once the Napoleonic Wars ended in 1815, missionaries and merchants resumed their drumbeat for Vietnam. Minh Mang lashed out against the proselytizing, ordering the executions of seven Christian missionaries between 1833 and 1838. He and his successor, Thieu Tri, failed to read the winds of change. Their intransigence and unwillingness to compromise agitated the Gallic temper.

After the British took Hong Kong in the 1840s, the French tired of playing second fiddle to the British, Spanish, and Portuguese, each of whom had won significant concessions in Asia. Oddly enough, though, it was the Americans, not the French, who first wielded Western military might in Vietnam. In 1845, after learning that the Vietnamese had imprisoned a French missionary in Hue, the captain of the U.S.S. *Constitution* seized three mandarins as bargaining chips in a negotiation for the European's release. The ploy failed, and the United States later apologized for meddling.

Several years later, King Tu Duc executed another missionary, raising a hue and cry for armed intervention from the 40 or so missionaries then at work in Vietnam. In 1858, the French attacked Tourane with purpose, landing soldiers as the vanguard of a people who meant to stay. The French evacuated the city in 1860, but by then the French at home in Paris had rallied around the notion of *mission civilisatrice*, justifying their actions against the Vietnamese as a means toward enlightenment of the "yellow race."

The Vietnamese kept hoping the French, worn down by heat and disease, would simply give up and go home. The old kings of Vietnam had rallied hundreds of thousands of troops to repel invaders, but Tu Duc was not cut from the same cloth. Instead, he legalized the import of opium and put mandarin degrees up for sale. In 1863, the impotent king agreed to give up the lower third of Vietnam to France as the colony of Cochinchina. After the deaths of notable French adventurers in the 1870s and 1880s, France established protectorates in the central and northern provinces of Vietnam, known respectively as Annam and Tonkin.

THE RESISTANCE

The loss of sovereignty spawned a resistance movement among the disenfranchised elite. Phan Dinh Phung (1847–1895) mustered a guerrilla force that would later serve as a model for resistance in the 1940s. Renowned poet Phan Boi Chau (1867–1940) first tried to restore the monarchy, then later, in exile, favored democracy as an antidote to colonialism. Others, like Phan Chu Trinh, favored a moderate approach. All the while, France propped up a series of handpicked kings and used its military might to douse the brushfires of revolt in the provinces.

Enter Ho Chi Minh (1890–1969). Ho was born Nguyen Sinh Cung in a village of Nghe An Province in central Vietnam. His father was a distinguished scholar who, for mildly revolutionary behavior, fell out of favor with the imperial court in Hue. In 1911, Ho shipped out of Vietnam on a French freighter and over the next several years called at ports in the Middle East, Africa, and America. In 1919, under the alias Nguyen Ai Quoc (Nguyen the Patriot), he dispatched an appeal to Allied leaders, then meeting at Versailles to hammer out the terms of the armistice. Ho's petition called for political autonomy, versus outright independence, for the Vietnamese people. His eight-point plan called for freedom of the press, association, and religion and reductions in taxes on salt, opium, and alcohol. It would not be the last time Ho's aims coincided with the precedent of America's Founding Fathers.

Although a member of Woodrow Wilson's delegation acknowledged Ho's plan, no action was taken. Wilson's 14-point plan

trust by the state. Vietnamese entrepreneurs and capitalists garnered far less esteem than did their Western counterparts. The colonial revolutionaries loathed capitalism not so much from a philosophical standpoint, as did Marx, but because capitalism had exploited their people.

Ho Chi Minh was a nationalist, a socialist by temperament, and a Marxist out of expedience. The Americans who knew him best between 1945 and 1954 liked and respected him.

addressed colonialism by calling for self-determination for all peoples. But it was a limp-wristed gesture compared to Vladimir Lenin's iron grip in 1920, when he declared that communist countries in the West should actively participate in the struggle for freedom by colonial peoples.

Attracted by Lenin's support, Ho traveled to Moscow in 1924 and cast his lot with the communists. The tenets of Marxism were not anathema to him or a people steeped in Confucian values. Private property was not a commodity in Vietnam but was held in

By way of China, Ho surreptitiously returned to Vietnam in February 1941 and linked up with Vo Nguyen Giap and Pham Van Dong (1906–2000). Dong was the son of a mandarin who served as Emperor Duy Tan's chief of staff. Born in 1912, Giap is also the son of a mandarin, and his maternal grandfather fought the French in the 1880s. The trio would soon become leading figures in modern Vietnam.

During World War II, the French Vichy government allowed Japanese forces to occupy Vietnam, a loss of face that broached the

CIA-sponsored civilian pilots resupplied besieged French forces at Dien Bien Phu in the spring of 1954 in an attempt to repel the Vietnamese, depicted in this painting by Jeff Bass.

possibility of liberation from a European power. But the Japanese won few friends among the Vietnamese, whose food they hoarded, leading to a famine that killed two million people. As he charted his country's fate through the closing months of the war, Ho courted the sympathies of U.S. military operatives, who supplied his movement with arms in the summer of 1945.

Following the Japanese surrender, Ho, as leader of the Viet Minh resistance movement, charged into the sudden vacuum of power with the presumption of control. A delegation accepted the abdication of King Bao Dai and the imperial seal at the Noon Gate in Hue, and the Viet Minh assumed provisional power in Tonkin, Annam, and Cochinchina.

Despite the politics he'd groomed in the Soviet Union, Ho continued to pursue the sympathies of the Americans. On September 2, 1945, before a crowd of 400,000 people in Hanoi's Ba Dinh Square, he declared independence for Vietnam, beginning his speech with these words: "All men are created equal. They are endowed by their Creator with certain inalienable rights, among these are

Life, Liberty, and the pursuit of Happiness."

Ho's deference to the U.S. Declaration of Independence fell on deaf ears in the West. Though the Viet Minh had seized power, the Allies had interim plans for Vietnam. At the Potsdam Conference in 1945, they'd agreed to partition the country at the 16th parallel. The British would disarm the Japanese in the South and transition the country from a wartime to peacetime footing; the Chinese would do so in the North.

Ho's bold declaration notwithstanding, the Viet Minh leader capitulated to the resumption of French power in 1946, if only as a means to rid Vietnam of the Chinese. For the promised withdrawal of French troops in five years, Ho chose the lesser of two evils. "I prefer to sniff French s— for five years than eat Chinese s— for the rest of my life," he said.

But the political winds in France again shifted, and overtures toward Vietnamese independence bowed to renewed interest in Cochinchina as a republic tied to the apron strings of Mother France. At negotiations in Paris, Ho quietly deferred to the French on Cochinchina, knowing his initials on a partial agreement would not deter war at home. The French and Viet Minh soon clashed in Haiphong. Hanoi erupted in December, and the First Indochinese War was on.

THE END OF FRENCH RULE

Until 1949, the United States pursued a hands-off policy with regard to the war in Indochina. After communist Mao Zedong took over in China and, like the Soviets, recognized Ho Chi Minh's regime, however, the Americans threw their support behind a government led by the on-again, off-again king of Vietnam, Bao Dai. As justification for underwriting the French war, the United States invoked the "domino theory": If Indochina were to fall, so would the other countries of Southeast Asia.

By 1953, the United States was funding 80 percent of the French war effort. It was a losing proposition. While the United States was game for total victory, the French had resigned themselves to a political solution. Between 1945 and 1954, some 100,000 French soldiers died in Indochina, mostly in Vietnam. The French public had lost interest in its dirty war; the Vietnamese resistance had not. "You can kill ten of my men for every one I kill of yours," Ho told a French visitor during the war. "But even at those odds, you will lose, and I will win."

General Giap made good on Ho's promise in a far-flung valley near the Laotian border, where he launched a series of human-wave assaults against the French garrison at Dien Bien Phu. The French repulsed these early advances but could not persevere against Giap's stranglehold. On May 7, 1954, the beleaguered French troops surrendered. The next day, peace talks got under way in Geneva.

The Vietnamese won their greatest set-piece battle of the 20th century at Dien Bien Phu. The French defeat set the stage for the 1954 Geneva Accords and a push toward autonomy.

With victory at Dien Bien Phu, the Vietnamese were in a strong bargaining position, but not so strong that they could demand immediate unification of the country. Negotiations bogged down on two points: where to draw the line of partition and when to hold unification elections. Eventually, the parties agreed on the 17th parallel as the dividing line between North and South and on a two-year run-up to a nationwide election that would unite the country. That election would never come.

EYE OF THE STORM

The United States chose not to sign the Geneva Accords, a gesture that would have limited its options in the region. The government led by former King Bao Dai also declined to sign the accords. Instead, with wholehearted support from the Americans, Bao Dai appointed Ngo Dinh Diem (1901–1963) prime minister of the Republic of South Vietnam. Ardently Catholic, monkish, and undiplomatic, Diem transformed the southern "regroupment" zone into a fledgling state. He won a loyal following among people who shared his faith, including some 600,000 Catholic refugees who fled south after Ho Chi Minh and other Viet Minh leaders assumed power in Hanoi.

Diem turned out to be a disastrous choice. He ruled South Vietnam without any pretense of democracy, despite the lip service paid to his U.S. benefactors. He canceled the 1956 elections, an election that Ho, who was popular throughout the country, would likely have won. With his brother Ngo Dinh Nhu as his right-hand man, Diem embarked on a campaign to purge the South of communist agents. To deny the enemy easy access to the population, Nhu displaced farmers from their ancestral homes and herded them into *agrovilles,* or strategic hamlets. The Diem regime alienated the villagers and non-Catholic religious sects, denied freedom of the press and freedom of assembly, and outlawed all political opposition. Yet Lyndon Johnson, as John F. Kennedy's vice president, would liken Diem to Winston Churchill.

Meanwhile, in the North, Hanoi was trying to get its own house in order. The government sanctioned a land reform campaign that ran amok. Roving people's tribunals harassed and humiliated countless thousands of people and executed several thousand landlords as more than two million acres were redistributed to two million farm families.

In 1959, Le Duan, a southerner who ascended to power in Hanoi, decided the time was ripe for revolution in the South. Northerners blazed the Ho Chi Minh Trail through the highlands of Vietnam, Laos, and Cambodia to ferry troops and matériel to their southern compatriots. In 1960, a coalition of anti-Diem forces formed the National Liberation Front (NLF), or Viet Cong.

In the spring of 1963, Buddhists rallied against Diem in a movement that commanded worldwide attention after a monk from Hue doused himself with gasoline and set himself ablaze in a Saigon intersection. That November, fed-up generals of his own regime, with tacit consent from the Americans, launched a coup against Diem and executed the prime minister and his brother.

AMERICA WEIGHS IN

Diem was gone, but the United States was no less committed to South Vietnam and the domino theory. After a skirmish with a North Vietnamese patrol boat in the Gulf of Tonkin, the United States retaliated with a congressional resolution that gave Lyndon Johnson, now U.S. president, a free hand to conduct military operations in Vietnam. Gen. William Westmoreland called for troops to protect U.S. airfields, and the first contingent of U.S. combat Marines waded ashore at Danang in March 1965, the vanguard of 72,000 troops that would arrive in the country that spring.

Fueled by the resources of a vast military-industrial complex and an overconfidence in the supremacy of airpower, the United States prosecuted the war with a hammer, ignoring the opinions of seasoned strategists who called for scalpels. In 1965, an American provincial adviser told journalist and historian Bernard Fall that the U.S. military was shooting a half million dollars worth of artillery onto unobserved targets in his region every month but spending a mere 300 dollars on intelligence gathering.

The U.S. Air Cavalry's signature UH-1 (Huey) helicopter ferried troops in and out of battle.

As the Marines settled in at Danang, the United States launched a bombing campaign that was supposed to stop the flow of supplies down the mountainous Ho Chi Minh Trail but never did. The bombing intensified and moved south, or "in country," as American servicemen referred to South Vietnam. By the end of that spring, B-52 bombers were obliterating oblongs of suspect targets across the south; in April 1966, the B-52s went to work on targets in the North.

Westmoreland believed he could win through attrition. If he could simply kill enough Vietnamese, they'd cry uncle and give up. But he faced a tenacious enemy of unwavering resolve. The more bombs dropped by the U.S. military, the deeper soldiers from North Vietnam and the National Liberation Front dug in.

By contrast, the South Vietnamese allies of the United States hardly seemed to have a dog in this fight. Their leaders were rickety and corrupt and more attuned to skimming shares of American largesse than fighting an enemy whom they didn't seem to loathe nearly as much as their Western allies. In 1966, Buddhists and other dissidents raged against the corrupt southern regime of Prime Minister Nguyen Cao Ky, as they had against Diem three years earlier. They seized power in Danang and Hue. While the larger war played on, Ky skirmished against his own army. In protest, ten more monks and nuns set themselves ablaze.

During the Tet lunar new year in 1968, the North Vietnamese and NLF coordinated a series of attacks on 31 of the 44 southern provincial capitals. The offensive surprised the Americans, who'd been expecting a pivotal battle in the central highlands at Khe Sanh, where the North Vietnamese had been building up forces for weeks. But Khe Sanh was a ruse that enabled the communists to sneak through back doors all over the

A mural at My Lai portrays the suffering of 504 villagers massacred by rogue U.S. troops.

country. In Saigon, communist infiltrators breached the U.S. embassy. In Hue, they wrested control of the city and held on for 25 days as the U.S. Marines battled back, street by street, house by house. At Khe Sanh, the ruse turned into a two-month siege, despite relentless bombings by wave after wave of B-52 bombers.

In the end, the communists lost 50,000 combatants at Tet and failed to spark the desired uprising. The ranks of the Viet Cong were shattered, never to recover, and North Vietnamese Army soldiers migrated south in greater numbers to pick up the batons dropped by their southern comrades.

In the United States, Tet was a turning point in the war. Americans had already begun to sour on a dirty war that had grown too big, with more than half a million U.S. troops on the ground in 1968.

Extensive media coverage of the battles confirmed mounting doubts and accelerated the antiwar movement. After America's preeminent newsman, Walter Cronkite, declared that the war was locked in a hopeless stalemate, Johnson saw the writing on the wall and withdrew from the 1968 presidential race.

Richard Nixon, who as a candidate claimed to have a secret plan to end the war, took office and then prolonged the fighting another three and a half years. In 1970, he widened the war with an invasion of Cambodia that sparked broad antiwar protests. The governor of Ohio aggravated unrest at Kent State University by calling in National Guard troops, who ultimately shot and killed four student protesters.

With the revelations of a 1969 massacre of some 500 Vietnamese villagers at My Lai, Americans had had enough. The United States turned over increasingly more military responsibilities to the South Vietnamese, who were less willing than their northern brethren to sacrifice themselves.

At the negotiating table in Paris, U.S. National Security Council adviser Henry Kissinger matched wits with Vietnamese negotiator Le Duc Tho, trying to achieve a so-called peace with honor. When talks bogged down at the end of 1972, Nixon ordered a renewal of bombing along the 60-mile (96 km) corridor between Hanoi and Haiphong, the main port in the North. The United States dropped 40,000 tons (36,000 metric tons) of bombs between December 18 and December 30, excluding Christmas Day, in the most intensive bombing campaign of the war. The action forced the North Vietnamese hand, and on January 27, 1973, the enemies formally signed a ceasefire agreement in Paris.

REUNIFICATION

In the spring of 1975, Hanoi launched its final offensive against the Saigon regime. The towns and cities of South Vietnam toppled as readily as dominoes, surprising even the North Vietnamese. Hundreds of thousands of refugees—fearful of reprisals like the massacres of 1968, when communist troops killed thousands during their occu-

Enduring war images

The Evacuation Helicopter. The Girl in the Picture. The Viet Cong Execution. The Burning Monk. These four potent images seared the front pages of newspapers worldwide between 1963 and 1975. Though decades have passed since their initial publication, such is the indelibility of their content that they need little introduction today.

The evacuation helicopter was not perched atop the roof of the U.S embassy in Saigon, as captions have repeatedly stated since 1975, but on the penthouse of an apartment building at 22 Ly Tu Trong that was home to a number of CIA employees (see p. 198). The refugees climbing the ladder were Vietnamese, not Americans. The precariously perched Huey would not be the last to ferry refugees from the city. That flight would take off 12 hours later. On this eleventh-hour run, the chopper pilot shuttled 14 or 15 passengers to Tan Son Nhat Airport.

Three years earlier, a South Vietnamese pilot had inadvertently dropped napalm near the Cao Dai temple in the town of Trang Bang, about 25 miles (40 km) northwest of Saigon. Gobs of the burning jelly splashed across the back of Phan Thi Kim Phuc, who tore off her flaming clothes and rushed into the road before the temple.

There's less certainty about the story behind the Viet Cong execution. Lt. Col. Nguyen Ngoc Loan pulled the trigger in front of Saigon's An Quang Pagoda in 1968. The executed man was a Viet Cong named Nguyen Van Lam. Loan justified the execution to photographer Eddie Adams by saying Lam had killed Americans and Vietnamese. Others defend Lam as a low-level fighter who didn't deserve the brutal punishment.

Did Thich Quang Duc commit suicide on June 11, 1963, or was it immolation? Duc submitted to a dousing by gasoline and struck the fatal match himself—certainly a desperate act. But the monk lacked neither courage nor hope, two hallmarks of suicide. He was protesting repressive anti-Buddhist measures enacted by South Vietnam's Catholic leader, Ngo Dinh Diem. ∎

Vietnamese evacuees board a chopper atop a CIA apartment building in downtown Saigon.

pation of Hue—fled south ahead of the advancing forces. They converged at ports, on airfields, and on beaches, desperately seeking evacuation. In the waning weeks of the war, nearly 60,000 Vietnamese and Americans bolted from the country, including some 7,000 people during a panic-stricken airlift out of Saigon in the last 48 hours. On April 30, North Vietnamese tanks crashed through the gates of the presidential palace in Saigon, and South Vietnam was history.

But while the communists and NLF won the war, they promptly set about losing the peace. The victors indulged in vengefulness, jailing hundreds of thousands of the South's best and brightest in gulags euphemistically called "reeducation camps." They nationalized businesses and usurped property. The vaunted "liberation" was tantamount to deprivation for the vanquished southerners.

By 1978, Vietnam was deep in a quagmire of poverty and hunger. The Khmer Rouge, by then embarked on a genocide of its own people in neighboring Cambodia, swerved into Vietnam and massacred thousands. The Vietnamese retaliated with invasion and occupation.

Already angered by Vietnam's postwar alliance with the Soviet Union, China invaded Vietnam in 1979. The Vietnamese drove back their age-old nemesis, but continual poverty and hopelessness precipitated an exodus of as many as two million disenfranchised people, many of them ethnic Chinese.

The boat people, as the refugees came to be known, took to the seas in rickety vessels, steering toward neighboring Southeast Asian nations and, ultimately, the promise of a better life in the West. Thousands died in the open ocean. Meanwhile, Hanoi struggled to make good on the promise of its victory, a promise ultimately fulfilled by the inauguration of a market economy and fiscal reform policy *(doi moi)* in 1986.

RENOVATION

After 1975, as preconditions for the normalization of relations, Vietnam insisted the United States make good on Nixon's secret promise to pay war reparations, and the United States insisted on a full accounting of its 2,400 soldiers still listed as missing

in action (MIA) in Indochina. Vietnam eventually backed off its demand for reparations and economic aid, but by then the United States was busy trying to normalize relations with China.

Throughout the 1980s, the U.S. justified its trade embargo and the ongoing enmity by pointing to Vietnam's occupation of Cambodia and its failure to provide the "fullest possible accounting" of America's MIAs. The latter issue was fueled by a small but powerful lobby of American families who held U.S. foreign policy hostage to their personal sorrow.

By the early 1990s, Vietnam had

Vietnamese soccer fans celebrate a goal during a recent Tiger Cup tournament.

decamped from Cambodia, and U.S. senators John McCain and John Kerry, both decorated veterans of the Vietnam War, were calling for an end to the trade embargo and a resumption of relations. In 1994, President Bill Clinton lifted the embargo, and the following year the United States normalized relations and opened an embassy in Hanoi. In the same year, Vietnam became a full member of the Association of Southeast Asian Nations (ASEAN).

Those landmarks released a flood of interest in this time-warped nation where labor costs were low, the market potential was enormous, and the sky was the limit. But an Asian financial crisis, coupled with governmental corruption and bureaucracy, stifled initial enthusiasm, and Vietnam watched its foreign investments plunge from eight billion dollars in 1996 to one billion in 1999.

Near the end of his presidency, Clinton visited Vietnam to lay the groundwork for a bilateral trade agreement that was signed in 2001. Membership in the World Trade Organization continued to elude Vietnam, though accession was anticipated in 2006. ■

The arts

IN VIETNAM, SOME SAY HALF OF THE COUNTRY IS POPULATED BY PAINTERS and the other half by poets. That may be true, though the actors, musicians, wood carvers, and artisans of ceramics and lacquerware might protest.

LITERATURE

Poetry enjoys a currency in Vietnam that's been largely lost in the West. Friends write each other poems to celebrate homecomings and holidays. A waiter may serve up a few lines of verse as he dishes up your entrée.

Because Vietnamese is a tonal language, a single word can have six different meanings, depending on the pitch of one's voice. Thus, the chance of lighting upon a rhyme increases by a factor of six, which may explain why poetry comes so readily to the Vietnamese.

Although the country's literary roots stretch back two millennia, Chinese invaders in the 15th century destroyed most of the early texts in an attempt to extinguish Vietnam's concept of itself as a nation apart from China. After occupation by soldiers of the Ming dynasty, Buddhist and Confucian scribes resumed work, using two scripts— Han, or classical Chinese, and *chu nom*, a homegrown ideographic script in widespread use by the end of the 14th century.

The dominant poet of Vietnam's golden age, Nguyen Trai (1380–1442), was a Confucian and profound humanist who withdrew from court life and its dispiriting intrigues to write nom poetry about society and nature. Many of Vietnam's kings also fancied themselves poets. While Nguyen Trai embraced the colloquial script for his verse, the greatest of all of Vietnam's kings, Le Thanh Tong (1442–1497), composed his annals in Han.

In the 18th century, Vietnamese poet Nguyen Du (1765–1820) penned "The Tale of Kieu," an epic narrative in six-eight verse that Vietnamese quote often and reverently. In Du's interpretation of a Chinese novel, he chronicles the story of a girl sold into slavery and prostitution in order to save her family. The tale is steeped in allusions to the Confucian classics, as well as Buddhist and Taoist scriptures.

In the early 20th century, as the educated elite rebelled against colonial oppression, publishers of verse, essays, novels, and journalism initiated widespread use of the *quoc ngu* script. Developed by missionaries in the 17th century, quoc ngu is a transliteration of Vietnamese speech into the Roman alphabet. Compared to the ideographic scripts, which included thousands of characters, quoc ngu was far easier to master and so a much better vehicle of communication as revolutionaries sought to rally the populace.

In the early 1930s, literature entered a golden age as writers rebelled against Confucian strictures and explored the role of the individual. These writers shifted their focus from the stilted prerogatives of duty and responsibility to explore love and other emotions in novels like *South Wind,* by Hoang Ngoc Phach and *Old Love,* by 21-year-old Luu Trong Lu.

Today, after decades of war and demands for writers to toe the party line, contemporary novelists Bao Ninh *(The Sorrows of War)* and Duong Thu Huong *(Paradise of the Blind)* have broken new ground in stories that resurrect the horror, not glories, of war and the harsh realities of life in postwar Vietnam.

ARCHITECTURE

The Vietnamese celebrate architecture as the most illustrious achievement of their arts. With geomancy, or feng shui, as one of its principal determinants, the country's architecture takes in both the physical and metaphysical, the terrestrial and the celestial.

The buildings themselves, whether used for religious or civil purposes, share fundamental characteristics: massive roofs of terra-cotta tiles lofted by pillars of jackfruit and hardwood; low sheltering rooflines; and an elevated brick foundation. The country's military architecture manifests itself in citadels—some as old as 2,000 years— peppered throughout the country.

Since stone was scarce, most buildings

The wood-carved door panels at the exquisite Perfume Pagoda date from the 17th century.

were constructed of wood. Thus, due to regional heat and humidity, the oldest extant examples of Vietnamese buildings—except for the brick citadels—date back only a couple of hundred years.

Military & imperial

The most imposing structures in historical Vietnam were the citadels, with high walls, ramparts, and moats (Co Loa, Hanoi Citadel). Later, the Nguyens, with help from French

The landmark Tortoise Tower rises from the midst of Hanoi's Hoan Kiem Lake.

room, banquet hall, sports venue, theater, and temple for local tutelary gods. Most were built 300 to 400 years ago and have been renovated once or twice a century since. Elaborate carvings often adorn the interior woodwork of the dinh's truss—along the beams, purlins, and panels. The Vietnamese have identified more than 700 dinh, mostly in the Red River Delta, as cultural and historical landmarks.

Unlike the dinh, the *den* is a dynastic temple reserved for Taoist deities or national heroes like Tran Hung Dao. While the dinh serves both civilian and religious functions, the den is a religious house. A dien is a den reserved for Taoist spirits. The *van tu* is another form of religious architecture, reserved for the cult of Confucius.

Religious

The country's most religious body of architecture is the Buddhist pagoda. Pagodas *(chua)* can be as small as a single structure, like Hanoi's One-Pillar Pagoda, or comprise temple compounds that include stupas, towers, galleries, bell towers, and stela houses, like the complex at Hue's Thien Mu. From the 13th to 17th centuries, one popular form of pagoda design positioned the sanctuaries and shrines along a single axis, connected by galleries, courtyards, bridges, and gardens. Another popular arrangement positions the sanctuaries around an interior garden filled with bonsai and other flowering plants.

Inside the main sanctuary, a succession of altars bears statues that conform to a set arrangement. The Buddhas of the past, present, and future reside on the highest altar. On the tier below is Amitabha, the Buddha of the pure land, flanked by bodhisattvas. Sakyamuni sits below this tier, represented in one of several forms—as a baby, as an ascetic, or as a recumbent Buddha on his way to Nirvana. Various other bodhisattvas and Taoist deities occupy the lowest tiers.

Modern foreign

With the arrival of French colonists in the mid-19th century came grandiose new edifices, in the neoclassic and art deco styles, with decidedly European flourishes such as pediments, quoins, and fluted Corinthian

advisers and European models, built citadels throughout their dominion, including the magnificent walled fortress city of Hue.

Hue is also home to the country's most marvelous collection of imperial structures. In the 19th century, the Nguyen kings used the Forbidden City in Beijing as a model for their own imperial capital, though the Nguyen versions of the Zenith Gate and Palace of Supreme Harmony are smaller, more sublime versions of the Chinese archetypes.

Civil

The epitome of vernacular architecture is the traditional *dinh*, a village's most important structure. It is a forum, court-

columns. Good examples are sprinkled throughout the country, but especially in Hanoi, Ho Chi Minh City, Dalat, and Haiphong. In the 1920s, French architect Ernet Hebrard popularized a fusion of French and Vietnamese architectural styles as the Indochinese style.

After the French War, the Soviets influenced Vietnamese architecture with functional rectangular buildings. Some interesting examples include the People's Committee building and Ho Chi Minh's Mausoleum, both in Hanoi.

Modern architectural influences can be seen in styles varying from Trang Tien Plaza shopping center's pseudo-classical facade to the futuristic Sofitel Plaza Hotel, both in Hanoi. Glass and concrete highrises in Ho Chi Minh City represent mainstream international traditions.

CHAM ART & ARCHITECTURE

From the 600s to the 1400s, Vietnam's south-central coast was dominated by Champa, a kingdom best known for its brick temple towers that dot the region and its Hindu-influenced sculpture.

The Cham tower is the most distinctive representation of that culture's architecture. The brick-built towers, known as *kalan,* rise in three stages—a base that represents the material realm, a square central section that evokes the realm of premonition, and a pyramidal top that symbolizes the spiritual realm. Inside the temple, worshippers pay homage to the chief divinity at a pedestal altar surrounded by corridors used by priests. The kalan was the centerpiece of a walled temple complex that included other towers and cult houses.

Brahma, Vishnu, and Siva reigned as the trinity of Cham gods and are liberally represented in statues and bas-relief on Cham temples and towers. Siva, who lorded over the cult of creation and destruction, is most frequently depicted in human form with one or more of his many wives.

PAINTING

Despite a relatively late jump on the fine arts, the modern art scene in Vietnam is conspicuous and as vibrant as any other community in Southeast Asia. Where the Chinese accorded equivalent artistic status to painting and literature, the Vietnamese always ranked literature as the higher art form. Until the founding of the Indochina School of Fine Arts in 1925, painting fell under the folk art category in Vietnam

Victor Tardieu's "Portrait de Femme Assise," painted in the early 20th century

and was most obviously practiced as an extension of wood carving.

In Red River Delta towns like Dong Ho, recognized by UNESCO as a traditional crafts village, artisans carve drawings into woodblocks and use these as printmaking templates, especially at holidays such as Tet. Motifs range from flowers to the Trung sisters to boys riding water buffalo or harvesting coconuts. Families pass down these woodcuts for generations.

Victor Tardieu (1870–1937) is widely regarded as the father of modern art in Vietnam. A Frenchman who provided more than lip service to the condescending notion of *mission civilisatrice*, Tardieu culled the most promising native talent from throughout the country and nurtured the first generation of serious fine artists. Students painted with oil and lacquer and to a lesser extent on silk. After the country was partitioned in 1954, the northern school continued to draw most of its inspiration from the village and traditional crafts, while the southern school ventured West for additional themes.

In the mid-1950s, the communist government ordained social realism as the preferred style for its painters. Those who found inspiration in politics and propaganda, like Ran Van Ca, depicted a muscular, well-fed peasantry at work in bountiful fields using tractors that never rust. The illustrations did not ask questions of its audience but provided examples of strength, tenacity, and optimism. Other painters responded by publicly dabbling in sanctioned art, but going underground to follow their own muse. Artists like Bui Xuan Phai painted on whatever they could, including cardboard, matchboxes, newspapers, and old schoolbooks.

In the mid-1980s, the government loosened its grip on the content of Vietnamese imagery, and by the mid-1990s the country was awash with painters. Today, artists such as Le Hong Thai, Le Quang Ha, and Dinh Y Nhi are respected for their honest depictions of the human condition.

Art galleries command the tourist hubs

For 600 years, the villagers of Bat Trang have mined local resources to turn out renowned ceramic pieces collected by museums worldwide.

of major cities, offering stunning reproductions of European masterworks and prime examples of homegrown art. Because their work is often plagued by copycat piracy, the best Vietnamese painters often keep their most affecting work out of the galleries and instead offer private showings.

CERAMICS

Vietnam's stoneware traditions are rooted in Neolithic times, but it wasn't until independence from China in the tenth century that ceramic arts and crafts really took off. In the 1300s, the country adopted the cobalt blue motif from China that remains prevalent on regional pottery. In the 1400s, after a Chinese emperor imposed a ban on certain "blue and white" motifs, the demand for Vietnam's work grew throughout Southeast Asia and as far away as the Middle East.

Where the Chinese applied a rigid hand to the ornamentation of vases and plates, Vietnamese potters cultivated a more spontaneous touch. They rejected the school that

a colorful enamel overlay, elaborate on the design, and then fire the piece again before glazing.

After Bat Trang's heyday in the 18th and 19th centuries, Bien Hoa, near Ho Chi Minh City, emerged as an important ceramics center. In 1903, the French opened the Bien Hoa College of Applied Arts. Artisans fused Oriental and Occidental techniques in

Beyond popular handicrafts and everyday objects, wood carving achieved its greatest glory in the form of pagoda statuary and sculpted structural beams.

adhered to "one color, one decor" and mixed motifs, combining chrysanthemums and dragons, for example, on the same piece.

In handicraft villages throughout the Red River Delta, especially at Bat Trang and Chu Dau, artisans turned out everyday objects, as well as such ceremonial objects as fluted vases, incense burners, and altar pieces. Active since the 15th century, Bat Trang is renowned for its lightness and the blurred intensity of its interpretations.

Historically, Vietnamese potters did not limit themselves to blue and white or to artistry dyed into the clay before firing. After an initial firing, a potter might add

pieces that won awards at international exhibitions throughout the mid–20th century. Unlike Bat Trang potters, who painted their works, Bien Hoa artisans incised motifs into their wares.

Both Bat Trang and Bien Hoa continue to produce ceramics for the domestic and export markets. The market is glutted with ceramics from all over Vietnam, so much so that it's become difficult to distinguish quality ceramics from cheap imitations.

LACQUERWARE

Travelers to Vietnam see so much lacquerware in tourist haunts that a natural bias

Vaudeville acts are a popular pastime at Ho Chi Minh City's Botanical Gardens and Zoo.

Because lacquer is an excellent defense against rot, the strategy was employed for the preservation of everything from bowls to teeth.

In the 1930s, under the tutelage of French painter Joseph Inguimberty, the medium rose from folk art status to the fine arts and achieved remarkably abstract intensity in the hands of such modern masters as Nguyen Gia Tri and Nguyen Lam.

The art form is an arduous process that requires months to prepare wood surfaces and months more to execute the painting. The techniques involve engraving, inlaying, polishing, and coloration. Usually, the palate is limited to earth tones—black, red, and "cockroach brown"—and to inlays of mother-of-pearl and crushed eggshells.

THEATER

Water puppetry is by far the most commonly encountered of Vietnam's performance arts (see pp. 80–81). In this thousand-year-old spectacle, carved and painted wooden puppets parade, splash, plunge, and whisk over a watery stage, manipulated by puppeteers concealed behind a gauzy scrim and accompanied by an orchestra of traditional musicians.

As distinctively Vietnamese as water puppetry, *cheo* is a form of folk opera that originated in the Red River Delta in the 11th century. Traditionally, the stage was no more complicated than a straw mat unfurled before the village communal hall in an open-air setting. A drum or a gong anchors an orchestra of traditional instruments, including a moon-faced lute and flute. Characters sing and speak in a declamatory style, interpreting familiar stories that often have roots in China, like "The Tale of Kieu." Actors accent the gist of their songs and speech with exaggerated foot and hand gestures. Flex a wrist one way, and the audience clues into a character's lewd intention; flex another way, and the audience understands the symbol for greed. Songs tend to praise women and deride men through sarcasm. The audience often banters with the actors, who are free to improvise and swerve the skit in a direction that feels right for the moment.

Folk opera eventually found its way to the courts, but the aristocracy and scholars denounced the form as vulgar and rejected

inevitably arises against mother-of-pearl on lacquered backdrops. Although lacquerware has been exploited for mass consumption and all too frequently indulges images of archetypes such as boys on water buffalo, the medium is a specialty of East Asia and, in the right hands, a highly evocative means of expression.

Not surprisingly, the tradition derives from earlier Chinese developments and first came to prominence during the Ly dynasty (1010–1225) when an ambassador returned from a trip north with lacquering skills. Lacquer is made from the sap of the *cay son* tree. The white sap is collected at night, as sunlight darkens it.

In the 1400s, the art matured in temples and communal halls (dinh), where jackfruit pillars were coated in vermilion lacquer and polished to a high sheen with pumice stone.

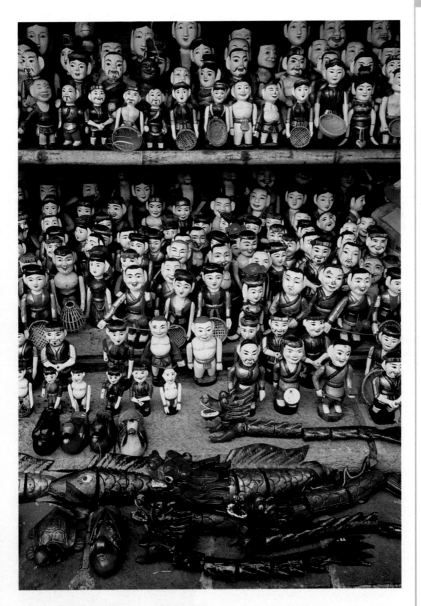

Carved from fig wood, water puppets are painted distinctive hues and coated with lacquer.

it, instead favoring a 700-year-old classical form of theater known as *tuong*. This theatrical style peaked during the Nguyen dynasty and, not surprisingly, reveled in epic tales of war, heroism, and court life in which virtue would inevitably prevail.

Tuong, like cheo, makes no feint toward realism. Red-faced actors are virtuous heroes, white-faced characters despicable villains. Costumes are colorful, and actors' movements are stylized. To embellish certain sentiments, actors peal off their lines in distinctive diaphragm-guttural and mouth-resonating timbres.

In the 1920s, the burgeoning middle class popularized a new form of classical theater known as *cai luong*. Founded in Saigon, cai luong drifted from the Confucian ethos that infused tuong theater and focused on modern stories from pop novels, Chinese swashbucklers, and such Western literature as Molière's *The Miser*.

MUSIC

While pop music, blaring out of karaoke bars and cafés, inundates Vietnam's contemporary soundscape with synthesized, melancholy love songs, deeper musical traditions quietly endure. The country celebrates a number of genres, including court music *(nha nhac)*, ritual gong music of the central highlands, folk songs *(quan ho)*, and chamber music *(ca tru)*. In 2003 and 2005, UNESCO recognized court music and gong culture as Masterpieces of the Oral and Intangible Heritage of Humanity.

Nha nhac means "elegant music," though "elegance" is hardly the right word for this ritual music that accompanied court ceremonies from the 15th to 20th centuries. It's more brash than sublime, freewheeling and sometimes chaotic. As in jazz, each musician orbits a commonly understood core, improvising within limits imposed by a commanding drum until called in by the cadence.

More instrumental than lyrical, the richly textured music evokes the landscape of an Asian ink brush painting. In the imperial era, the Nguyen retained both a light orchestra and a grand orchestra whose instruments consisted of lutes and flutes, clappers, and a broad array of percussion instruments such as a lithophone, cymbals, and hide drums. Today, nha nhac is performed daily in the Royal Theater of Hue's Imperial City.

In the central highlands, villagers bang gongs to commune with the supernatural world when celebrating births, weddings, housewarmings, buffalo sacrifices, and harvests. Groups of 3 to 21 musicians pound the flat or dish-shaped gongs in rhythm or in dialogues. The primitive music is not so much a masterpiece as a curious relic from human prehistory. In the villages of the

Bahnar (Ba Na), E De, and Giarai, the highlanders often perform gong music to welcome guests to the communal house.

The "ho" in quan ho is rooted in the Vietnamese word for "raise the voice." These folk songs originated on the rice paddies of the Red River, where farmers used music to stimulate labor. Ho naturally evolved into songs sung at rest and songs sung at festivals in call-and-response competitions. It is as call-and-response music that quan ho is most frequently performed today.

Monochords and bamboo flutes cushion lyrics that skirt melancholy tones and celebrate love in a more cheerful manner. Quan ho is as rooted to Bac Ninh Province as *pho* is rooted to Hanoi. Bac Ninh remains one

of the premier venues, especially during the Quan Ho Festival, held every year after Tet.

Like quan ho, ca tru chamber music no longer appeals to young people, who complain that it doesn't play well in the modern era. It was born of the Vietnamese aristocracy that matured in the 11th century.

Ca tru singers, who are invariably female, performed in the royal courts, in aristocrats' homes, and, like geishas, for male audiences at special inns. The singer's voice is high-pitched and nasal. Her songs make music of the country's poetry. While she strikes a bamboo clapper to keep time, a musician on a long-necked lute provides the only instrumentation, though a judge in the seats does beat a small drum to express his appreciation for the singer's performance. The audience dispenses bamboo sticks, known as *tru*, to the singer as tokens of their approval.

SILK

While its annual silk output of 2,000 tons (1,800 metric tons) makes Vietnam a relative lightweight in an industry where China spins out 60,000 tons (54,000 metric tons) per year, its gorgeous silks are highly coveted. The village of Van Phuc is the cradle of sericulture, though Lam Dong Province in the central highlands now produces the bulk of the industry's cocoons.

Most of Vietnam's vaunted silk cocoons are processed in small factories near Dalat.

The high-collared *ao dai* silk dress is both an homage to tradition and an everyday garment.

After fattening up larvae on mulberry leaves, silkworm farmers turn over the cocoons to the factories. These are plunked in hot water to loosen a natural glue that binds the wrap. Weavers can tease 2,000 to 3,000 feet (600–900 m) of filament from each cocoon, twisting a half dozen filaments together for a single fiber. These fibers are wound onto spools, dyed in rich colors, and applied to looms, where they are fed through templates to create a variety of motifs.

FASHION

The *ao dai* (long shirt) is a high-collared silk dress that Vietnamese women wear over blousy trousers. The long-sleeved garment flatters the feminine physique, molding to the arms, bosom, and waist, divulging every curve and yet exposing nothing. The dress splits at the hips and flows as far as the ankles in a pair of front and rear panels.

The ao dai made its debut in Hanoi in 1934 as women rebelled against stodgy Confucian mores. In this modern age, women began to indulge in makeup, fancy hairdos, high heels, and—thanks to a reinterpretation of an older style dress by a graduate of the Fine Arts College—the ao dai.

Even more distinctively Vietnamese than the ao dai, the *non la* (conical hat) shelters farmers from tropical sun and monsoon rains like a mobile parasol. The hat is made from latania palm leaves woven about a bamboo lath. ■

The capital of Vietnam since A.D. 1010, Hanoi has washed up on the shores of the 21st century with much of its charm intact. Its bustling Old Quarter, colonial architecture, and age-old traditions kindle one of the most powerful spells in Asia.

Hanoi

**A colonial jailer at
Hoa Lo Prison**

Hanoi

WHILE MUCH OF THE WORLD BOOMED IN THE WAKE OF WORLD WAR II,
Hanoi hunkered down for another half century of hot war, cold war, and privation. This
sacrifice of the city's residents is our boon, for today Hanoi is one of Southeast Asia's
most captivating cities. Its Old Quarter, colonial French districts, thousand-year-old
temples, and spate of lakes can feel more conjured than real.

Motorbike-dominated traffic speeds down Trang Tien in central Hanoi.

The city lies on the Red River in the midst of Vietnam's second most fertile region and at the heart of the country's ancient culture. In the sixth century, during Vietnam's tenure as a vassal state, the Chinese founded a settlement here known as Tong Binh, then Dai La. Ly Thai To, the founder of Vietnam's first great dynasty, moved his capital here in 1010 and renamed the settlement Thang Long ("ascending dragon") after apparently spotting a golden dragon in flight over the river. The Nguyen kings moved the capital to Hue in 1804 and renamed Thang Long Hanoi, but Ho Chi Minh and modern Vietnam's founding fathers anointed the northern city as the nation's capital once again in 1945.

The bulldozer of the 20th century made few incursions here. In the bustling Old Quarter, life spills from the maws of 19th-century tube houses onto splendidly crowded sidewalks and streets. The French districts, with their Indochinese architectural marvels and art moderne villas, evoke a pinch of nostalgia for colonial days, no matter how you feel about colonialism.

The Vietnamese regard Hanoians as more austere than southern citizens, though that distinction is likely to be lost on the typical traveler. As you walk these teeming streets, you'll ward off all-too-frequent

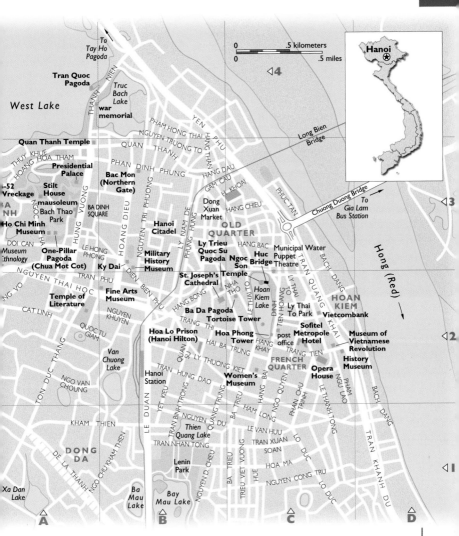

Map labels:
To Tay Ho Pagoda · Tran Quoc Pagoda · Truc Bach Lake · war memorial · West Lake · THANH NIEN · Quan Thanh Temple · THUY KHUE · HOANG HOA THAM · PHAM HONG THAI · YEN PHU · HANG THAN · Long Bien Bridge · Hanoi · NGUYEN TRUONG TO · QUAN THANH · HANG DAU · GAM CAU · Presidential Palace · PHAN DINH PHUNG · Bac Mon (Northern Gate) · H. KHOAI · HANG CHIEU · Chuong Duong Bridge · To Gia Lam Bus Station · B-52 Wreckage · Stilt House · mausoleum · BA DINH SQUARE · Bach Thao Park · HOANG DIEU · NGUYEN TRI PHUONG · Dong Xuan Market · OLD QUARTER · PHUC TAN · Ho Chi Minh Museum · BA NH · DOI CAN · Museum of Ethnology · One-Pillar Pagoda (Chua Mot Cot) · Ky Dai · Hanoi Citadel · PHUNG HUNG · HANG BAC · Municipal Water Puppet Theatre · Ly Trieu Quoc Su Pagoda · Huc Bridge · Ngoc Son Temple · TRAN QUANG · BACH DANG · Hong (Red) · Military History Museum · St. Joseph's Cathedral · NHA THO · Hoan Kiem Lake · HOAN KIEM · NGUYEN THAI HOC · TRAN PHU · DIEN BIEN PHU · HANG BONG · Fine Arts Museum · NGUYEN KHUYEN · Ba Da Pagoda · Tortoise Tower · Ly Thai To Park · Vietcombank · Temple of Literature · CAT LINH · QUOC TU GIAM · TRANG THI · Hoa Lo Prison (Hanoi Hilton) · Hoa Phong Tower · Sofitel Metropole Hotel · Museum of Vietnamese Revolution · TON DUC THANG · Van Chuong Lake · HAI BA TRUNG · HANG KHAY · post office · TRANG TIEN · History Museum · NGO VAN CHUONG · Hanoi Station · LY THUONG KIET · FRENCH QUARTER · Opera House · PHAM NGU LAO · TRAN HUNG DAO · Women's Museum · NGO QUYEN · PHAN CHU TRINH · LE THANH TONG · KHAM THIEN · YET KIEU · TRAN BINH TRONG · NGUYEN DU · HAM LONG · BACH DANG · DE LA THANH · CHU VAN AN · THIEN QUANG · Thien Quang Lake · LE VAN HUU · LO DUC · TRAN KHANH DU · DONG DA · TRAN NHAN TONG · TRAN XUAN SOAN · Lenin Park · BA TRIEU · HOA MA · Xa Dan Lake · Ba Mau Lake · Bay Mau Lake · TRIEU VIET VUONG · HUE · NGUYEN CONG TRU · LO DUC

Scale: 0 – .5 kilometers / 0 – .5 miles

solicitations from motorbike and cyclo drivers. Such earnest friendliness presents a challenge here and all over Vietnam.

Since the late 1980s and the advent of the *doi moi* (fiscal renovation policy), Hanoi's infrastructure has upgraded from the deplorable to the grandiose. Local chefs are whetting the world's appetite with some of the most creative East-meets-West concoctions, yet at reasonable prices. Museums showcase the country's most precious artifacts, covering anthropology, dynastic relics, ethnography, revolutionary history, and the fine arts. You could easily spend a week in this metropolis of three million people and never eat a drab meal or lapse into a dull moment.

A number of sites in the north (see pp. 85–110), including the region's most remarkable pagodas and a number of handicraft villages, are most conveniently experienced in day trips from the capital. ■

Visitor information

✉ Hanoi Toserco, 98 Hang Trong

☎ (04) 928-6631

Business still spills out onto teeming sidewalks in Hanoi's Old Quarter.

A walk around the Old Quarter

Hanoi's Old Quarter is a warren of merchants' shops, still bustling 600 years after dozens of guilds claimed different stretches of road to market their wares. No longer are the Old Quarter's byways a venue for an exclusive kind of product, but the streets are still named for the merchandise *(hang)* purveyed during imperial times. Traditionally, each guild was associated with an outlying village and raised a temple to pray for prosperity.

From **Hoan Kiem Lake**'s north end ❶, walk up Luong Van Can and turn left on Hang Quat (fans). At No. 64, an inauspicious doorway opens onto a **guild temple** ❷, where members worship the mothers of water, mountains, and forests in grottoes at the back of a high-chambered room. The interior is a jam-packed potpourri of anything and everything—a stuffed tiger, a massive ceramic plate—that locals have mustered to appease their patron deities.

Moving north again on Luong Van Can, turn right, then left on Hang Ngang to No. 48, **Ho Chi Minh's residence** ❸ during the summer of 1945. In an apartment on the second floor, Ho invoked the United States' Declaration of Independence while writing a speech he would deliver in Ba Dinh Square on September 2, 1945, declaring independence for Vietnam. As late as 2005, Ho's former landlord still safeguarded his chair and table as a shrine to the national hero.

Farther along, Hang Ngang becomes Hang Duong (sweets). At No. 65 is a typical **tube house,** most of which date from the late 19th century. Because there was so little space in the old city, and because merchants were taxed according to street frontage, they limited the width of their facades to 7 to 10 feet (2–3 m) and instead built 60 to 200 feet (20–60 m) deep, and sometimes as much as 330 feet (100 m). The country's feudal laws limited tube houses to a single story as a way to thwart would-be assassins in second-floor windows, as well as to prevent anyone from looking down on the king.

At 21 Hang Duong is a **merchant's shop** that has remained true to its street's ancient charter. Since the 1930s, but for a hiatus from 1975 to the 1990s, this shop has been peddling an array of candied fruits—star fruits, apricots, tamarinds, etc. Not merely treats, such fruits are also prescribed as remedies by practitioners of traditional medicine.

Straight down Dong Xuan, the street's eponymous **market** ➍ fronts a small plaza where colonial authorities built five tin-roofed halls in 1889. The market was rebuilt in 1990, with its preserved original front, but it burned to the ground in 1994. The present structure dates from 1996. A plaque by the main entrance commemorates a 1947 battle between the French and Viet Minh, during which the latter destroyed four tanks and sustained one hundred casualties.

Walk through the market, turn right on Nguyen Thien Thuat and then left on Thanh Ha (or Hang Chieu) to approach the **Quan Chuong Gate** ➎. Built in 1749, this triple gate is the only surviving example of 16 gates into a Vietnamese citadel the French destroyed at the end of the 19th

---

- 🗺 See area map p. 61
- ► Hoan Kiem Lake
- ↔ 1 mile (1.6 km)
- 🕐 90 minutes
- ► 87 Ma May

NOT TO BE MISSED
- Ho Chi Minh's residence
- Quon Chuong Gate
- traditional two-story home

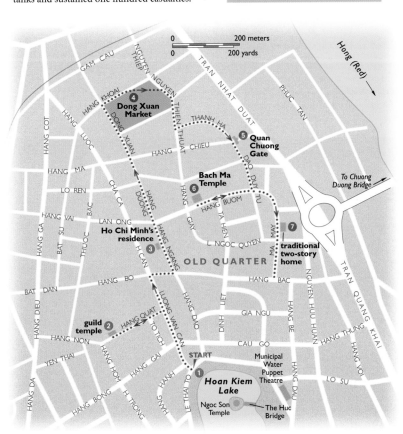

century. The gate was originally named Dong Ha, which means "east gate to the Red River."

On Hang Buom (sail), merchants sold sails for boats that plied the To Lich River, a nearby Red River tributary the French later paved over. At 76 Hang Buom is **Bach Ma** ("white horse") **Temple** ❻ *(closed 11 a.m.–1:30 p.m.)*, one of four temples that protected Hanoi on the north, south, east,

Above: Trendy spots like this salsa bar breathe new life into the Old Quarter. Below: Narrow shopfronts ensured commercial opportunities for myriad tube-house merchants.

and west. Dating from Hanoi's founding in 1010, this eastern guardian is the quarter's oldest structure. The temple is named for the legendary white horse that showed King Ly Thai To how to orient the walls of his citadel. In the middle bay is a red palanquin that porters tote about the quarter on festival days. Bach Ma has been repeatedly renovated, most recently in 2000. Along the inner walls, the names of those who've provided for the temple's upkeep are inscribed on stone tablets, some as old as the temple itself. The streetside inner wall bears tablets from more recent patrons who, for as little as $35, have had their names etched for posterity.

Backtrack along Hang Buom to Ma May. At 87 Ma May is a **traditional two-story home** ❼, built in the late 19th century by a well-to-do practitioner of Chinese medicine. From 1954 to 1999, when the Hanoi People's Committee acquired it, five families lived here. The typical tube house is divided into five bays. The streetside bay is for commerce; the second bay is for storage; the third bay is an open courtyard, also called a heavenly well by the Vietnamese; the fourth bay is for living quarters; and the fifth bay is the kitchen. This house largely follows this plan, though it includes a second story. ∎

Hoan Kiem Lake

HOAN KIEM LAKE IS A MEDALLION OF AVOCADO GREEN water in the midst of the city's hustle and bustle. The northern section brushes the city's storied Old Quarter, while its southern fringe borders the colonial French Quarter. This 25-acre (10 ha) oasis is rimmed by a shady promenade that's abuzz with peddlers and hustlers, lovers, chess players, tourists, and other city folk from dawn to dusk. A stroll around this soulful place, celebrated in poems, songs, and legends of the Vietnamese people, is the best introduction to Hanoi, a city that locals say you can't know unless you know Hoan Kiem.

Hoan Kiem was once part of the Red River, but sometime after 1490, the river shifted, leaving this stretch. The lake achieved legendary status during the 15th-century reign of Le Loi when a giant tortoise seized a sword the emperor had used to oust Chinese occupation forces. Formerly known as Luc Thuy ("green water"), the lake was thereafter dubbed Hoan Kiem ("lake of the restored sword").

The main attraction here is **Ngoc Son** ("jade mountain") **Temple,** on a tiny island at the lake's northern end. Rising from a mound between its two entrance pillars is the five-story **Ink Brush Tower.** The pillars are inscribed with the Chinese characters for happiness and fortune, while the tower itself bears the inscription *Ta Thanh Thien*, which translates as "writing on the clear blue sky."

Now cross the red arc of the **Huc Bridge,** passing the **Dac Nguyet** ("receiving the moon") and **Tran Ba Ding** ("wave-calming") **Pavilions,** which shield the temple from the lake. Beyond Ngoc Son's rather dull entry hall, the middle bay commemorates the temple's three patron saints—Van Xuong, guardian of literature; Quan Vu, master of martial arts; and Lac To, protector of medicinal arts. The innermost bay honors Tran Hung Dao, the 13th-century hero who conducted naval exercises on the lake prior to his celebrated rout of the Mongols.

On an island to the south, the landmark **Tortoise Tower** is reputed to summon the lake's resident giant softshell tortoises. One preserved and gilded 550-pound (250 kg) specimen is on display in the temple. ■

After the Red River shifted its course, this lake remained as a "souvenir" for the people of Thang Long.

Hoan Kiem Lake
- 61 C2
- Entrance to Ngoc Son Temple near Dinh Tien Hoang at Lo Su
- $

French Quarter

French Quarter

🅰 61 C2

HOWEVER YOU MAY REGARD THE FRENCH COLONIZATION of Vietnam, there's much to admire in the magnificent buildings that survived the occupation. In Hanoi, the French clustered their architectural gems in two districts and on two scales—residential and municipal. Even if you have no sympathy for the *mission civilisatrice* (civilizing mission), you can't help but be bowled over and perhaps feel a bit sentimental as you gaze at these buildings.

Start at the south end of Hoan Kiem Lake, where the French started to build shortly after their bombardment of the Hanoi Citadel in 1882. Note the date (1886) in bas-relief at **3 Hang Khay,** perhaps the city's oldest extant colonial building.

Up the east side of Hoan Kiem Lake, you'll pass the **Hoa Phong** ("peaceful wind") **Tower,** a remnant of Bao An Pagoda, which the French razed to make room for colonial structures. Across Dinh Tien Hoang, the whole face of this urban block is consumed by the post office, a rather grim Soviet-inspired edifice sandwiched between two colonial buildings.

Check out the colonial-era octagonal bandstand in nearby **Ly Thai To Park.** In 1954, the Vietnamese named this space Chi Lang Park in honor of Le Loi's victory over Ming Chinese invaders in 1427. In 1986, to recognize India's long friendship, they renamed it Indira Gandhi Park. They recently changed the name again to Ly Thai To Park, in preparation for the city's thousandth anniversary in 2010.

Just off the park on Ngo Quyen is the **Vietcombank,** formerly known as the Banque d'Indochine. This 1930 art deco structure is a no-nonsense symbol of financial stability. Note the fusion of East and West in the Chinese characters for happiness and longevity on the building's upper reaches.

Turn right on Ngo Quyen, and on the right you'll find the former palace of the French governor of Tonkin. Shuttered and idle, this 1918 beaux arts structure with a remarkable many-petaled portico now serves as a **government guesthouse.** Ho Chi Minh slept here for a short time in 1946.

History aside, visitors today would rather book a room across the street at the posh **Sofitel Metropole Hotel** (see p. 246; *15 Ngo Quyen),* whose guests have included Charlie Chaplin, Graham Greene, and Jane Fonda; they all stayed on the second floor of the 1901 colonial building. Note the immaculate white exterior, the Ionic pilasters, balustraded balconies, and green shutters, a hallmark of colonial French aesthetics.

At the end of the block, turn left on Trang Tien to reach the grande dame of the city's French architectural legacy—the **Opera House.** Built between 1902 and 1911, the still active space is the most opulent of Vietnam's three French-designed municipal theaters. After the Japanese surrender in 1945, some 20,000 locals rallied outside the Opera House, and the Viet Minh seized control of the rally—its boldest demonstration of power to that point.

Across town, the city's second French district is anchored by the **Ministry of Foreign Affairs** *(Nuits 1 Ton That Dam St.),* a 1931 blend of European beaux arts and

NHÀ HÁT LỚN HÀ NỘI

Asian aesthetics. Note the two-tiered pagoda-style roofs on the gatehouses that flank the entrance and the vaguely Chinese motifs that bracket the main entrance. Renowned French architect Ernest Hebrard designed the building as the Banque d'Indochine's treasury in the 1920s. He also designed many of the nearby villas; once home to merchants and officials, these now serve as embassies and ambassadors' homes.

Wander the wide sidewalks of this neighborhood to appreciate the architecture from the 1920s and 1930s. Check out the art deco masterpiece at **10 Ba Huyen Thanh Quan,** which centers on a three-story front stairwell with a long glass panel in the middle of the facade. At **10 Le Hong Phong** is a beautifully restored, jazzy art moderne house. The German and Swiss ambassadors live at **47** and **49 Dien Bien Phu,** respectively; the former is bracketed and gabled, with a steeply pitched roof. ∎

A bride borrows the majesty of the colonial Opera House as a backdrop for her wedding photos.

History Museum

61 C2

1 Trang Tien

(04) 825-3518 or
(04) 825-7753

Closed Mon.
& 11:30 a.m.–
1:30 p.m.

$

History Museum

THE HISTORY MUSEUM (BAO TANG LICH SU) IS THE MOST powerful French colonial building in Vietnam, a masterpiece of the Indochinese style developed by Ernest Hebrard in the 1920s and '30s. Fortunately, the museum's exhibits, which survey Vietnamese history from 500,000 B.C. to the 1940s, are a worthy complement to the promise of the building's grandeur.

The History Museum, housed in one of French architect Ernest Hebrard's elegant masterpiece, ranks as Hanoi's best museum.

Upon completion in 1932, the building housed artifacts collected by members of the École Française d'Extrême-Orient, whose emblem is embossed on the upper facade of the octagonal tower. Before entering, stroll past the stelae, stupas, and stone gongs on the building's right side for a broad view of its long, balconied back.

Inside, you'll begin your finely presented, artifact-rich journey in the **Stone Age,** with adzes, axes, and skulls, soon encountering the museum's finest objects, the Dong Son drums. Cast in the Red River Delta as far back as two millennia, these bronze drums were used at festivals, to pray for rain, and to rally for war. Note the four frogs perched on the tympanum of the 2,000-year-old Thon Bui drum. To the left of the drum collection is a 2,000-year-old bronze burial jar from Yen Bai, capped with tiny copulating figures.

Also on the first floor, the **Ly exhibits** include a turtle stela with an upright stone slab, raised by Ly Thuong Kiet at the opening of the Linh Xung Pagoda in 1126, some 350 years before Le Thanh Tong inaugurated this genre of statuary at the Temple of Literature (see pp. 72–75). The **Tran exhibits** glorify the battle of Bach Dang River in 1288 with a panoramic 1979 painting and some of the actual stakes used to impale the Mongol fleet. Also look for the collection of goggle-eyed terra-cotta dragons with Jaggeresque lolling tongues.

Upstairs, sandstone **Cham art** rims the rotunda. Look for a replica of Vietnam's most significant piece of Buddhist statuary, the Thousand-Hand, Thousand-Eye Goddess of Mercy from But Thap Pagoda in Bac Ninh; it's not marked as a replica, a common oversight at Vietnamese museums.

At the end of the hall is a fine collection of **Nguyen dynasty artifacts,** including screens, urns, a mandarin's robes, decree boxes, and colored illustrations of the Nguyen Court done in 1895. ∎

Hoa Lo Prison

HOA LO PRISON IS BETTER KNOWN TO AMERICANS AS THE Hanoi Hilton, a grimly ironic moniker coined by American pilots incarcerated here from 1964 to 1973.

In the 1890s, the French drafted plans for Maison Centrale prison, obliterating a village to make room. Originally built to house 450 inmates, the prison held some 2,000 between 1950 and 1953. A high-rise now occupies most of the former prison grounds, but the old jail's south-east corner was preserved in 1993 as a memorial, primarily to Vietnamese prisoners who struggled against French colonialism.

Beyond the main doorway— through which released POWs were pictured marching in 1973— turn right into **Detention Camp D,** where a diorama and photos detail a colonial-style compound that, at least at this distance, looks more quaint than menacing. One picture on the wall shows inmates fettered to wide benches following a 1908 poisoning incident in Ha Thanh; the actual benches are in the next room. In the aboveground cells, jailers shackled prisoners to sloped concrete slabs; oily stains from inmates' hands and buttocks testify to long periods of detention.

Outside, an excavated sewer canal reveals the means of escape for a hundred prisoners at the end of World War II. On Christmas Eve in 1954, 16 death-row inmates sawed through an iron sewer grate and also escaped.

In two small **POW exhibit halls,** the museum makes its case for how well the North Vietnamese treated U.S. prisoners and displays "detainees'" toothbrushes, sweaters, beds, and even a volleyball net. The room to the right offers photos of POWs.

The **Death Cell sector** holds several cells, one of two guillotines used by the French, and a metal barrel used for water torture. Upstairs, gold plaques memorialize the 1,624 "revolutionary patriots" once held here. ■

Hoa Lo was named for a pottery village the French razed to build this prison in the 1890s.

Hoa Lo Prison

- 🅰 61 B2
- ✉ 1 Hoa Lo, Hoan Kiem District
- ☎ (04) 824-6358
- 🕐 Closed Mon. & 11:30 a.m.–1:30 p.m.
- 💲 $

St. Joseph's Cathedral

**St. Joseph's
Cathedral**
- 61 B2
- 40 Nha Chung
- (04) 828-5967
- Closed noon–2 p.m.

ST. JOSEPH'S CATHEDRAL STANDS AT THE HEART OF HANOI, anchoring the archdiocese's 480 Catholic churches and chapels and 113 parishes. Built between 1882 and 1886, the Gothic church is both an emblem of onetime colonial prerogatives and a vibrant place of worship for the 400,000 Catholics living in Hanoi. Nearby, two notable Buddhist pagodas—Ly Quoc and Ba Da—reflect a lighter countervailing religious influence.

The imposing Gothic facade of St. Joseph's Cathedral, at the end of Hanoi's trendy Nha Tho, evokes medieval Europe.

The facade is bracketed by two square, 103-foot (31.5 m) towers hung with five bells each. Tall stained-glass windows, pointed arches, and high rib-vaulted ceilings call to mind medieval Europe.

The nave is slightly unkempt, a casualty of the tropical climate, but the sanctuary is a glistening spectacle of red- and gilt-trimmed wood carving reminiscent of Phat Diem Cathedral and the imperial aesthetics of Hue architecture. In a further nod to native customs, a red-and-gilt palanquin bearing a statue of the Virgin Mary occupies the left side of the nave.

The cathedral lies at the end of Nha To ("church") Street, a short, trendy thoroughfare of boutiques selling home goods, upscale silks, and other items. Tucked between two shops, a simple doorway opens onto the compound of **Ba Da Pagoda,** whose roots stretch back to 1056 and the reign of Ly Than Ton. In 1946, Ho Chi Minh paid a visit and urged the monks to become engaged in the struggle for independence.

A short distance up Ly Quoc Su from the cathedral is **Ly Trieu Quoc Su Pagoda,** another secluded sanctuary in central Hanoi. In the main temple, long tangerine-colored parallel sentences hang from tall hardwood columns. In the right bay is a gallery of deceased monks, while the left bay contains a gallery of candy-colored statues. ∎

The cathedral was built by a French missionary, Monsignor Puginier, who wheedled permission from the colonial French government to hold two lotteries as fundraisers for the building's construction. Despite its seeming stone-slab edifice, St. Joe's is made of brick faced in cement.

Hanoi Citadel

AFTER HUNDREDS OF YEARS AS THE EXCLUSIVE DOMAIN of Vietnam's imperial elite, followed by a 50-year military occupation, the Hanoi Citadel lowered its bars and opened to the public in 2004. Unlike the Hue Citadel (see pp. 134–135), which remains intact, the 12-acre (5 ha) Hanoi Citadel, located just west of the Old Quarter, is a fragmented collection of monuments that nevertheless manage to collectively convey some of the imperial city's vanished grandeur.

Hanoi Citadel
- 61 B2–3
- (04) 734-2862
- Closed Mon.
- Ky Dai tower: $ (pay to Army Museum). Doan Mon: $

After moving the capital to Hanoi in 1010, Ly Thai To added to the citadel first erected by Chinese governors more than two centuries earlier. Some of the 11th-century building blocks stand outside **Hau Lau,** aka Lau Cong Chua ("palace of the princesses"; *entrance on Hoang Dieu*), where imperial maidens stayed when the Nguyen emperors traveled to Hanoi.

In the 15th century, the Le built the **Doan Mon** ("central gate"; *entrance on Hoang Dieu*), a massive U-shaped stone gate that served as an entrance to the king's forbidden realm. Wooden doors on wooden casters still bar the archways. Inside, archaeologists have unearthed a roadway of flower-shaped yellow bricks that date from the Tran dynasty. The Le also built **Kinh Thien Palace** (*entrance on Nguyen Tri Phuong*), which was demolished in the late 1800s, except for two dragon balustrades on a flight of stairs.

In 1805, the first Nguyen king, Gia Long, added the **Ky Dai** (*28 Dien Bien Phu*), a 60-foot (18.2 m) flag tower with six fan-shaped windows and 36 flower-shaped windows. Visitors can access the tower via the Army Museum for limited city views. Gia Long's son, Minh Mang, razed part of the citadel to spite a Chinese ambassador who, refusing to travel as far as Hue, forced Minh Mang to travel to the "only recognized capital" for his investiture.

The French continued the destruction between 1894 and 1897, sparing the flag tower and the **Bac Mon** ("northern gate"; *entrance on Phan Dinh Phung*), which still bears the cracks and gouges of artillery fire from 1882 when the French sacked the citadel and took command of the city. The gate's mirador is now a temple dedicated to a pair of imperial leaders—Nguyen Tri Phuong and Hoang Dieu—who chose death over submission to French forces in 1873 and 1882. ∎

Gia Long, the first Nguyen king, complemented the work of his imperial predecessors by adding a flag tower to the Hanoi Citadel.

Temple of Literature

Temple of Literature

🅰 61 A2

✉ Entrance at 58 Quoc Tu Giam

☎ (04) 823-5601

💲 $

WHILE OTHER TEMPLES AND PAGODAS INSPIRE DEEPER reverence in visitors, Van Mieu (Temple of Literature) is an extraordinary place of worship and a rarified expression of the Vietnamese esteem for education and literature in general and Confucianism in particular. Between 1070 and 1919, Vietnam's best and brightest gathered in this 14-acre (5.6 ha) compound of temples, pavilions, courtyards, and dormitories to study the master's teachings and strive for recognition as a *tien si* (doctor laureate). Some scholars say the fullest flowering of the philosopher-king was achieved by the Vietnamese.

Modeled after the Temple to Confucius in Qufu, China, the Temple of Literature was founded by King Ly Thanh Tong in 1070. Six years later, his successor, Ly Nhan Tong, established the nation's first university (Quoc Tu Giam, or "school for the sons of the nation") here, initially for the sons of royalty, but progressively for the sons of mandarins and then for any educationally qualified candidate. In the 14th century, the school's most revered rector, Chu Van An (1292–1370), ushered the university into its golden age. In 1484, the school started to honor each of those who achieved a doctorate laureate by inscribing his name and birthplace on a stone stela, a tradition that would continue through 1779.

In a country that has lost so much to war, it's remarkable that the temple has survived. The Mongols or the Ming Chinese could have razed the shrine during their incursions in the 13th and 15th centuries but didn't, out of respect for Confucius.

VISITING THE TEMPLE

The temple complex is an oblong of five courtyards accessed via the **Great Portico,** a two-story, three-gated entrance guarded by two mythical lion-dogs that let the good in and keep the bad out.

A Chinese inscription on the 300-year-old gate reads, "Among the doctrines of the world, ours is the best and is revered by all culture-starved lands."

Upon entering, you are standing in the **Entrance to the**

Way Courtyard, divided into symmetrical halves by a tiled path. Follow the path to the **Great Middle Gate** (Dai Trung Mon), whose name not only refers to its placement between the **Accomplished Virtue Gate** to the right and the **Attained Talent Gate** to the left, but also alludes to a pair of books written by two of Confucius' disciples. The obeisant fish atop the gate represents the deference of students who aspire to become laureates, as carp aspire to become dragons.

The **Great Middle Courtyard** comes next, leading to the **Constellation of Literature** (Khue Van Cac). In 1802, King Gia Long moved the university to Hue, where he built his own temple of

Mandarin exams

Between 1076 and 1919, Vietnam conducted a series of 185 examinations to identify its best minds. To earn a *cu nhan* (bachelor's degree) or become a *tien si* (doctor laureate), candidates had to master the Chinese language and its 5,000 characters. The exams covered philosophy, ethics, poetry, history, and political science; knowledge of exact sciences was unnecessary. Though some scholars retired to their villages as esteemed sages, most went on to join the country's mandarinate. In fact, this largely democratic system was the only road to public office in Vietnam. ∎

The Gate of Great Success leads into the temple precinct.

literature. That loss was ameliorated by the erection of this elegant two-story pavilion. The four wooden circles in each window of the belvedere represent the sun.

The third courtyard is the **Garden of the Stelae,** site of the beautiful **Well of Heavenly Clarity** (Thien Quang Tinh) and home to some of the country's most precious relics. The names of 1,306 doctor laureates, who achieved fame between 1442 and 1779 are inscribed on 82 stelae. Each stela details the name, birthplace, and sometimes age of each laureate; the youngest was 16 years old, the oldest 61, though most scholars earned degrees in their late 20s and early 30s. The laureates also chiseled maxims for the ages, including this nugget from 1442: "Virtuous and talented men are the life breath of the nation."

During the Vietnam War, authorities entombed the stelae and turtles in sand and concrete to guard against bombings. After the war, the stelae lay more or less abandoned, cracked and sinking into the earth, until 1993, when conservationists built eight elevated pavilions to shelter the relics on either side of the Well of Heavenly Clarity.

Constellation of Literature

Great Middle Gate

Attained Talent Gate

Entrance to the Way Courtyard

Great Portico

Accomplished Virtue Gate

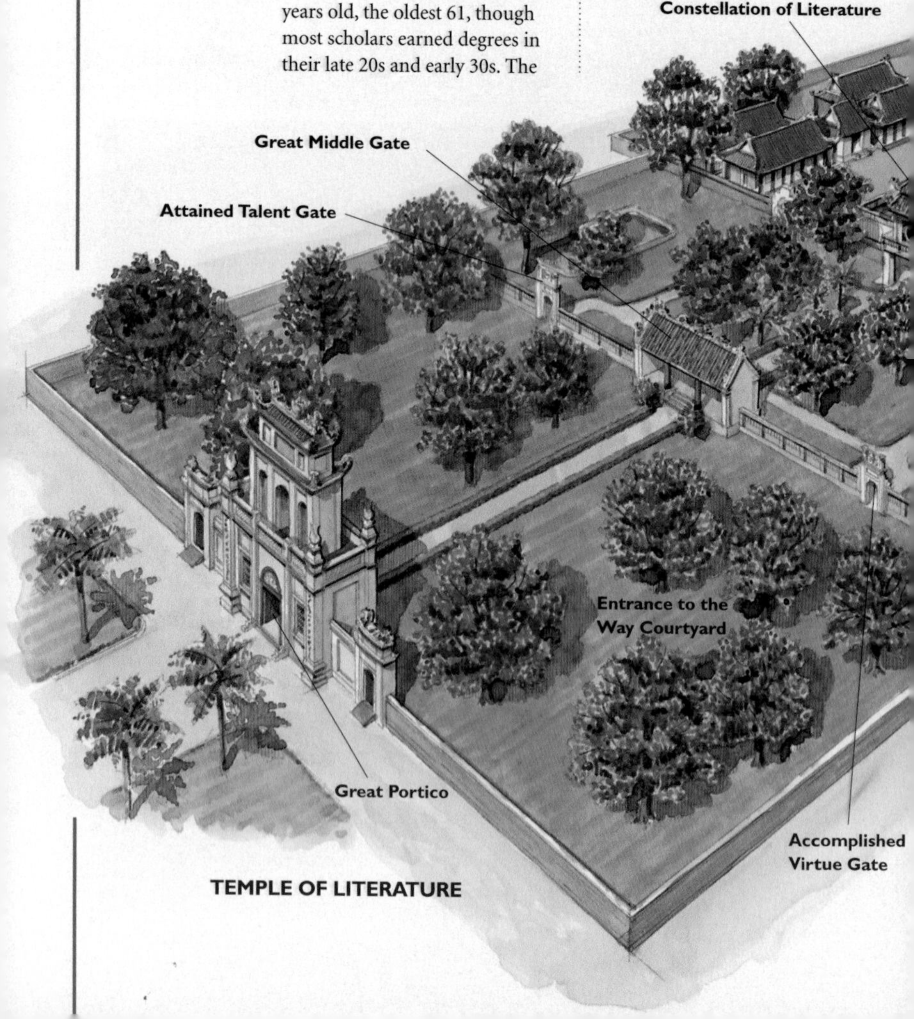

TEMPLE OF LITERATURE

Proceed through the **Gate of Great Success** (Dai Thanh Mon) to the **Courtyard of Sages,** flanked by two rebuilt side buildings where the contemplative spell is broken by shopkeepers' entreaties to buy souvenirs. Across the courtyard is the **Great House**

In 2000, the courtyard was resurrected as the site of **Thai Hoc Hall,** a magnificent ironwood-timbered museum and sanctuary for the veneration of three great Vietnamese kings. It also holds a bronze of rector Chu Van An, Vietnam's preeminent educator. ■

Thai Hoc Hall

Well of Heavenly Clarity

Gate of Great Success

Khai Thanh

Great House of Ceremonies

Courtyard of Sages

Garden of the Stelae

To guard against U.S. bombing during the war, temple overseers entombed the stelae and stone tortoises in sand and concrete.

of Ceremonies, with its nine-pillared bays and the sanctuary where a statue of Confucius—the "Teacher of Ten Thousand Generations," as a placard reads—holds eternal court, flanked by statues of his four closest disciples.

After Gia Long skipped town with the Quoc Tu Giam, the temple's fifth courtyard, **Khai Thanh,** was dedicated as a shrine to Confucius' parents. In 1947, the French accidentally shelled Khai Thanh and destroyed the shrine.

Ba Dinh Square

Ba Dinh Square
🅰 61 A3

ON SEPTEMBER 2, 1945, HO CHI MINH PROCLAIMED INDE-
pendence for the Democratic Republic of Vietnam in a speech at Ba
Dinh Square. Today, a cluster of high-profile attractions—the Ho Chi
Minh Mausoleum, Ho Chi Minh Museum, Presidential Palace, Stilt
House, and One-Pillar Pagoda—are powerful draws for domestic and
foreign tourists alike. The lines are long, and the crowds preclude
much soulful communion with the sites, but this is the holiest place
in modern Vietnam and a required call on any visit to Hanoi.

**Ho Chi Minh's
final resting
place, a site of
pilgrimage**

Ho Chi Minh's preserved body lies
in a refrigerated viewing chamber
in the marble mausoleum that
commands the square. If you're

unfamiliar with his life story, start
your tour instead at the neighboring **Ho Chi Minh Museum**
(*3 Ngoc Ha, tel (04) 846-3752, $*).
The design of this massive, stark
white building is a brutal Soviet
interpretation of a lotus flower.
Opened in 1990, it is the most
prominent of the many Ho Chi
Minh museums scattered about
the country. Its vast interior holds
photos, handwritten letters, dioramas, and yellowed newspaper
clippings. Unfortunately, there's
far more edifice than content.

The museum's third floor is
the most satisfying. Check out the
loom, bed, and hammock supposedly used from 1890 to 1895 by
Ho's father, the prominent Confucian scholar Nguyen Sinh Sac.
Later in life, after a personal rebellion against the ruling clique, Ho's
father became a practitioner of
traditional Chinese medicine. His
pestle and other tools of the trade
are on display. Also look for Ho's
exercise equipment. Other cases
hold a tape recording of his declaration of independence and the
Chinese costume Ho wore in an
escape from Hong Kong in 1930.

HO CHI MINH
MAUSOLEUM
Thus primed, now join the long
line of devotees who've come to
see Ho's remains, laid to dubious
rest in a gargantuan mausoleum

of marble quarried from the Viet Cong redoubt of Danang's Marble Mountains. In a number of revisions to his will, Ho repeatedly included a provision for the cremation of his remains and their distribution at undisclosed spots in the country's north, south, and center. The ruling clique had other ideas. Before Ho's 77th birthday, they secretly dispatched a delegation to Moscow to research the possibility of embalming the venerable leader. After Ho died of a heart attack in 1969, his custodians subscribed to the Soviet template and embalmed their founding father for public display, as the Soviets had enshrined Lenin.

The mausoleum, on the west side of the square, opened on August 29, 1975. To see Ho, join the procession up the steps for a brisk pilgrimage through a series of passages and the vault. Loitering and photos are prohibited. You're in, you look, and you're out.

Inscribed prominently on the mausoleum is Ho's most famous maxim: "Nothing is more precious than independence and freedom." This universal ideal emphasizes Ho's nationalism and echoes the first lines of the declaration that he cribbed from Thomas Jefferson and uttered on Ba Dinh Square in 1945: "All men are created equal. They are endowed by their Creator with certain inalienable rights, among these are Life, Liberty, and the pursuit of Happiness."

MORE SIGHTS

After exiting the mausoleum, wind around the right side to adjacent **Bac Thao** (closed Mon. & Fri. p.m.), home to a cluster of historically compelling buildings. Anchoring the grounds is the **Presidential Palace** ($), an Italianate Renaissance château

built in 1906 as the residence and headquarters of Indochina's governor-general. The palace would become known as the

Uncle Ho

Though Ho Chi Minh is the founding father of modern Vietnam and the preeminent member of the Vietnamese pantheon, he is paradoxically known as Bac Ho (Uncle Ho), not Father Ho, to the Vietnamese. Kindly, avuncular portraits of the man are plastered everywhere in Vietnam, and it is true that Ho never had children of his own. But that's not the principal reason he's known as uncle. In Vietnamese families, children refer to a father's younger brothers as *chu* (uncle) and to the eldest brother as *bac*, which also means "uncle." A father's eldest brother is the most prestigious member of the clan, thus Uncle Ho is a more esteemed form of address than Father Ho. ∎

After coming to power in Hanoi, Ho Chi Minh eschewed residence in this grandiose 1906 Presidential Palace and set up housekeeping in a modest stilt house nearby.

Ho Chi Minh Mausoleum

✉ Entrance at corner of Hung Vuong & Le Hong Phong

☎ (04) 845-5128

🕐 Closed Mon. & Fri., most of Sept., & all of Oct. & Nov.

💲 $

house the ascetically minded Ho declined to live in. Today, it is reserved for affairs of state and is off-limits to the merely curious. Its golden ocher color speaks to its colonial French origins.

Shunning the palace in 1954, Ho moved into three

As its name suggests, the One-Pillar Pagoda is supported by a single pillar (of concrete).

modest rooms in the green-shuttered servants' quarters beyond. Behind the bungalow is a pair of sober-gray cars—a French Peugeot 400 and a Russian M20 Pobieda—that the Vietnamese president used in the 1950s and 1960s. In 1963, expatriate Vietnamese living in Moscow presented Ho the M20 as a gift.

From the bungalow, stroll around the fishing pond to the square-columned **Stilt House** (Nha San) that was Ho's home from the time it was built in 1958 until his death in 1969. The house was a tribute to Vietnam's ethnic minorities, for whom Ho long had a beneficent interest. When he returned to Vietnam from China in 1941, after 30 years abroad, he wore the costume of the Nung minority and lived briefly in a Nung home.

Today, you can climb a stairway beside the Stilt House and view the second-floor interior from a walkway that skirts its length. One room holds Ho's office and desk. A second room contains his straw bed, a fan, clock, radio, hat, and books in a glass display case. The open-air ground floor is where Ho often met with colleagues.

From the Stilt House, the inexorable stream of visitors meanders across the palace grounds past the **One-Pillar Pagoda** (Chua Mot Cot). As quaint as a tree fort, the pagoda is built around a single pillar of concrete, like a lotus flower blooming on a stem. A board inscribed with Chinese characters over the entrance reads *Lien Hoa Dai* ("lotus flower shrine"). The pagoda was the fancy of King Ly Thai Tong, who dreamed that the goddess of mercy, Quan Am, led him to a lotus flower and told the king he would soon be the father of a son. After the king married and sired a son, he erected the pagoda in 1049 in a gesture of gratitude. The French military spitefully razed the original pagoda as they abandoned the country in the 1950s. ∎

West Lake

Mat Dung
Pagoda, on West
Lake

LIKE HOAN KIEM LAKE, WEST LAKE (HO TAY) IS ANOTHER "orphan" of the Red River, formed after the river shifted course and abandoned this vast body of water. The city's oldest pagoda and one of its four guardian temples lie off either side of a short, leafy causeway that divides the larger expanse of West Lake from Truc Bach Lake, a smaller fragment partitioned by road-building locals.

At the south end of the Thanh Nien Causeway, **Quan Thanh Temple** *($)* honors Huyen Thien Tran Vo, guardian of the northern approach to the city of Thanh Long. Established during the reign of Hanoi founder Ly Thai To (1010–1028), the temple is known for its four-ton (3.6 metric ton) bronze statue of Tran Vo, cast in 1677. It stands in the back compartment. Devotees lay money at the statue's base, rub its feet, and anoint themselves with blessings.

More impressive are the wooden substructure and 180 panels of gilded landscapes and Chinese poems inscribed in mother-of-pearl on black lacquered wood. The middle compartment is home to a statue of Trum Trung, the 17th-century artisan who upgraded Tran Vo from wood to bronze and forged a 5-foot (1.5 m) bell that hangs in the mirador of the triple-gate entrance. In the first compartment, two phoenixes flank a frieze of warriors engaged in battle

West Lake
🅰 61 A4

before a temple and a netherworld of mythical beasts.

Farther north on Thanh Nien, a **war memorial** honors an antiaircraft battery that downed a number of planes during the Vietnam War. On October 26, 1967, they shot down an A-4 piloted by future Sen. John McCain, who would endure five years as a POW in the notorious Hanoi Hilton (see p. 69) and later champion the normalization of relations between the U.S. and Vietnam.

Just a little farther along the causeway on the left is **Tran Quoc** ("protecting the nation") **Pagoda,** founded in the sixth century during the reign of Ly Nam De. Its axis extends from an 11-story octagonal tower through a sitting room to the main temple, which holds seven successively higher tiers of bodhisattvas and Buddhas. In the courtyard is a bodhi tree cut from the tree under which Sakyamuni received his enlightenment. ∎

Water puppet skits exalt the folklife—its culture, traditions, and beliefs—of rural Vietnam.

Water puppets

Water puppetry is a thousand-year-old Vietnamese performance art with deep roots in the wet rice agriculture of the Red River Delta. Carved from fig wood, then painted and lacquered to a high, distinctive sheen, the madcap puppets career over a watery stage, enacting skits drawn from Vietnam's treasury of folklore and history.

Historically, the paddy water of a rice field or communal pond of a village served as the stage, but today most shows play out in basins of water at theaters like the Thang Long in Hanoi. Unlike marionettes or hand puppets, which are controlled from above and below, water puppets are manipulated by submerged rods and strings operated by puppeteers standing in thigh-deep water behind the scrim of a stage set. For some of the more rigorous acts, several people work a single pole.

In bygone eras, water puppeteers formed guilds and closely guarded the tricks of their trade from artisans in neighboring villages. They were especially secretive with regard to the complicated apparatus that gives a puppet its dramatic flair. What you don't see in the opaque water are the 10- to 13-foot (3–4 m) bamboo rods with pincerlike tools built into each puppet's float.

Though the puppets can be as tall as 40 inches (102 cm) and weigh up to 35 pounds (16 kg), most are slighter, standing about 16 inches (41 cm) high on a buoyant wooden base or float that plows along just beneath the water's surface. Like marionettes, the lyrically expressive characters are fashioned in linked segments to maximize their agility and flair, especially through the arms and the head, which occasionally flies off in a scripted decapitation!

At the Thang Long (see p. 263), Vietnam's premier venue for the art, a 45-minute performance skitters through 17 episodes drawn from legends and myths, such as Le Loi's return of the magic sword to the golden tortoise of Hoan Kiem Lake and the dance of the four Holy Animals (dragon, lion-dog, phoenix, and tortoise) of Vietnamese mythology. Most sketches also pay tribute to the trials, tribulations, and triumphs of common folk going about their daily business. All the while, a traditional orchestra conducts a clamorous soundtrack while *cheo* (popular opera) singers narrate the dialogue and action in song.

In nearly every water puppet performance, you'll meet a poor farmer who brags about the pedigree of his ducks until one is snatched by a fox that runs up a tree. You're also likely to see boy puppets swimming after frogs and playing flutes from a perch on the back of a water buffalo.

The most beloved character in water puppetry is Teu, an ever smiling buffoon, not unlike the Punch of British puppetry, who wears a loincloth and waistcoat and styles his hair in three tufts that sprout from an otherwise bald pate. Uncle Teu is the sharp-tongued master of ceremonies and something of a clodhopper, though he also stands as a symbol of Vietnam's indomitable spirit.

Above: A system of submerged rods and pulleys control the water puppet's antics on the watery stage. Below: The puppeteers wade out from behind the scrim to salute the audience at the end of a performance.

Popular in the north, water puppetry was seldom practiced in the south until modern times. On special occasions, performances at Thay Pagoda outside Hanoi (see p. 91) are held on a *thuy dinh* (stage set) that's more than 300 years old. ■

The museum
commissioned a
number of ethnic
structures for its
outdoor exhibits,
including this
Giarai tomb.

Museum of Ethnology

THE ART AND CULTURE OF VIETNAM'S ETHNIC MINORITIES
are lionized in this modern museum on the city fringes. The museum
makes for a grand prelude to deeper exploration of the highlands,
or a worthy surrogate if you plan to skip them.

**Museum of
Ethnology**

- 61 A3
- Nguyen Van Huyen
- (04) 756-2193
- Closed Mon.
- $

Allow plenty of time to take in
the stunning open-air exhibitions.
In fact, after paying admission, go
straight out back to the faithfully
reconstructed minority homes.

The path leads first to a fenced
compound of five **Cham houses.**
At the central Thang Lam, peer
inside the *garong,* a wheeled
trunk used to preserve a dead
ancestor's belongings and a box
containing his/her forehead bone.

The most commanding structure is a 62-foot-high (19 m)
Bahnar (or Ba Na) **communal
house,** with pitched roof panels
of 1,800 square feet (170 sq m)
each. Climb any of the four hewn
logs onto the 970-square-foot
(90 sq m) bamboo-planked floor,
where villagers met for war
councils, rituals, and celebrations.
Forty-two Bahnar villagers from
Kontum built the house over a
period of five weeks in 2003.

The 138-foot-long (42 m) **Ede**
(or E De) **house** is remarkable for
both its length (some such homes
near Buon Me Thuot stretch an

astounding 650 feet/200 m) and
its roots in a matrilineal ethnic
group, as underscored by none-
too-subtle breasts carved into
one of the hewn stairways.

As conspicuous are carved
penises on the servants of the
dead who form a wall of statuary
around the nearby **Giarai tomb.**
Four lonely, moping servants
squat at the corners of the tomb,
one a ringer for Frankenstein.

Inside the museum, dioramas
of ethnic activities—funerals,
initiation rites, etc.—accompany
videos of the actual events.
Highlights include a cultural
exploration of Vietnam's ethnic
majority, the Kinh, or Viets, and a
diorama that shows how to make
traditional conical hats from the
blanched leaves of latania palms.

Galleries group the remaining
53 ethnic minorities into linguistic
families. As for artifacts, check
upstairs for the elaborately carved
windows from a Black Thai stilt
house and a water buffalo cart
made by the Cham in 1956. ∎

Other museums

BEYOND THE MUSEUMS OF HISTORY AND ETHNOLOGY, Hanoi boasts a respectful second tier of museums that indulge the fine arts and military history, as well as a suite of lesser museums about women, revolution, and more peculiar subjects. In general, curators are not always precise about authenticity; reproductions are not always marked as such. But these museums make for great rainy day diversions.

The Fine Arts Museum showcases ceramics, stone and wood sculpture, paintings, and patriotic exhibits.

The best of the bunch is the **Fine Arts Museum,** home to the country's foremost collection of ceramics, sculpture, and painting. Much of the art on the ground floor originated in Red River Delta pagodas and communal houses. The wood carvings of village festivals, wrestling, and tiger fighting are masterpieces of the form and may inspire deeper exploration of the delta. Also look for the intricately carved pairs of doors from Pho Minh and Keo Pagodas.

The two upper floors survey fine art painting, which didn't really get off the ground in Vietnam until the 1930s. The lacquer and silk paintings are particularly interesting, but the subject matter bogs down in overt nationalism. Pottery buffs will dig the ceramics gallery in an adjoining annex.

A short walk away, the **Military History Museum** is a tribute to national defense, from the ancient days of arrowheads and breastplates, through the medieval wars with the Chinese and the Mongols, up to the recent wars with the French and the Americans. A highlight is the T-54 tank that crashed through the gates of Saigon's Presidential Palace during the city's fall in 1975. If you plan to visit Dien Bien Phu (see p. 108), be sure to check out the second-floor diorama of the battle site. Outside, a well-preserved UH-1 (Huey) helicopter stands amid assorted aircraft wreckage,

including an F-111 and the upended tail of a downed B-52 bomber.

South of Hoan Kiem Lake, the **Museum of Vietnamese Revolution** *(Map 61 C2, 25 Tong Dan, tel (04) 825-4151, closed Mon.)* is too much space for too little actual stuff. Enlarged, poorly exposed photos clutter the walls and make one wonder why they didn't just publish a book. If you're still curious, look for the Hoa Lo guillotine and a 20th-century lathe used to make weapons.

Nearby, the **Women's Museum** *(Map 61 C2, 36 Ly Thuong Kiet, tel (04) 825-9935, closed Mon., $)* is also long on fervor and wartime relics: a sword used to capture a French lieutenant, an oil lamp used to signal comrades. The highlight is the top-floor gallery of traditional dress worn by Vietnamese women, including ethnic minority styles. ∎

Fine Arts Museum
- 61 B2
- 66 Nguyen Thai Hoc
- (04) 823-3084
- Closed Mon.
- $

Military History Museum
- 61 B3
- 28 Dien Bien Phu
- (04) 823-4264
- Closed Mon. & Fri., & 11:45 a.m.–1:30 p.m.
- $

More places to visit in Hanoi

B-52 WRECKAGE

In the Ba Dinh District, just east of the Ho Chi Minh Mausoleum, the wreckage of a B-52 bomber remains partially submerged in the vegetable green waters of Huu Tiep Lake as a memorial to the antiaircraft gunners who brought the plane down on December 27, 1968. The plane is one of more than a dozen B-52s shot down during the Tet Offensive. Wreckage includes the rear landing gear and mangled undercarriage, which fell into this small lake as the plane broke up over Hanoi. Surrounding the oddly affecting memorial are posh town homes and Ngoc Ha Elementary School.

61 A3 ⊠ From Ba Dinh Square, travel east along Hoang Hoa Tham, turn left at the sign for B-52, and continue about 100 yards (100 m) down the alley to lake.

LENIN PARK

Every morning, Lenin Park swells with aging tai chi practitioners. Joggers circuit the pathways throughout the day, and couples take to the benches in the evenings. Anchoring the park is a large lake, once known as Seven-Hectare Lake. During the colonial era, the site was used as Hanoi's dump.

Hanoi is one of the last places in the world where the founding father of 20th-century communism is publicly lionized.

After the French War, Ho Chi Minh played an active roll in the site's rebirth as a public space.

61 B1 ⊠ Entrance on Le Duan Boul

LONG BIEN BRIDGE

Crossing the Red River, this span was designed by the French architectural firm Dayde & Pill. Three thousand Vietnamese laborers erected the Long Bien Bridge between 1898 and 1902. Its mismatched trestles are graceless reminders of the damage wrought by repeated wartime bombing runs by the U.S. Air Force. Until further restoration, the bridge remains limited to bicycle and pedestrian traffic.

61 C3 ⊠ Spanning the Red River in downtown Hanoi

TAY HO TEMPLE

Founded in the 17th century, this temple sits atop a spit of land that juts into Ho Tay (West Lake), where the mother goddess, Thanh Mau, is said to have revealed herself as pretty girl to a local mandarin, recited poetry, and then vanished. She's enshrined today in a man-made grotto in one of two temple buildings. Check out the 1.6-ton (1.4 metric ton) bronze bell, an industrial stove in which to burn paper offerings, and banyan roots that stretch across the temple grounds. Walking in, you pass by stalls purveying temple offerings and food and a string of seafood restaurants. You enter through a three-entrance gate roofed with tube tiles. The panels on either side depict the meeting between Phung Khac Khoan and Goddess Lieu Hanh. Divided into three sections of worship, the temple contains many valuable objects, including panels and frescoes from the 19th century. Worshippers flock here on the 1st and 15th of each lunar month in the hopes of decreasing risk and receiving good fortune.

61 B4 ⊠ Beyond the Sheraton Hotel on Xuan Dieu, turn left on Dang Thai Mai. The pagoda is at the end of the road, 2.5 miles (4 km) from downtown. ∎

From the limestone wonders of Ha Long Bay to exotic highland villages to the ancient seat of Vietnamese civilization on the Red River Delta, the north of Vietnam is diverse, culturally deep, and scenically marvelous.

The north

A shrine in bas-relief at one of Ha Tay's pagodas

The north

BEYOND HANOI, THE RED RIVER FLOODPLAIN IS A SKEIN OF RIVERS, tributaries, canals, and dikes. Vietnamese culture began percolating here 3,000 years ago and continues to do so today as archaeologists unearth bronze drums, funeral pirogues, and other relics of ancient civilization. To the northeast, Ha Long Bay lives up to the wonders promised by sirens who sing its song in Hanoi's traveler's cafés. To the north and northwest, the interior is rumpled by fantastic limestone and granite mountains inhabited by some of Asia's most colorfully costumed ethnic minorities.

For all of Hanoi's charms, the area's most compelling pagodas are nestled among the limestone mountains about 20 miles (30 km) from the city proper. The most popular day trip takes in the Perfume Pagoda (Chua Huong). Although its architecture and statuary don't match those of other nearby pagodas, its setting and grottoes are astonishing. In Bac Ninh,

But Thap Pagoda holds Vietnam's best examples of Buddhist art, from both an architectural and statuary standpoint, though it stands amid a lackluster landscape. Thay and Tay Phuong Pagodas occupy more picturesque surroundings.

Be sure to visit the enticing handicraft villages of Van Phuc and Bat Trang, even if they don't live up to

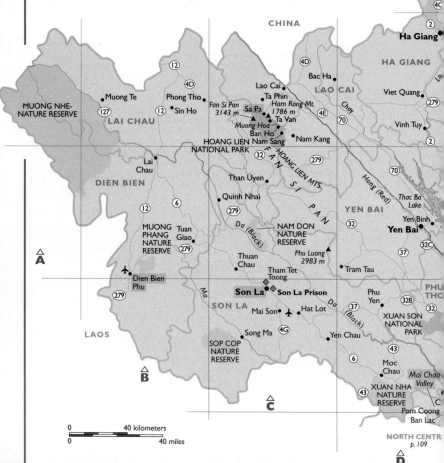

NORTH CENTR
p.109

preconceived notions of what a village should look like. Day trips from Hanoi access all of these villages and pagodas, and you can visit them independently, though it's far easier and more rewarding to hook up with a guide or a tour.

With its fascinating communal house and chockablock French architecture, Haiphong is an interesting gateway to the spectacular Ha Long Bay. The world paid scant attention to this region as Vietnam spent decades mustering resources for war, but Ha Long's star is now rising. Skip the hotels and spend your nights on the water in any of a selection of air-conditioned boats.

Due north from Hanoi, the limestone karst mountains east and west of Cao Bang make for some of Vietnam's most fantastic inland scenery. For the best perspective, ply the region's blue highways, preferably by motorbike, where one awe-inspiring vista after another will rise up before you. The most popular sights are the Ban Gioc waterfalls and the Pac Bo Cave, though again, the journey is the destination.

In the far northwest, Sa Pa is a trekker's mecca. Though slightly tarnished by its popularity, the region remains among Vietnam's top five travel destinations, and deservedly so. Its massive granite mountains shelter ethnic minority villages whose costumed denizens look like they've walked through a time warp from the 18th century. Go see them now, as those wardrobes may not be long for this world. ∎

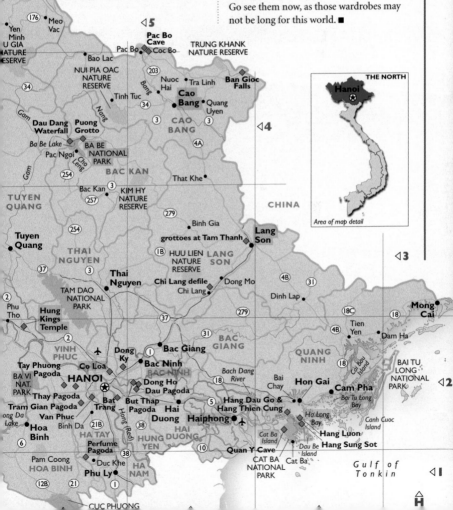

Perfume Pagoda

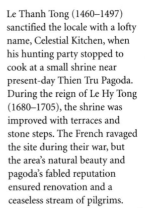

Perfume Pagoda

🗺 87 E2

✉ 38 miles (62 km) SW of Hanoi via Hwy. 6 and Rte. 21B. Boats to the pagoda *($)* travel up Swallow Tail Stream from Ben Duc Wharf in Duc Khe.

💲 $

Perfume Pagoda

THE PERFUME PAGODA (CHUA HUONG) IS A COMPLEX OF 16 separate halls, temples, and grottoes amid a craggy karst landscape 38 miles (62 km) southwest of Hanoi. No other landscape in Vietnam so closely mirrors the preternatural world of a Chinese ink painting. Nor is any pagoda as popular. International travelers flock to the site on daily outings from Hanoi, while domestic pilgrims swarm the pathways and halls during a 300-year-old festival held annually from the 6th to 15th day of the first lunar month (January or February).

Impressed by the area's natural beauty, the great Vietnamese King Le Thanh Tong (1460–1497) sanctified the locale with a lofty name, Celestial Kitchen, when his hunting party stopped to cook at a small shrine near present-day Thien Tru Pagoda. During the reign of Le Hy Tong (1680–1705), the shrine was improved with terraces and stone steps. The French ravaged the site during their war, but the area's natural beauty and pagoda's fabled reputation ensured renovation and a ceaseless stream of pilgrims.

Three clusters of pagodas and shrines are grouped along two tributaries of the Day River. By far, the most popular route ascends Swallow Tail (Yen) Stream. From Ben Duc Wharf in **Duc Khe,** female paddlers ferry tourists 2 miles (3 km) up this shallow tributary in aluminum skiffs amid an increasingly beautiful karst landscape.

On the way, you pass the **Trinh Temple,** dedicated to a legendary general under the sixth Hung king who saved the Van Lang Kingdom from Yin invaders. You'll also pass beneath a red bridge, from which a road leads up to a pair of pagodas that form one of the pagoda clusters.

The ferries drop passengers at a wharf below **Thien Tru Pagoda.** It's mostly new since the French War. The Triple Gate was built in 1989, and the beau-

tiful bell tower inside was rebuilt in 1986. Inside the main sanctuary, a pair of bas-relief panels of netherworld monkeys and devils are worth a look.

From Thien Tru, you can either walk 2 miles (3 km) up to Huong Tich, one of Vietnam's most spectacular grottoes and the most attractive element in the pagoda complex, or you can ride up by cable car (*$*).

If you skip the hike, you'll miss a pair of mildly interesting pagodas. A little more than a kilometer from Thien Tru, a small path to the left leads to the pagoda of **Giai Oan** ("absolution") and its collection of gilded Buddhist statuary in a niche of limestone. A narrow crevice to the right opens into a shallow chamber with some polychromatic statuary.

Back on the main path to Huong Tich, you'll reach **Cua Vong,** a 200-year-old shrine to the green-robed Holy Mother of the Mountains and Forests, where Ho Chi Minh stopped for lunch one day in 1958.

As the climb to Huong Tich wears on, the Buddhist faithful occasionally seek relief by prayerfully clasping their palms to greet other pilgrims with the phrase *Nam Mo A Di Dat Phat* (Glory to the Buddha Amitabha).

The vast maw at **Huong Tich's** entrance is singularly marvelous. A 1770 inscription of Chinese characters by a Trinh lord describes Huong Tich as the "most beautiful grotto in the southern sky." The entrance is said to resemble the mouth of a dragon; the giant stalagmite inside is the dragon's tongue.

Deeper inside this grotto, dedicated to Quan Am, two more stalagmites serve as altars for women praying for children.

Would-be mothers pat the rocks and mumble, "Come along with me my little boy (or girl)."

After a survey of the grotto's statuary and typically fanciful limestone formations, go back down the path and make yourself climb the far less arduous stairway to the grotto of **Tien Son** ("fairy mountain"), 650 feet (200 m) north of Thien Tru. The cave entrance is an alluring triangular-shaped passageway of runnelled stalagmites, some of

which sound like drums when beaten. The French torched a 1903 pagoda here during the war, as well.

Upon your return to Ben Duc, be prepared to tip the ferry boat women. They'll ask for one, and they'll aggressively haunt you if you don't pony up.

On the return to Hanoi, remain alert for the great numbers of communal houses (*dinh*) off the right side of the dike road. If you're traveling independent of a group, make a point of detouring for the two dinh in **Binh Da** village, about 12 miles (20 km) southwest of Hanoi. ∎

Above: Devotees have come to kneel before Huong Tich's statuary for more than 200 years. Left: Mystical Huong Tich Grotto is the premier attraction at the Perfume Pagoda.

A Bat Trang artisan brings forth a rice bowl from the lump of clay on her pottery wheel.

Handicraft villages

HUNDREDS OF HANDICRAFT VILLAGES DOT THE NORTH, specializing in a diversity of trades—ceramics, silk weaving, wood-carving, woodcut printing, hatmaking, bronze casting, and others. Some craftspeople, especially those closer to Hanoi, welcome tourists into their cottage industry workrooms and, of course, into their shiny new showrooms.

Handicraft villages visitor information

✉ Hanoi Toserco, 18 Luong Van Can, Hoan Kiem District, Hanoi

☎ (04) 828-7552

The best handicraft villages, Bat Trang and Van Phuc, are also the closest to Hanoi. On the Red River 9 miles (14 km) southeast of town, **Bat Trang** ("bowl workshop"; *map 87 E2)* is a 500-year-old village of thatched huts whose pieces are among the collections at the Louvre. Reaching its artistic peak in the 18th and early 19th centuries, Bat Trang was nearly razed in the 1950s during construction of an irrigation works. It has since become Vietnam's best-known pottery center. A narrow road lined with shops and pottery works winds a half mile (1 km) through the village to an open-air ceramics market. The black paddies stuck to brick walls about town are a coal-clay mix used in the kilns.

For a thousand years, villagers in **Van Phuc** *(Map 87 E2)*, 7 miles (12 km) southwest of Hanoi, have been harvesting silkworm cocoons from waffle-like brackets of mulberry branches. One of the best silk workshops is Trieu Van Mao's, a four-generation family operation. Watch their looms weave an industrial choreography of cogs, belts, and paperboard templates.

Northeast of Hanoi, the road to **Dong Ky** *(Map 87 E2)* is lined with four- and five-story homes above showrooms that traffic heavily in garish dragon-backed furniture. Beyond its open-air wood market, the village sawmills churn out furniture. Stop to watch the process, as craftspeople chisel and inlay mother-of-pearl motifs.

Only a few houses actively make woodcut prints in **Dong Ho** *(Map 87 F2;* see p. 51), 22 miles (35 km) east of Hanoi in Bac Ninh Province. Among the most famous is Nguyen Dang Che. ■

Ha Tay pagodas

THAY PAGODA AND TAY PHUONG PAGODA IN HA TAY, A suburban province of Hanoi, display a feast of Buddhist statuary art in lovely limestone landscapes and offer the best one-two pagoda punch in the country. Farther afield in Ha Tay, the venerable Tram Gian Pagoda used to generate a sublime aura in an equally attractive setting, but ill-advised renovations have ruined the atmosphere.

Nineteen miles (30 km) west of Hanoi in the village of Sai Son, **Thay Pagoda** was built in the 11th century at the base of a limestone outcrop. The pagoda forged enduring fame as the *Thay,* or master's pagoda, under the stewardship of the legendary Tu Dao Hanh, a founding father of water puppetry. Water puppet shows are still held during holidays and festivals on a specially built stage in the center of a pond.

The complex features three parallel pagoda buildings that resemble the Chinese character Tam ("three"). Before entering, pause by the singular kidney-shaped stone perched on a lung-shaped pedestal—there to draw badness from the bodies of passersby. The inscribed Chinese characters offer well wishes for health and happiness.

The outer section, used for ceremonies, is a celebration of Tu Dao Hanh, a statue of whom in the middle bay is draped in yellow robes. In the left bay, a pair of Cambodian ambassadors bow at the feet of Ly Than Tong, a 12th-century king believed to be a reincarnation of Tu Dao Hanh. In the right bay, a closed altar house shelters a macabre statue of Hanh, allegedly fashioned from the ashes of his bones and limestone mineral deposits. The jointed statue was rigged to stand on the one festival day of the year when the door is

Thay Pagoda's Thuy Dinh stage has been hosting water puppetry performances for centuries.

Ha Tay pagodas
▲ 87 E2
Visitor information
✉ Handspan Adventure Travel, 23 Phan Chu Trinh, Hanoi
☎ (04) 933-2377

Getting there
Hire your own car and driver to visit Thay and Tay Phuong Pagodas.

Children exit a weathered stone gate between parallel sentences at a Ha Tay pagoda.

opened. However, a Tay Son general halted the spectacle 200 years ago, arguing that so lofty a saint as Tu Dao Hanh should not stand for commoners. Don't miss the two 16th-century phoenixes, each carved from a single chunk of jackfruit wood.

The middle pagoda features another gallery of impressive statuary. The corpulent guardians of Buddhism *(ho phap)*—known to the Vietnamese as Mister Sternness and Mister Benevolence—date from the 17th century. You'll also find the eight diamond-king bodhisattvas *(kim cuong)*, fierce protectors of the meditating Buddha.

The third part is largely open space where monks teach.

Four miles (6 km) farther west on Tay Phuong mountain in Yen village, **Tay Phuong Pagoda** was established sometime between the third and sixth centuries A.D. In the ninth century, a Chinese proconsul and wizard named Cao Bien refurbished the pagoda to serve as a symbolic jail for a dragon

that dwelled within the hill and that might otherwise escape and empower the Vietnamese people. Its present arrangement, also laid out according to the Chinese Tam character, took shape in the 17th and late 18th centuries, with Tay Son dynasty renovations.

In the first hall, or Hall of Prostrations, eight armor-clad diamond kings share tight quarters under a double-tiered roof—common to all three of the pagoda's halls and to Buddhist architecture in general.

In the middle hall, or shrine, terraced altars hold two of the pagoda's 18 arhats, as well as a masterful depiction of the Buddha on Snowy Mountain. The shrine is lit by circular *thi* windows, a form of architecture that plays on both visible and corresponding invisible components. Take note of the truss of ironwood columns on blue stone pedestals, with carved mulberry and banyan leaves, dragons, phoenixes, and tiger heads.

In the back hall, or sanctuary, the remaining arhats provide the pagoda's most interesting congregation of statuary. These statues date from a renovation in the early 20th century. Each represents a story in the annals of Buddhism. Look for Hiep Ton Gia, the old man who began studying Buddhism late in life and vowed never to lay down until he had learned the entire doctrine.

Tram Gian Pagoda, 12 miles (20 km) southwest of Hanoi in Tien Lu Village, is laid out in the *noi cong ngai quoc* style, notable for flanking corridors that frame interior halls. The 800-year-old pagoda's picturesque setting and buildings have long been regarded as a high-water mark in Buddhist architecture, and the bell tower remains captivating, but the modern-day interior renovations are deplorable. ∎

Bac Ninh pagodas

Bac Ninh pagodas
 87 F2
Visitor information
✉ Bac Ninh Tourist, Ninh Xa
☎ (0241) 821-296 (no English spoken)

BAC NINH IS A SUBURBAN PROVINCE OF HANOI AND ONE of three ancient centers of Buddhism in Vietnam. The province is home to the country's oldest pagoda, Chua Dau, though a recent renovation has erased the patina of its venerable charm. Nearby, But Thap Pagoda is a masterpiece of architecture and contains the finest ensemble of Buddhist statuary in the country.

On an inspection tour of Ninh Phuc Tu Pagoda in 1876, Emperor Tu Duc dubbed the 230-year-old pagoda **But Thap** ("pen stupa") for its 45-foot (13.5 m) octagonal tower that resembles a pen. From the triple-gate bell tower, a succession of seven houses aligns on a 110-yard (100 m) axis flanked by two corridors of 26 columned bays.

From the **Incense Burning House,** a covered gallery leads to the treasures of the **Superior House,** including the Thousand-Hand, Thousand-Eye Goddess of Mercy, a true masterpiece of Vietnamese wood carving, with 11 faces, 994 arms, and 994 eyes. A trinity of carved Buddhas *(Tam the)* reigns over the hall from the central bay, flanked by a fascinating gallery of emotionally expressive, polychromatic Buddhist deities.

Across an arched stone bridge, a nine-story lotus tower rises from the 17th-century **Virtue Hermitage.** This tower rotates on its axis like a prayer wheel, enabling contemplation of bas-relief depictions of the Pure Land. Outside the right corridor, the bell tower honors the Zen master who inspired the pagoda's founder. Stone balusters girdle the first of its five stories, setting off engraved scenes of fighting tigers, dragons, buffalo, clouds, and a Zen master.

Not far from But Thap in Dau, Thuan Thanh District,

Dau Pagoda is Vietnam's oldest pagoda, probably built in the third century A.D. It once was the most important center of Vietnamese Buddhism. Its three-story Hoa Phong tower houses an 1817 bronze gong and a 1793 bell, accompanied by the statues of followers of the goddess of mercy. ■

Seven sacred structures align along the central axis at But Thap Pagoda.

Haiphong

Haiphong

⛰ 87 F2

**Visitor
information**

✉ Haiphong Tourism,
44 Lach Tray

☎ (031) 852-720

HAIPHONG, VIETNAM'S THIRD MOST POPULOUS CITY AND largest port, is the gateway to Ha Long Bay. The city suffers from this proximity, as most travelers skip its temptations to take in nearby natural wonders. Its own lures are cultural and include a communal hall *(dinh),* a fascinating pagoda, and a city center replete with French colonial structures in various states of ruin and repair.

Haiphong's French colonial Opera House is one of three in Vietnam.

During the French and Vietnam Wars, Haiphong took it on the chin. The French shelled the city in late 1946, killing many civilians, and Nixon had its harbor mined in 1972 to strengthen his position at the bargaining table. Today, the city offers increasingly better accommodations and a contagiously energetic spirit.

If you haven't visited any of Vietnam's 700 dinh, most of which lie scattered around the Red River Delta, be sure to visit the **Hang Kenh Communal House,** on Hang Kenh near the city center. The temple is 106 feet (32 m) wide and 43 feet (13 m) deep, with a roof that sags from the weight of its thousands of tiles. The central bay honors Tran Hung Dao, who routed the Mongols at the nearby Bach Dang River in the 13th century. Though Vietnam Tourism dates the dinh to 1856, a caretaker claims it stretches back to 1718. Regardless, the 308 carved wooden dragons on the building's ironwood truss are well preserved.

Across town, at 121 Chua Hang, the traditional **Du Hang Pagoda** (aka Phuc Lam Pagoda) includes flourishes from an idiosyncratic monk named Thong Hanh, who dwelt here in 1899. Ten marble statues of distinctive, slightly Gothic arhats ring a pond that percolates with the gulpings of fat carp. Look among the statues for the exultant bronze Happy Buddha, arms raised in a touchdown-like celebration. Behind it stands Thong Hanh's bell tower. In the main temple, pillars split the central bay into five segments, each adorned by a successively higher altar and a wonderful assortment of religious statuary.

A long sweep of park dominates the **city center.** The French legacy is apparent in much of the surrounding distinguished architecture. Off one edge of the park on Tran Hung Dao is Haiphong's lavish **Opera House,** restored in 2005. ∎

Cat Ba Island

Cat Ba is a popular seaside resort among Hanoians.

CAT BA IS ALSO THE NAME OF THE TOWN AND NATIONAL park on this karst isle at the southern end of Ha Long Bay. Historically a fishing village, the town has spruced up for tourists with a wall of new five- and six-story waterfront hotels. While a few boat operators offer tours of the bay out of Cat Ba, most cast off from the town of Ha Long.

From the town of Cat Ba, a paved road winds through a scenic narrow valley in the mountainous interior. Just past Hai Son, a stairway climbs to **Quan Y Cave** (*$*). In 1960, the Vietnamese and Chinese teamed up to build a concrete hospital compound in this spacious cave. The groundskeeper is a veteran in his 70s named Vu Dinh Khoi who spent a decade working in the cave and now guides visitors, rendering placenames in English—kitchen, surgery, swimming pool, movie theater. In the wonderfully acoustic conference room, Khoi will sing his rendition of "Vietnam, Ho Chi Minh." Settle tour rates in advance to avoid being overcharged.

Quan Y is the most interesting of a number of limestone caves throughout **Cat Ba National Park,** a 24,000-acre (9,800 ha) reserve that covers about a third of the island. The rugged hills rise as high as 1,000 feet (300 m) and shelter the world's last troop of golden-headed leaf monkeys.

The park entrance lies along the island's main north-south artery, 9 miles (14 km) north of Cat Ba. From here, a short trail summits 660-foot (200 m) **Ngu Lam,** where a watchtower offers park vistas. A more ambitious four-hour trek through the park leads past Frog Lake to the village of **Viet Hai,** from which a ferry returns to Cat Ba.

You'll find several appealing beaches along a promontory east of town. Tourism boosters have run a precarious boardwalk along the cliff, while stairways and paths lead to so-so offshore vistas. ■

Cat Ba Island
Ⓜ 87 G2
Visitor information
✉ Haiphong Toserco, Tran Quang Khai, Hong Bang District, Haiphong
☎ (031) 745-415

Getting there
Every morning hydrofoils leave from the pier at the end of Cu Chinh Lan in Haiphong for a 45-minute sprint down the Bach Dang River to Cat Ba.

Cat Ba National Park
✉ Hai Son
☎ (031) 888-741
Ⓢ $

Ha Long Bay
🅜 87 G2
**Visitor
information**
✉ Vietnam Tourism,
Ha Long Bay Hotel,
Ha Long, Bai Chay
☎ (033) 845-210

Getting there
Most tour boats operate
from the piers in Ha Long.
From Ben Beo tourist port
in Cat Ba, one or two
junk ferries depart for Ha
Long every morning.

Ha Long Bay

HA LONG BAY, WITH ITS SWEEPING SEASCAPE OF CRAGGY karst towers that rise hundreds of feet from jade-green bay waters, is a spellbinding wonder and a must-see destination on any trip to Vietnam. Nearly 2,000 distinct islands stud this 620-square-mile (1,553 sq km) offshoot of the Tonkin Gulf. In 1994, UNESCO designated 174 square miles (434 sq km) of the bay a World Heritage site, a long overdue accolade for one of the world's most stunning natural marvels.

According to legend, the bay formed when a dragon plunged into the sea, whipping its tail from side to side in a frenzy that carved the region into a grand archipelago. (The name Ha Long means "dragon descending.") Geologists tell a different story,

of course. Over the past 230 to 280 million years, rainwater and the ocean have eroded the landscape into an array of towers, known as *fenglin*, and clusters of conical crags, known as *fengcong*. At the same time, rising and falling tides have chiseled notched bands into their karst bases, lending a tottering appearance to these primeval expressions of rock. In 2000, UNESCO again inscribed Ha Long Bay on its World Heritage List, citing its geomorphology as a unique asset worthy of mankind's preservation.

Humans moved into the bay area some 25,000 years ago, and several cultures—the Soi Nhu, Cai Beo, and Ha Long—evolved here during the prehistoric era. In 1149, a trading port was established on the coast at Van Don. By the 15th century, when Emperor Le Thanh Tong extolled the bay in verse, the region was firmly rooted in the Vietnamese imagination.

VISITING HA LONG BAY

The bay is best approached from Ha Long town, a Janus-faced port split by the Cua Luc River and linked by an impressive new suspension bridge in 2006. On one side of the bridge, **Hon Gai** is a grimy exporter of coal; on the other side, **Bai Chay** is a gussied-up importer of tourists that sports a bank of new waterfront hotels. The bay is also accessible from Cat Ba (see p. 95). While technically an island within Ha Long Bay itself, the latter is so vast, it can feel tangential to the archipelago.

Although Ha Long tourism authorities make much of the islands' grottoes—several of which are admittedly striking—the preeminent Ha Long experience is waterborne. It's about being afloat as much as possible amid a landscape as fantastic as one dreamed up by a five-year-old with a box of Crayolas. Many travelers take to the bay on day-tripping tour boats. For a richer experience, book a night's passage on the *Emeraude* (see p. 249), a faithful replica of a 1920s French paddle wheeler that crystallizes the romance of colonial Indochina in three stories of terrace-topped splendor. For a more indigenous, if less luxurious, overnight cruise, sign on for a tour aboard one of the junks that suckle up to the tourist pier at Bai Chay.

A fleet of junks and a replica colonial French paddle wheeler host travelers on overnight cruises in the bay.

A junk's bamboo-ribbed sails aren't necessary for propulsion, but they do add a romantic cultural note to a bay excursion. Overhead, eagles soar and dive, plucking fish from a population of a thousand different species. Though eagles seem as common as butterflies, the islands' resident langurs and other monkeys are more elusive.

zon or as boundaries to sight, towering up on all sides like the walls of an arena.

SIGHTSEEING

Tours afford plenty of time for the most popular pastime— mere gazing—but for those who crave the particular, there's no shortage of sights. In recent years, the overnight tour boats have

The typical tour of Ha Long cruises past several waterborne fishing villages.

But animals aren't the highlight of Ha Long Bay. One comes here for the fantastical karsts, frizzed with short, gnarled vegetation and sculpted over the eons into shapes that resemble swans, kettles, toads, saddles, monsters, incense burners, and other likenesses. The most dramatic towers are six times higher than they are wide. More breathtaking than individual formations, however, are the karsts from a distance—as a line on the hori-

lapsed into a greatest hits collection of stops, so you'll have to shop around for boats willing to ply lesser known waterways. Whatever your itinerary, be sure to visit **Hang Sung Sot** ("grotto of surprises"), generally regarded as one of the two most beautiful caves in the bay. This cave opened to tourists in 1995, though the French pioneered the route for Westerners in the early 1900s, as evidenced by graffiti painted on and inscribed in the limestone.

A trail leads a half mile (800 m) through the 135,000-square-foot (12,000 sq m) cave, threading through three chambers, each larger than the previous. Grotesque stalagmites and stalactites reveal the usual suspects—turtles, junk sails, monkeys, a Happy Buddha, the roots of molars—and one "special part" of a dragon, luridly lit in red and aimed at a hole in a pocked ceiling of smoothbore craters. The third chamber is breathtakingly cavernous and, while not rivaling Phong Nha (see pp. 118–119) as Vietnam's most magnificent, it does play a worthy second fiddle.

Off the overnight boat track, **Hang Thien Cung** ("grotto of the heavenly palace") challenges Sung Sot as Ha Long's most beautiful cave and offers up a stone breast in answer to Sung Sot's "special part." In **Hang Dau Go** ("grotto of the wooden stakes"), 13th-century warrior-hero Tran Hung Dao stockpiled the legendary iron-tipped wooden stakes he'd later use to impale the Mongol fleet.

At **Hang Luon,** tenders from the bigger boats and, better yet, kayaks, skim the waters beneath its low-slung roof to emerge in a lagoon of sheer-walled majesty that contains some of the bay's best underwater coral gardens. Salt water's corrosive influence also gouged six lagoons at **Dau Be Island.** At **Than Tho Island,** where flying squirrels sail over riotously vegetated slopes and monkeys hoot from unseen perches, legend has it that two star-crossed lovers drowned together rather than submit to arranged marriages. Their act of love imbued these waters with a magical potency, and in past ages, only those borne of royal parentage were allowed to swim here.

Though beaches don't come naturally to these karst islands, swimming is a pastime to be indulged, as the high saline content supports even the leanest bathers with remarkable buoyancy. Depths range from 25 to 40 feet (8–12 m) and can be as shallow as 15 feet (5 m) at many moorings. Most boats dip ladders over their sterns for swimming and, in this

land of limited liability, encourage those brave enough to jump in from the boat's rooftop.

While the beach at **Titov Island** looks suspiciously man-made, the real thrill here comes at the top of a 420-step climb to the summit for a 360-degree, postcard-perfect vista of the bay. The island is named for a Russian cosmonaut who shared this same view with Ho Chi Minh in 1962.

One last cultural note regarding Ha Long Bay: In 1991, a French production company filmed scenes in Ha Long Bay for its epic masterpiece *Indochine*, a hymn to the waning days of the lost colony, starring Catherine Deneuve. Tour boats cruise past one of the movie sets. ■

Figureheads of fierce dragons ward evil spirits away from bay-borne fishing boats.

Cao Bang

Cao Bang

🅜 87 F4

Visitor information

✉ Cao Bang Tourist, Phong Lan Hotel, Kim Dong

☎ (026) 858-229; request info by fax: (026) 852-258

Pac Bo Cave & Ban Gioc Falls

✉ Ha Quang District

☎ (026) 862-140

💲 $ (mandatory permit from Cao Bang police station)

The Quy Xuan river rises in China and tumbles into Vietnam at Ban Gioc Falls.

Near the China border, Cao Bang is a bustling market town on the fringes of some of Vietnam's least traveled but most spectacular scenery. From Pac Bo Cave in the west to Ban Gioc Falls farther east, the region is a mass of craggy limestone mountains that provide one striking vista after another. Probing the blue highways amid these limestone mountains by motorbike, bicycle, or 4WD is a must.

In February 1941, after 30 years abroad, Ho Chi Minh trekked 40 miles (65 km) from his base in China to **Pac Bo** ("the source") **Cave.** He spent his first week in a hut just inside the border. The hut is gone, but you can climb a steep limestone stairway to see the spot. More interesting is the nearby cave, where Ho lived that February and March, plotting revolutionary activities with Vo Nguyen Giap and Pham Van Dong, who'd begun to blaze their own legendary paths across modern Vietnam. They ate fish from a stream that Ho named for Lenin, and at night, beneath the glowering bulk of Karl Marx Mountain, Ho lectured on history and politics.

The shallow cave contains a copy of Ho's wooden bed, and signs below point to where he fished, drew water for tea, and worked at a limestone slab desk. In a museum that's as likely to be staffed as not, exhibits include Ho's bamboo suitcase and Hermes typewriter, and the Nung tunic he wore in 1941.

Farther east, **Ban Gioc Falls** thunders out of China, churning up an ever present mist. Lately, the Vietnamese and Chinese have been bickering over ownership of the falls. ■

Ba Be National Park

Most visitors to Ba Be explore the 5-mile-long (8 km) lake on sampan tours.

HO BA BE, NORTH OF HANOI IN BAC KAN PROVINCE, IS Vietnam's largest natural lake and the centerpiece of this national park. The 5-mile-long (8 km) lake is hemmed in by dramatic limestone bluffs, smothered by lush flora, and "guarded" by Pac Ngoi, a 2,597-foot (787 m) sheer promontory to the south.

The park is home to bears, lorises, and the rare François' langur, a small, reclusive black monkey with distinctive white sideburns. Ba Be is also one of the country's richest butterfly habitats, hosting more than 350 species.

Just over a mile (2 km) from the park entrance, skiffs depart from a ferry landing for tours of the lake, which is fed by three rivers and drained by one. Two five-hour boat trips ply separate rivers, bound for the 1,000-foot (300 m) **Puong Grotto** on the Nang River and **Dau Dang Waterfall.** A leisurely two-hour trip (*$*) tours the lake from end to end. At the north end, the trees are cocooned in tangles of viny growth and rise from the ground like grotesque stalagmites.

At the south end, the clear waters of the Cho Leng River course beneath **Pac Ngoi** and past a Tay village of the same name, which means "mouth of the lake." The Tay settled this area two millennia ago and still occupy wooden stilt houses in the valleys and river bottoms. All told, 3,000 ethnic minority people inhabit 13 villages in the park; more than half are Tay. The Dao, who moved into the area a century ago, live at the mid-elevations, while the Hmong inhabit the uplands.

A paved road rims the lake's south end, opening up beautiful vistas of Pac Ngoi as you reach the bridge. In **Pac Ngoi village,** the Tay provide guest facilities in two stilt homes. Alternatively, you could stay in the state-run guesthouses by the park entrance, but they're nothing special, and you'll have to listen to karaoke on weekend nights. ∎

Ba Be National Park

🅰 87 E4

✉ Park entrance: 27 km (44 km) W of Na Phac on Hwy. 279

☎ (0281) 894-099 or (091) 550-1916

💲 $

Among some hill tribes, one's wardrobe is more important than household trappings.

Hill tribes

Beyond the Viet, Chinese, Khmer, and Cham ethnic groups, Vietnam's highlands are home to an additional 50 distinct ethnic minorities with a total population of four to five million. Since 1993 when authorities opened Sa Pa's colorfully costumed hill tribes and their picturesque villages to tourism, trekking in the highlands has become a major draw. While the most popular treks comb the hills of Sa Pa, even the farthest flung highland provinces are now open to exploration.

Called *moi* (savages) by ethnic Vietnamese and *Montagnards* (mountain dwellers) by the French, the highlanders were largely ignored until the early 20th century, when French growers discovered the rich red earth was excellent ground for coffee cultivation. During the Vietnam War, southern and central highlanders suffered tremendously from bombings and herbicides as the United States tried to stanch the flow of matériel along the Ho Chi Minh Trail. One prominent ethnographer, Gerald Hickey, estimates the war killed 200,000 central highlanders and destroyed 85 percent of their villages.

After the war, authorities encouraged lowland ethnic Vietnamese (Kinh) to resettle in the highlands in New Economic Zones. As worldwide demand for coffee boomed, so did the demand for coffee plantations. In this climate, highlanders accused ethnic Vietnamese of encroaching on their land and religious persecution. The resentment occasionally flared into deadly protests.

When the French first made contact in the late 19th and early 20th centuries, they met a primitive people who had one foot in the world of the hunter-gatherer and one in the world of the peasant farmer. Even today, many hill tribes straddle the boundary between ancient ways and modern methods.

Across Vietnam—and a broad swath of Southeast Asia—ethnic minorities share many similarities. Many farmers practice swidden (slash-and-burn) agriculture. They dwell in stilt homes for protection against dangerous wildlife (though threats from tigers and other cats are no longer what they were). They drink rice wine from communal jars. And they perform blood sacrifice of water buffaloes as a way to assert status in the community or mark the inauguration of a new communal hall or house. The kind of ritualistic buffalo sacrifice that provided a dramatic parallel to the death of Kurtz in the film *Apocalypse Now* still happens in parts of the Central Highlands.

Through the centuries, the Vietnamese and highlanders have allied over common causes. In fact, the first historically verifiable king of Vietnam, An Duong, was a Tay chieftain who founded the state of Au Lac late in the third century B.C. The Tay remain one of Vietnam's longest standing ethnic minorities. Today, about 1.2 million Tay live across the north, with the greatest concentrations near Cao Bang.

The tribes are most visibly distinguished by dress, especially women's dress. While men readily don contemporary clothes, the women often cling to traditional costumes. Among the Hmong and Dao women, the elaboration of dress is more important than the elaboration of home. Red Dao women wear ornate red headdresses, often decorated with long strings of coins, while Black Hmong women favor black leggings, embroidered tunics, huge loop earrings, and brimless hats.

The Hmong, like many ethnic minorities, branch into subgroups. There are the Black, Red, White, and Flower Hmong. There are the White Thai and the Black Thai. The distinctions have as much to do with differences of customs and dialect as dress. Unlike the Tay, who absorbed the belief systems of the Vietnamese, most Thai maintained their traditional religious beliefs, which focus on ancestor worship and genii, not Confucianism, Buddhism, or Taoism.

In the southern and central highlands, home to 44 distinct ethnic groups, the great attraction to the hill tribes is not a matter of dress but architecture. The matrilineal E De (Ede) people near Buon Me Thuot live in thatched stilt homes that stretch as long as 165 feet (50 m), with common areas and sleeping compartments for related families. The communal houses of the Bahnar

Above: Hill-tribe children perform a cultural dance. Below: The Red Dao, identifiable by their red headdresses, emigrated to Vietnam from China 300 years ago.

(Ba Na) people soar 50 to 60 feet (15–19 m) in dramatic thatch pitches. Husbands in both the Bahnar and Giarai tribes live with their wives' families and have no rights of inheritance. ■

Sa Pa & around

Sa Pa
△ 86 C4
Visitor information
www.sapatourism.info.vn
✉ Sa Pa Tourism & Information Center, 28 Cau May, Sa Pa
☎ (020) 871-975
🕐 Closed Sun.

NESTLED AMONG THE BIG-SHOULDERED MOUNTAINS OF the northwest, Sa Pa is the boomtown hub of Vietnam's most color-fully exotic ethnic minorities. The town is thronged by domestic and international visitors who've come to see the elaborate costumes of the Hmong, Red Dao, and Tay people. The town also serves as a base for treks into the region's far-flung villages, where the minorities eke out a living as farmers of rice, cardamom, and corn.

First, a caveat about Sa Pa: It has been corrupted by its popularity. Black Hmong women, especially, crowd the doorways of hotels and glom onto passers-by, hawking sales of "blankies" in feathery light voices. Hotel rooms have multiplied exponentially since authorities opened the region to tourism in 1993. But go anyway. Hire an inexpensive guide and trek, motorbike, or 4WD your way into the hinterland villages. The ethnic wardrobes are a wonder, and years from now, when traditional dress has fallen further out of fashion, you can say you were there and show some stunning photographic evidence.

On the Red River, **Lao Cai** serves as the gateway town. You can hop a minibus for the 19 miles (30 km) to Sa Pa. The 90-minute drive unveils steep mountain flanks corrugated by terraced rice fields, Sa Pa's signature topographical feature. While other landscapes in Vietnam are more dramatically pitched—the limestone karsts of Cao Bang, for example—residents of those regions lack the allure of Sa Pa's captivating costumes.

Despite its gold rush feel, cloud-bathed Sa Pa retains much of the appeal that prompted a French building boom here in the 1930s. Its mile-high (1,586 m) elevation keeps the heat at bay, though the town is often fogged in. When it clears, the views are tremendous, especially from **Ham Rong** ("dragon's mouth"), whose rocky summit sits nearly 700 feet (200 m) above Sa Pa. To reach it, take the trail that starts behind the stone church in the center of town. From the summit, look south into the Muong Hoa Valley, north into the Trung Chai Valley, northwest to Ta Phin, and west to O Quy Ho. Visible in the distance is **Fan Si Pan,** Vietnam's highest peak (see p. 107).

Sa Pa is best known for its **market** for area villages, whose costumed residents arrive hauling huge bamboo hampers on their backs. Historically, they've traded with each other, though these days, tourists are the better quarry. Off Cau May, a stairway flanked by fresh vegetable vendors descends to an attractive market largely dominated by ethnic Vietnamese (Kinh). Turn left at the bottom to find a graphically jarring suite of butcher's blocks that display trays of beet-red livers, hearts, and severed heads of cows.

Of greater interest to tourists is a separate upstairs room where the region's minorities sell clothes and jewelry. Heavily brocaded blankets, waistcoats, indigo-dyed bolts of hemp, men's caps, and silver bracelets are the big sellers, but shop with discretion. The embroidery on that brocade bag may have been mass-produced in Hanoi. If the more beautiful

Opposite: The residents of Sa Pa are the beneficiaries and casualties of a thriving tourist trade.

As this view from the Topas Eco-Lodge suggests, Sa Pa's greater glories await outside of town.

objects are cheaper, it's probably because they are. The markets in such remote villages as Bac Ha, east of Lao Cai, and Ban Ho, in the nearby Muong Hoa Valley, are less popular and thus more traditional.

Farther up Cau May is a new open-air tourist market, across from the sunken public square, and another market on the apron of the **stone church** *(Ham & Phan Xuan Huan),* built by the French in 1935. You'll likely spot young ethnic minorities flirting here in a so-called love market.

The tourism bureau shills for **Cau May,** a rattan bridge over the Ta Van River south of Sa Pa. The bridge is now closed, replaced by a ubiquitous cable-stay span. Nearby are the pic-

turesque stone ruins of a colonial-era church, blanketed in a fine orange moss, as well as Sa Pa's **ancient sacred stones,** a collection of smooth granite boulders faintly inscribed with inscrutable lines and shapes of houses and figures. The carvings are reputed to be 3,000 years old, but Easter Island this is not.

SA PA HILL TOWNS

You won't be able to sing Sa Pa's praises fully unless you trek for several days among the country's highest mountains. Note that authorities recently closed a number of villages, so be sure to ask which are accessible, hire a guide, and go there.

Sa Pa offers easy access to

comfortable mattressed lofts. As you stroll village paths, look for bamboo saucers of drying purple cardamom buds, an aromatic spice of the ginger family. Or catch the scent of fragrant white smoke from kilns at the village entrance.

Up the valley is the Xa Pho village of **Nam Sang,** whose 400 residents occupy simple huts and speak a unique language. They are diminishing rapidly because, like most regional minorities, they won't marry outside their group.

Still farther up the valley is **Nam Kang,** a more prosperous village that's off-limits to tourists, allegedly for security reasons. Stop atop a bluff just short of the village to admire one of the region's truly beautiful waterfalls.

Sa Pa is also a base for treks to 10,312-foot (3,143 m) **Fan Si Pan,** which anchors the Hoang Lien range and national park south of town. Treks to the peak leave from **Cat Cat,** a village 2 miles (3 km) south of Sa Pa, and other nearby hamlets. Though the distance is only 11 miles (19 km), this is rough terrain and will take three or four days for a round-trip hike.

LAI CHAU PROVINCE

West of Sa Pa, the road to Lai Chau climbs past the Silver Waterfall to 6,600-foot (2,000 m) **Heaven's Gate,** Indochina's highest pass. From here you can trek to the Hmong village of Sin Chai.

A spectacular region, Lai Chau is a remote province with little but the prospect of serendipity to offer travelers. The town of **Lai Chau** sits south of the confluence of the Song Da and Nam Na Rivers. The town is destined to undergo dramatic change once the government dams a nearby river in 2010. In the meantime, check out the White Thai villages, clustered off the main road. ■

Ta Phin, a Red Dao village about 7 miles (12 km) north, where the local tourist bureau touts a so-so granite cave.

To the southeast is the Tay village of **Ban Ho,** on the Muong Hoa River. As you approach town, you'll spot windowless Hmong homes. After the Xa Pho people, the Hmong are the region's poorest ethnic minority, though the most fancifully attired. Each house centers on the family's simple altar, little more than a sheaf of handmade paper hung from a hook and tacked with the family's recent good fortune, such as feathers or horns from downed game.

In Ban Ho, guided trekkers can stay in a bamboo-floored Tay stilt home, bunked in reasonably

An old-timer pays his respects to the fallen at Dien Bien Phu.

Dien Bien Phu

AT DIEN BIEN PHU IN 1954, THE VIETNAMESE SCORED THEIR greatest victory in a modern, set-piece military battle and decisively set the stage for the French withdrawal from Vietnam. Today, the sprawling town that sprouted in the wake of conflict is largely visited by domestic pilgrims and French War buffs.

Dien Bien Phu
⊠ 86 B3
Visitor information
⊠ Lai Chau General Tourist Agency, 7 Thang 5
☎ (023) 825-103

Dien Bien Phu Museum
⊠ 7 Thang 5
☎ (023) 830-874
$ $

In late 1953, French soldiers parachuted into this remote valley to cut Vietnamese supply lines and draw out the guerrillas. Gen. Vo Nguyen Giap took the bait and marshaled 55,000 combatants to counter a French force of 16,000. On May 6, 1954, Giap mounted an all-out attack, defeating the French after a 55-day siege and strengthening Vietnam's hand at peace talks in Geneva.

Start your tour at **Dien Bien Phu Museum,** a half mile (1 km) from the town's main fork near the market. One outdoor pavilion displays artillery pieces of the kind used by Giap's forces, though their provenance is suspect. Another pavilion holds a graveyard of French matériel, including rusted Willys Jeeps, battered aircraft fuselage, and tanks.

Inside is a panoramic diorama of the valley floor, including the suite of low-lying hills at the core of the French garrison. You'll also find miscellaneous battle relics, including an iron bathtub French commander General de Castries used in his bunker.

Across the street, ranks of unmarked tombs fill one of several **cemeteries** that hold the 10,000 Vietnamese casualties. Its white granite gate with a mirador bell tower is reminiscent of the triple gates of Vietnam's imperial past. Just inside are listed the names and hometowns of the dead, most from Nghe An and Thanh Hoa, the home provinces of Vietnam's two greatest heroes, Ho Chi Minh and Le Loi, respectively.

Above the museum is a recently restored hilltop redoubt known to the Vietnamese as **A1** and to the French as Eliane 2, with tunnels, trenches, and a massive bomb crater. Across town, **de Castries' command bunker** endures as a more pristine vestige of the battle. ■

Mai Chau Valley

Mai Chau

📍 86 D2

Visitor information

✉ Hoa Binh Tourist, Rte. 6, Hoa Binh, near Mai Chau

☎ (018) 854-374

THOUGH THE WHITE THAI VILLAGES NEAR MAI CHAU LACK the colorfully costumed inhabitants of Sa Pa (its rival for trek-minded customers), this valley's bucolic charms, proximity to Hanoi (84 miles/135 km to the northeast), and stilt-house architecture all make for an enriching ethnic minority experience. Nearly every visitor to this fairly remote locale overnights in Ban Lac or Pom Coong, Thai villages situated on the outskirts of Mai Chau town.

With about 75 stilt houses, **Ban Lac** is slightly larger and more popular with travelers than neighboring **Pom Coong.** Both villages are touristy, especially Ban Lac, where the space among the stilts is frequently made over as shops for local handicrafts. Beyond these villages, the commercialism gives way rapidly to more pristine villages.

Most visitors come to the area as part of an organized tour, with a homestay at the heart of any visit. Usually, host families sleep in a seg-regated wing of the house, and tourists bunk communally under mosquito tents on thin mattresses. As you carry your baggage upstairs, look for the fishtails carved into the wooden doorframe of the main entrance. Traditionally, an unmar-ried son carved a tail for every fish caught, showing off his skills as a provider to prospective in-laws who come calling.

Trekking is another popular thing to do. One good hike: Seven and a half miles (12 km) from Ban Lac, the Ma River flows between Hoa Binh and Thanh Hoa Provinces. Ferry 2 miles (3 km) down and across the river to **Co Luong Village** and trek 2 miles (3 km) back along a foot-path. This hike threads a pair of hamlets, **Chieng Anh** and **Than Pong.** The first language spoken is Thai, though nearly all speak Vietnamese as well. Look for tombs of deceased Thai in the foliage above the path, built on stilts and posi-tioned with due regard to feng shui. ∎

Harvest hampers in this rural region can weigh as much as 90 pounds (40 kg).

More places to visit in the north

BA VI NATIONAL PARK
The landmark mountains of 28-square-mile (73 sq km) Ba Vi National Park rise from a fairly level plain and top out at 4,251 feet (1,296 m). A road summits cloud-wreathed **Ngoc Tan,** where worshippers at **Thuong Temple** pray to the mountain god Tan Vien. On clear days, soak in vistas of the Red River Delta and Hanoi, 31 miles (50 km) east. The French built 200 villas at Ba Vi during the colonial era. The ruins of a Catholic church and its 36-foot (11 m) bell tower, now smothered by forest, remain popular with photographers. The Muong minority live at the mountains' base, while the Dao dwell higher on the slopes. These forests are also renowned for medicinal plants.

▲ 87 E2 ☎ (034) 881-205 **Hanoi office** ✉ 144 Hoang Quoc Viet, Cau Giay District ☎ (04) 836-2323

BAI TU LONG BAY
Northeast of Ha Long Bay (see pp. 96–99), a similar batch of limestone islands speckle the emerald waters of Tu Long Bay. Designated a national park in 2001, the bay lacks Ha Long's sweep, but the secluded setting is a welcome trade-off.

▲ 87 G2 **Visitor information** ✉ Ha Long Bay Hotel, Ha Long, Bai Chay ☎ (033) 845-210

CO LOA
Although Hue is known as the ancient imperial capital of Vietnam, that designation rightfully belongs to Co Loa, founded in the late third century B.C. by King An Duong and occupied by the Ngo dynasty in the middle tenth century. Co Loa means "old snail" and refers to a likeness between the city's concentric walls and the rings of a snail shell. Nine miles (14 km) of earthwork ramparts remain discernible at the original site, 11 miles (18 km) from Hanoi. Inside the citadel, the **Co Loa communal house** stands on the site of the old royal court. Nearby is a **shrine to My Chau,** the king's daughter. Archaeologists have unearthed bronze drums, stone stelae, and tens of thousands of arrowheads, axes, and knives.

▲ 87 E2 ✉ 10 miles (16 km) north of central Hanoi in Dong Anh District $ $

HUNG KINGS TEMPLE
This complex at Nghia Linh Mountain in Phu Tho venerates the legendary Au Co, whose hundred eggs hatched at the site of Ha Temple, thus forming the people of Vietnam. One of those eggs held the first of 18 Hung kings, who worshipped at the site of present-day **Thuong Temple.** At **Trung Temple,** the youngest son of the 18th Hung king presented his father with *banh chung,* the sticky rice cake at the heart of every Tet table. After defeating invaders, the sixth Hung king died and was buried in a hillside tomb. At the foot of Nghia Linh, the 18th king's daughters used the surface of the **Gieng Temple well** as a mirror when they combed their hair.

▲ 87 E2 ✉ Tran Phu, Viet Tri ☎ (0210) 846-756

LANG SON
Eleven miles (18 km) from the border, Lang Son bore the brunt of Vietnam's 1979 conflict with China, hence the relatively new look to a rather old town. Primitive peoples dwelled in caves here 500,000 years ago, and caves remain the attraction. In the three **grottoes at Tam Thanh** ($), look for the 18th-century poem inscribed by mandarin border guard Ngo Thi Si.

▲ 87 F3 **Visitor information** ✉ Hoang Vu Hotel, 240 Tran Hung Dao ☎ (025) 873-738

SON LA
In 1908, the French built a penitentiary in this remote province, 203 miles (328 km) northwest of Hanoi. Between 1930 and 1945, **Son La Prison** *(Tien Le, $)* housed thousands of revolutionaries, thus consecrating its status as a memorial. Though partly destroyed by a 1952 bombing, its underground cells evoke the torturous past. An on-site **museum** explores the cultures of the province's dozen ethnic minority groups.

▲ 86 C2 **Visitor information** ✉ Trade Union Hotel, 6 Thang 4 ☎ (022) 852-804 ■

Long overlooked but now up and coming, north-central Vietnam boasts the country's most magnificent cave system, fantastic limestone landscapes, and the home villages of the nation's greatest heroes.

North central

A mandarin statue at Pho Minh Pagoda, near Nam Dinh

North central

THE NORTH-CENTRAL PROVINCES OF VIETNAM FORM A LONG, slender stem between the great bulge of the Red River Delta and highlands to the north and the beefy belt of the central highlands to the south. The coast offers long stretches of white dunes and unexploited beaches. Inland, limestone mountains crumple the terrain into an alluring landscape of caves, karsts, and bastions of Vietnamese nationalism.

The temptation for tourists traveling the main north-south axis is to leapfrog by plane or by train over north-central Vietnam, from Hanoi to Hue or vice versa. To do so would mean bypassing the UNESCO World Heritage site at Phong Nha and the marvelous landscapes and temples around Ninh Binh. That said, you could tackle both sets of attractions on tours from Hanoi or Hue.

Southeast of Hanoi, Nam Dinh Province is a fertile tract of the Red River Delta that warrants a visit for its pagodas and temples. Tran Hung Dao, who repelled the Mongol invasions in the 13th century, hailed from Nam Dinh and expanded a palace at the present site of Thien Truong Temple.

The attractions in Ninh Binh Province have broad appeal. The local tourist bureau touts the karsts of Tam Coc as an inland Ha Long Bay. They're not, but only because Ha Long is in a league of its own. More intriguing is the Phat Diem Cathedral, a hybrid of Oriental and Occidental architecture designed by an eccentric Catholic priest in the latter part of the 19th century. In this picturesque landscape, the temple complex at Hoa Lu is an architectural tribute to the

Dramatic limestone karsts define the inland landscape near Ninh Binh.

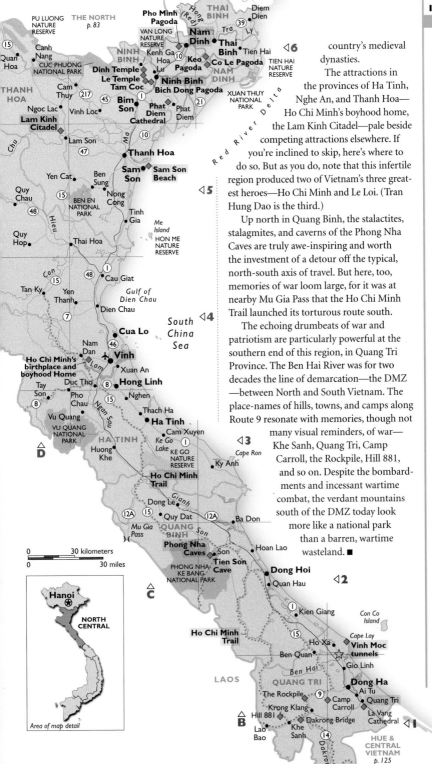

country's medieval dynasties.

The attractions in the provinces of Ha Tinh, Nghe An, and Thanh Hoa—Ho Chi Minh's boyhood home, the Lam Kinh Citadel—pale beside competing attractions elsewhere. If you're inclined to skip, here's where to do so. But as you do, note that this infertile region produced two of Vietnam's three greatest heroes—Ho Chi Minh and Le Loi. (Tran Hung Dao is the third.)

Up north in Quang Binh, the stalactites, stalagmites, and caverns of the Phong Nha Caves are truly awe-inspiring and worth the investment of a detour off the typical, north-south axis of travel. But here, too, memories of war loom large, for it was at nearby Mu Gia Pass that the Ho Chi Minh Trail launched its torturous route south.

The echoing drumbeats of war and patriotism are particularly powerful at the southern end of this region, in Quang Tri Province. The Ben Hai River was for two decades the line of demarcation—the DMZ —between North and South Vietnam. The place-names of hills, towns, and camps along Route 9 resonate with memories, though not many visual reminders, of war— Khe Sanh, Quang Tri, Camp Carroll, the Rockpile, Hill 881, and so on. Despite the bombardments and incessant wartime combat, the verdant mountains south of the DMZ today look more like a national park than a barren, wartime wasteland. ∎

Nam Dinh
& around

 113 C6
Visitor
information
 Vi Hoang Hotel,
 21 Nguyen Du
 (035) 849-290

Nam Dinh & around

NAM DINH IS A MAJOR CITY ON THE RED RIVER DELTA, where tourist traffic is light despite centuries-old pagodas and temples that rank among the country's oldest surviving examples. Tran Hung Dao, one of the top three heroes in the Vietnamese pantheon, was born in Nam Dinh, and a cult of his energetic devotees remains prosperous and hard at work, as is amply witnessed by the bustle at area temples.

Pho Minh's 14-story tower has loomed over the pagoda since 1305.

A pleasant city of 230,000 with lively, shaded streets, Nam Dinh has made few concessions for travelers. A gargantuan statue of Tran Hung Dao lords over a lake at the city center, looking remarkably like another legendary hero, Le Loi, whose statue stands in downtown Thanh Hoa.

Nineteen miles (30 km) east of Nam Dinh in Thai Binh Province, **Keo Pagoda** (*$*) is the region's star attraction. Dating from between 1133 and 1154, the pagoda was moved to its present site in 1611 after the Red River flooded its former grounds. Today, the pagoda is celebrated for its architecture and fanciful wooden statuary. More than 20 statues of Buddhist deities occupy the T-shaped entrance to the main temple, and more than 50 statues festoon a succession of altars along the pagoda's main axis. The second temple holds a lacquered miniature boat that's brought out during a major festival here in the ninth lunar month.

Across the Red River, **Co Le Pagoda** is a 1920 restoration of a pagoda built during the Ly dynasty. Lining the sanctuary walls are the most impressive relics—a series of devotional tablets, inscribed with Chinese characters in the 12th century. The 95-foot-high (29 m) main chamber is presided over by a painted ironwood Buddha, set on an altar near the ceiling. In front of the pagoda, a 105-foot (32 m) tower of nine tiers stands atop the undulate shell of a tortoise.

Two miles (3 km) northwest of Nam Dinh is **Pho Minh Pagoda,** whose 700-ton (630 metric ton), 14-story tower has somehow kept from sinking into the surrounding floodplain. The 1305 tower dates from the original Ly-built pagoda. Beside it stands **Thien Truong Temple,** where locals fervently worship Tran Hung Dao. ∎

Ninh Binh & around

THE FIRST KING OF THE DINH DYNASTY PUT THIS AREA ON the map in the 11th century when he moved his government from the ancient capital at Co Loa to this karst landscape 56 miles (90 km) south of present-day Hanoi. Today, Ninh Binh is best known as the jumping-off point for Tam Coc, an inland water world of precipitous karst crags reminiscent of the formations in Ha Long Bay. Beyond Tam Coc, several temples and a masterpiece of a cathedral in this very Catholic part of Vietnam warrant at least one long day of exploration.

The Dinh set their capital amid the limestone crags at **Hoa Lu,** just north of Ninh Binh town, because it was farther from China and easier to defend. The Ly abandoned the site in 1010 when they moved the capital to Thang Long, now Hanoi. Ruins are limited to a few unearthed sections of citadel wall, palace tiles, simple statues, bones, and porcelain. But the site is worth visiting for two temples built in the 17th century to commemorate the ephemeral dynasties.

Fragrant with jasmine joss and architecturally sublime, the **Dinh** and **Le Temples** boast stout ironwood pillars, lacquered to a high vermilion sheen and gilded with dragons. The pillars stand on stone plinths because, though insect resistant, the wood rots in water. Gilded wood carvings on the trusswork are richly detailed.

The T-shaped temples feature recessed bays on either side of the entrance, while their axes bustle with altars, urns, and platform beds. Ceremonial weapons represent the mandarins who flanked the throne during ceremonies. Statues of the king and his sons are enthroned in three bays at the rear of the Le Temple; the king, his son, and his wife occupy the rear bays in the Dinh Temple.

East meets West in the design of Phat Diem Cathedral.

Ninh Binh
113 C6
Visitor information
✉ Ninh Binh Tourism, Tran Hung Dao
☎ (030) 881-958

Hoa Lu
113 C6
✉ 7 miles (11 km) N of Ninh Bnih via Hwy. 1; turn left at Cau Huyen crossroad to Truong Yen commune
☎ (030) 620-044
💲 $

Tam Coc's karst landscape is best admired by boat.

Tam Coc

🗺 113 C6

✉ From Ninh Binh, 2.5 miles (4 km) S on Hwy. 1; turn right toward Ninh Hai in Hoa Lu District for 2 miles (3 km)

☎ (030) 848-006

💲 $

Kenh Ga boat tour

🗺 113 C6

✉ From Ninh Binh, 6 miles (10 km) N on Hwy. 1 to Gian Khau crossroad; turn right 6 miles (10 km) to Me; turn left 1.25 miles (2 km) to Dong Chua pier in Gia Vien.

☎ (030) 868-560

💲 $

South of Hoa Lu at **Tam Coc** ("three caves"), you can take a sedate trip up the Ngo Dong River through its eponymous three caves. The rowboats are typically skippered and crewed by women. The distant karst mountains come into high relief, and soon the river tunnels through 417-foot (127 m) **Hang Ca,** the first of the caves, followed by **Hang Giua** and **Hang Cuoi,** respectively. The farther you travel upriver, the more dramatic the scenery, as sheer crags rise from either bank.

Just over a mile (2 km) north of Tam Coc via Highway 1 is **Bich Dong Pagoda,** which occupies an interesting if over-hyped limestone grotto. To reach this shrine to the Buddha, you'll climb two sets of slippery stairs.

Farther north along Highway 1, another inland boat trip plies the muddy waters of the Hoang Long River from Ninh Binh to the village of **Kenh Ga** ("chicken canal"), its name a reference to nearby 127°F (53°C) hot springs

where locals douse chickens for easier plucking. Village homes perch beneath the crags and on miserly spits that flood during high water. After a quick tour of the watery main street, the sampan will meander into deeper water past limestone hills that supply cement factories.

Seventeen miles (28 km) southeast of Ninh Binh off Highway 1, hundred-year-old **Phat Diem Cathedral** was the brainchild of Tran Luc, an indomitable Catholic priest more popularly known as Father Six. Parishioners prepared the unstable site by driving thousands of bamboo stakes into the floodplain, followed by layers of earth, gravel, and bamboo rafts.

Today, the 5-acre (2 ha) compound comprises the cathedral itself, four chapels, and three man-made grottoes. It was from the 85-foot (26 m) bell tower that novelist Graham Greene watched the Viet Minh battle the French during the First Indochina War, a scene captured in his 1955 masterpiece, *The Quiet American.* A two-ton (1.8 metric ton) 1890 bell on the tower's upper mirador is audible for miles. From this height, 20 visible church steeples testify to the inroads Catholicism has made here over the past 400 years.

That said, the cathedral looks as much like a Buddhist pagoda as a Catholic sanctuary. Framing the entry is a garland of stone lotus blooms, symbolic of Buddhism. Inside, 52 ironwood columns support a roof that shelters 1,500 for Mass. The vermilion altarpiece has gilt woodwork reminiscent of Hue's Imperial City. Statues of Matthew, Mark, Luke, and John perch atop four pagoda-like turrets that frame the central tower. A massive drum on the tower's lower mirador is another nod to Vietnamese traditions. ∎

Vinh

THE CAPITAL OF NGHE AN PROVINCE, VINH STILL LIVES UP
to its reputation as the nadir of the North, though that's changing as
a rising tide of prosperity reinvigorates a city once infamous among
travelers for its downtown ghetto of six-story East German–designed
apartment complexes. Still, the main—and only—reason to lay over
in Vinh is for access to Ho Chi Minh's birthplace and boyhood home,
two bucolic compounds just west of town.

Vinh
🅰 113 C4
**Visitor
information**
✉ Nghe An Tourist,
13 Quang Trung
☎ (038) 844-692

Nghe An factors greatly in Vietnam's history. Among the country's
most densely populated and least
arable provinces, it has long been
a hotbed of discontent, giving rise
to generations of revolutionaries,
including the great nationalists
who came to prominence in the
1920s and 1930s. Ho Chi Minh,
the most famous of all, was born
in Hoang Tru hamlet, 9 miles
(14 km) west of central Vinh.

Ho was born Nguyen Sinh
Cung on May 2, 1890, in a simple
home his maternal grandfather
built in 1883 as a wedding gift
for Ho's parents. The thatched
home did not survive, but the
government reconstructed the
birthplace in 1959 in homage to
the president of what was then
North Vietnam.

Today, the **Ho Chi Minh
birthplace** is light on exhibits—
a few simple wooden furnishings
are all—and none of the explana-
tory text is in English. But the
spacious, rural compound gives
a good feel for how Vietnam's
rural mandarins lived in the
late 19th century.

Adjacent to Ho's birthplace
are a temple his maternal grandfather built for the veneration of
his ancestors and his grandfather's larger, five-bay thatched
home. In this wattle-walled
house, Ho's father, Nguyen Sinh
Sac, studied the Confucian classics for an exam that won him
a doctoral degree, the highest

**Ho Chi Minh
was born in a
thatched house
near Vinh in 1890.**

literary honor in Vietnam.

After Sac won the prestigious
degree, villagers built a new home
for him and his family, just over
a mile (2 km) away in Kim Lien.
Ho Chi Minh lived here as a boy
from 1901 to 1906. With fewer
exhibits than the birthplace, **Ho's
boyhood home** is somewhat
less interesting. It sits across the
road from an equally lackluster
Ho Chi Minh Museum, which
is also light on exhibits.

If you're in Vinh and curious,
explore the area around the vast
athletic complex at the city center
and look for three restored gates
of the citadel built here in 1831.
Literary pilgrims can journey 10
miles (16 km) east across the river
into Ha Tinh Province, where
Nguyen Du, Vietnam's answer to
Shakespeare, was born in 1765. ■

**Ho Chi Minh
birthplace &
boyhood home**
✉ From Vinh, follow
Phan Dinh Phung
to Rte. 46. After
about 6 miles
(10 km), look for
signs to Kim Lien.
Ho Chi Minh's
birthplace is in
Hoang Tru hamlet.
His boyhood home
is about a mile
(2 km) away in Kim
Lien.
💲 $

Phong Nha Caves

**Phong Nha–
Ke Bang
National Park**

🗺 113 B2–C2

✉ Son Trach Village

☎ (052) 675-021

💲 Boat tour: $$

THOUGH CELEBRATED BY NATIVES FOR CENTURIES, THE Phong Nha Caves are only now taking their rightful place among the world's most spectacular caverns. A UNESCO World Heritage site since 2003, these limestone grottoes are the centerpiece of Phong Nha–Ke Bang National Park and border the largest contiguous tract of forest in Vietnam, where the age of discovery has yet to end.

As far back as the ninth and tenth centuries, the Cham were using these vast subterranean chambers as temples. In the 19th century, Nguyen emperor Minh Mang memorialized the caves on one of nine dynastic urns in the Mieu compound of Hue's Imperial City. Léopold Cadière, a prominent French Jesuit from Hue, explored the grottoes in 1899.

During the Vietnam War, North Vietnamese troops used the caves as a garrison and weapons cache just off the Ho Chi Minh Trail, a fact not lost on the Americans, who heavily bombed the area. Look for scars on the limestone face above the cave entrance.

The national park lies 30 miles (50 km) west of **Dong Hoi,** a town of little interest to travelers other

The sampan puts in at a sandy beach within a stunningly vast chamber, 165 feet (50 m) high and bristling with stalactites and stalagmites. Growing at a rate of half an inch (1 cm) per year, one massive stalagmite stands 56 feet (17 m) high and is 21 feet (6.5 m) in diameter. Over this fantastic formation, an 82-foot (25 m) stalactite tumbles like a woman's hair falls, as locals say. Inscribed in a wall farther upstream is a thousand-year-old Cham religious tract comprising 97 characters and a reference to the Buddha.

Back outside, 600 steps climb to the mouth of **Tien Son Cave,** a 1,000-yard (1 km) chamber, nearly half of which is open to visitors. Where Phong Nha overwhelms with its vastness, Tien Son is all about fantastic rock formations. As in Phong Nha, the crannies of this cave are illuminated by fluorescent reds, greens, and blues. While the Vietnamese penchant for garish colors trends toward kitsch (e.g., the disco halo about the Buddha's head in venerably old pagodas), in Phong Nha this impulse actually enhances the drama of the formations.

Looping into this upper cave, you'll pass the **Love Grotto,** so named for a stone formation that resembles a wedding umbrella, beneath which prospective brides and grooms often pause to pray for endless love. Beyond, a series of hollow stone ribs elicits a range of tones when drummed.

A fence at the halfway mark restricts further access. As you turn around for the sampan ride back to the visitor center, the return pathway loops past four ceramic basins filled with water dripping from stalactites. Dipping a hand in such "lucky water" is thought to beautify women and strengthen men. ∎

Neon highlights the stalactites and stalagmites within Tien Son ("fairy mountain") Cave, one of two great systems in Phong Nha–Ke Bang National Park.

than the ruins of a 17th-century gate the Nguyen lords built to defend against Trinh rivals to the north. The city's hotels, energized since the UNESCO designation, can arrange transport to the park, or you can rent a motorbike *($$)* to make the round-trip journey.

From the visitor center, sampans ferry travelers 3 miles (5 km) up the Son River amid a picturesque karst crags, soon entering **Phong Nha Cave** through a slot at the base of a sheer, 492-foot (150 m) limestone cliff. In the dry season *(Feb.–Aug.),* low water levels limit tour boat access 2,000 feet (600 m) into the cave via a 330-foot (100 m) chamber known as Bi Ky. Spelunkers have surveyed nearly 30 miles (48 km) of this cavern.

Ho Chi Minh Trail

The Ho Chi Minh Highway rolls over long stretches of the former Ho Chi Minh Trail.

During the Vietnam War, North Vietnam spirited a million soldiers into South Vietnam along the Ho Chi Minh Trail, an elusive, 12,000-mile (19,000 km) web of jungle paths and primitive roadways. The road's principal artery plunged south from Mu Gia Pass near the Phong Nha Caves through Laos and Cambodia, where spurs branched eastward toward staging areas for attacks against southern targets. Today, the government has linked sections of the trail as the Ho Chi Minh Highway, a north-south corridor of dubious benefit to the region's ecology and economy.

In 1955, after it became obvious that Ngo Dinh Diem would thwart countrywide elections planned for the following year, a North Vietnamese major began to survey a north-south supply line for the inevitable war. In 1959, more than 400 volunteers started to extend a network of primitive pathways, originally cut by highlanders, as the Truong Son ("long mountain") Trail.

In the early 1960s, the trail comprised simple footpaths, a lane winding through a bamboo groves. North Vietnamese soldiers took six months to reach their destinations. By 1968, after years of upgrading, they'd whittled a few months off the transit, but still had to hustle along for 11 to 12 hours a day. By war's end, trucks completed the relatively brisk journey in 23 days.

The U.S. military detected the presence of the supply route almost immediately but was unable to stanch the tide of matériel funneling south for more than a few days at a time. Attempts to interdict soldiers and supplies along the trail precipitated the momentous battles at Ia Drang and Hamburger Hill, the siege at Khe Sanh, the air campaigns of Rolling Thunder, Nixon's Cambodian incursion of 1970, and the South Vietnamese incursion into Laos in 1971.

In 1969 alone, the United States pummeled the trail with 433,000 tons (390,000 metric tons) of bombs. By war's end, the Americans had dropped 1.7 million tons (1.5 million metric tons) of explosives, killing one enemy for every 300 bombs dropped, according to a CIA estimate. Between 1965 and 1971, antiaircraft batteries downed 43 U.S. airmen over Mu Gia Gate. In all, Hanoi claims its soldiers downed 2,500 U.S. planes over the trail; the Pentagon says the Vietnamese brought down 500.

There's no consensus as to why the bombing failed, except that it did. That became obvious to the Americans as early as 1966, when they began to mull the option of using tactical nuclear weapons. Strategists discarded the option, figuring that the political downside would far outweigh the upside on the battlefield.

So the B-52s rolled on, obliterating huge tracts of the highlands. The campaign killed countless thousands of communist soldiers and petrified everyone else, including the 300,000 laborers who toiled to keep the trail open. As perilous were the snakes, drownings, accidents, and disease. During the early years on the trail, nearly 10 percent of the porters succumbed to malaria. The

A typical porter along the Ho Ch Minh Trail would keep moving as much as 12 hours a day.

adversity forged a camaraderie that helped steel the communist forces.

In 2000, Vietnam broke ground on an inland highway along the former Ho Chi Minh Trail to link Hanoi with Saigon. Some suggest the money would be better spent upgrading Vietnam's IT infrastructure, education system, narrow-gauge railway, and existing north-south Highway 1 corridor. To many others, though, paving of the legendary trail is tantamount to consecration of the old jungle footpath. ■

Except for a brief respite in 1968, villagers lived in the underground tunnels from 1965 to 1973.

Vinh Moc tunnels

113 A2

From Hue, travel 60 miles (100 km) N along Hwy. 1 to Ho Xa, turn E (right), and travel several more miles to the tunnels at Cape Lay

(053) 823-238

$

Vinh Moc tunnels

FOR SIX YEARS OF THE VIETNAM WAR, THE MILE-LONG (2 km) tunnel complex at Vinh Moc was home to hundreds of refugees from a fishing village that had been decimated by U.S. bombing. On three levels, 40 to 75 feet (12–23 m) below the surface, families lived in cramped cells gouged from either side of a 4- to 5-foot-wide (1.2–1.5 m) passage. A testament to the fortitude and resourcefulness of a besieged people, Vinh Moc is one of 14 tunnel systems in the region north of the former demilitarized zone but the only one accessible today.

Villagers dug their refuge in 19 months and moved underground in December 1967. Except for a brief respite in 1968, they lived here without interruption until January 1973, enduring a barrage of 500 rockets per day on average.

Today, a quarter mile (400 m) of the complex is open to tours. Though some of the uppermost level has collapsed, the deepest sections remain intact. From the visitor center, flashlight-guided tours enter one of 13 portals. Bring your own light to inspect the various bays.

Unlike Cu Chi's claustrophobic tunnels (see pp. 214–215), Vinh Moc's corridors are a relatively roomy 5 to 6 feet (1.5–1.8 m) high, where planked walls give way to cocoa-colored laterite that looks almost edible. The corridor passes small bays that served as family quarters, larger conference chambers, and a maternity ward where 17 children were born. In the deepest chambers, residents drew water from two wells and warehoused supplies that had come down the Ho Chi Minh Trail. At night, they risked discovery by U.S. Navy patrols to ferry supplies to Con Co Island, 17 miles (28 km) offshore. From Con Co, food and ammunition were relayed south.

You'll wind in and out of the tunnels, also taking in a bluff above a beach that King Bao Dai used to frequent and an esplanade from which you can see Con Co Island. Tours end atop the bluff. ∎

Quang Tri

QUANG TRI, MORE THAN KHE SANH, IA DRANG, OR HUE, resonates painfully in the ears of Vietnamese who recall the ferocious 81-day battle in 1972 that reduced the town to rubble. Today, the principal attractions—two churches, a Buddhist school, and the 1824 citadel—are dilapidated remnants of the onetime provincial capital.

Quang Tri
🅰 113 A1
Visitor information
✉ Sepon Travel, 189 Le Duan, Dong Ha
☎ (053) 855-289

In the spring of 1972, as North Vietnamese forces advanced on Quang Tri, the South Vietnamese Army decamped from the citadel and joined thousands of refugees fleeing along Highway 1 toward Hue, 35 miles (56 km) south. The communists shelled the melee, wreaking havoc that inspired one correspondent to dub the road the Highway of Horrors. In the early 1950s, after frequent attacks by the Viet Minh, the French had called this stretch of Highway 1 the Street Without Joy. French historian Bernard Hall later immortalized the road in a prescient book of the same name.

Approaching Quang Tri from the south, one first notices the ruins of a Catholic church to the right of the highway—a photo op on popular DMZ tours out of Hue. Turn right on Tran Hung Dao, and you'll pass a bombed-out **Buddhist school** whose pocked walls speak to the firepower rained down on Quang Tri. Farther on, the **Cong Trong Gate** breaches the **citadel,** whose shattered brick walls still rim the grounds. A war memorial stands within, while a decent museum exhibits before-and-after photos of Quang Tri.

Back on Highway 1, near the white bridge, take Le Loi 2.5 miles (4 km) to its dead end at **La Vang Cathedral.** This 1928 church was upgraded to a basilica in 1962. Its bell tower and facade survived the 1972 campaign and are now complemented by a glass-walled nave. ∎

Patriotic art hangs from the walls of a museum inside the shattered Quang Tri citadel.

Quang Tri Citadel
✉ Ly Thai Tho
💲 $

Perilous terrain

Though the war ended in 1975, Quang Tri remains the most perilous ground in Vietnam. In this province alone, accidental detonations of old bombs and mines have killed 2,600 people and maimed 4,300 since the end of hostilities. That's an average of 7 deaths and 12 casualties every month. Half the victims are farmers, and a third are children born long after the war. Half the province's farmland is unsafe for cultivation. In 2001, American veterans of the war and the Vietnamese government launched a project to educate locals about ordnance and to recover as many buried munitions as possible. Though much of the ordnance is American, the U.S. Congress has made only modest contributions toward cleanup efforts. ∎

A drive along the DMZ

Though the former DMZ (demilitarized zone) and nearby mountains fell under the greatest deluge of bombs in the history of warfare until the late 1960s, nature has so persuasively regenerated the landscape that it takes a savvy eye to detect wartime scarring. Still, from the Ben Hai River to Khe Sanh, a tour through this country is a haunting journey through place-names that are resonant for people with even cursory knowledge of the Vietnam War.

Most DMZ tours originate in Hue (see pp. 130–145) and include a side trip to the Vinh Moc tunnels (see p. 122). The tour picks up a local guide in Dong Ha, then stops 9 miles (15 km) north at the **Ben Hai River ❶**, the former line of demarcation between North and South Vietnam along the 17th parallel.

A no-man's-land during the war, the DMZ stretched north and south of the riverbank for 3 miles (5 km) in either direction. On the north bank, the restored station of the International Control Commission, jointly staffed by Poland, Canada, and India, stands before a restored gateway to the **Hien Luong Bridge.** U.S. bombers knocked out the French-built planked bridge in 1967. The restored bridge serves as a memorial.

From **Dong Ha,** the tour heads west on Route 9, a road blazed by the French in 1904, toward the Truong Son Mountains. Just shy of **Cam Lo,** a onetime American firebase, a road veers right for **Con Thien ❷**, another U.S. firebase 7.5 miles (12 km)

north. In the midst of grueling summer combat in 1967, both *Time* and *Life* splashed images of besieged soldiers at Con Thien on their covers.

West of Cam Lo, a visible trail climbs to the 1,785-foot (544 m) summit of a hill once known as **Firebase Fuller ❸**, from which U.S. artillery hurled shells as far as Khe Sanh, 25 miles (40 km) southwest. Farther along Route 9, a short road to the left leads up to a pepper plantation at the former **Camp Carroll,** named for a Marine captain killed by friendly fire in 1966. Its 22 artillery pieces represented the largest firebase in the hills around Khe Sanh.

Beyond, Route 9 veers around a denuded crag to the **Rockpile ❹**, a 755-foot (230 m) hill off the right side of the road. In 1966, U.S. recon troops set up an observation post on the hill. Until abandoning the post in 1968, Marines here directed artillery in support of passing ground troops.

Climbing past the farm villages of the

Cement-filled sandbags replicate a typical American bunker during the battle for Khe Sanh.

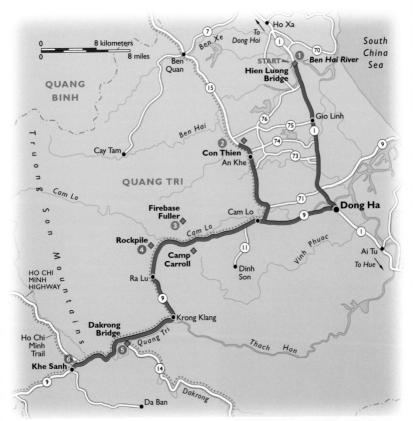

Bru highlanders, the highway beyond Krong Klang now serves trucks hailing from Laos and points farther east on a new route to Burma. At the **Dakrong Bridge** 5 over the Quang Tri River, a marker memorializes a spur of the Ho Chi Minh Trail that once intersected Route 9 here.

Eight miles (13 km) farther west, the road twists into **Khe Sanh** 6, site of the largest U.S. combat base in the DMZ and red- hot center of the war between January and April 1968. In late 1967, the North Vietnamese massed an army of 20,000 in the surrounding hills, diverting American attention from the Viet Cong's multipronged Tet offensive in 1968. Over nine weeks, the United States dropped 75,000 tons of bombs on North Vietnamese positions, killing 10,000 soldiers. Incoming mortars and artillery claimed 200 American lives.

Today, a **museum** ($) stands at the center of the onetime combat base and airstrip.

> 🗺 See area map p. 113
> ► Ben Hai River
> ↔ 63 miles (102 km)
> ⏱ 2.5 hours
> ► Khe Sanh
>
> **NOT TO BE MISSED**
> - Rockpile
> - Dakrong Bridge
> - Khe Sanh
>
> **TOUR OPERATOR**
> Sepon Travel, 189 Le Duan, Dong Ha, tel (053) 855-289

Outside, next to several helicopters and a tank, cement-filled sandbags replicate American bunkers. Exhibits inside include flak jackets, helmets, weapons, and mess trays salvaged from the base.

Guided tours return to Hue from here. ■

More places to visit in north-central Vietnam

CUC PHUONG NATIONAL PARK

Established in 1962, Cuc Phuong was Vietnam's first national park. Seventy-five miles (120 km) south of Hanoi and 40 miles (65 km) west of Ninh Binh, this is one of the more accessible and visitor-friendly places to experience the country's diverse flora and, with luck, fauna. The park's big draw is the **Endangered Primate Rescue Center,** a breeding facility that houses 120 primates comprising 15 species of gibbons

Langurs—slender, long-tailed monkeys—are rehabilitated at Cuc Phuong National Park.

and langurs. The park also breeds the rare Owston's civet, as well as weasels, otters, and big cats rescued from the wildlife trade. Trails meander past magnificent trees to caves in limestone outcrops and to Muong villages, where guests can overnight in a stilt house. Visitors can also stay at park-owned bungalows on **Mac Lake.** The best time to visit is in the dry season *(Oct.–March);* in April and May, millions of butterflies breed here.
⚠ 113 C6–D6 ✉ 28 miles (45 km) west of Ninh Binh via Hwy. 1. Follow the road to Kenh Ga and Van Long Nature Reserve. ☎ (030) 848-006 💲 $

LAM KINH CITADEL

From the Lam Son forests, Le Loi launched a ten-year campaign to oust the Ming from Vietnam. After reestablishing the capital at Hanoi in 1427, the new king ordained construction of a royal citadel, Lam Kinh ("blue capital"), near his birthplace, 31 miles (50 km) west of Thanh Hoa. Today, the ruins include ramparts, trenches, dragon balustrades on a flight of stone steps, and a carved stone turtle bearing a stela inscribed by Nguyen Trai that details the life and work of Le Loi. In 1994, the Vietnamese government dedicated two million dollars toward ongoing site restoration; as of press date, much of the citadel remains temporarily closed to visitors. ⚠ 113 D5 **Visitor information** ✉ Thanh Hoa Tourist, 25A Quang Trung, Thanh Hoa ☎ (037) 852-517 (no English spoken)

SAM SON BEACH

Ten miles (15 km) east of Thanh Hoa, Sam Son is one of the better known beaches along the north-central coast. The French colonial government popularized these shores and dunes with a holiday resort in 1907. Today, young Vietnamese couples flock to **Trong Mai** ("cock and hen") **Rock,** a natural landmark that memorializes a legend about a fairy who fell in love with a mortal. Before the god of thunder could punish her for this violation, she transformed herself and her lover into stone.
⚠ 113 C5

VAN LONG NATURE RESERVE

Like nearby Tam Coc and Kenh Ga, Van Long is often invoked as another terrestrial Ha Long Bay. The 7,410-acre (3,000 ha) reserve surrounds karst formations that rise abruptly from extant wetlands enlarged by local irrigation efforts. Boats probe the wetlands on tours popular with birders. Amid this natural splendor, the endangered Delacour's langur is making a last stand. ⚠ 113 C6 ✉ From Ninh Binh, 6 miles (10 km) north via Hwy. 1; at Gian Khau turn right and after 3 miles (5 km) look for signs to the reserve ☎ (030) 868-798 💲 Boat tour: $ ■

Within a radius of 50 miles (80 km), Hue, Hoi An, and My Son encompass Vietnam's most appealing constellation of attractions, flush with splendid imperial architecture, an ancient Southeast Asian port, and the ruins of a vanished kingdom.

Hue & central Vietnam

Closed silk lanterns await a buyer's touch.

Neighbors still gather along Hue's sidewalks for Chinese chess and the latest gossip.

Hue & central Vietnam

THE CHIMERA OF *INDOCHINE* IS RENDERED MOST TANGIBLE BY THE central provinces of Vietnam. The cities' imperial and colonial vestiges, the idyllic villages and garden houses, ever present mountains, and pregnant rivers seem to flow as much from an illusion of Vietnam as from the soil and water itself. Vietnam is firing on all cylinders here. When the weather's right, it's as good as good can get.

Thua Thien and Quang Nam (home provinces to Hue and Danang, respectively) entered the dominion of the Viets in 1306 after a smitten Cham king ceded a huge chunk of his kingdom for the hand of a Vietnamese princess. In the 16th century, a disaffected Nguyen aristocrat heeded the prophecy of a Nostradamus-like character named Nguyen Binh Khiem and migrated south from Thanh Hoa to settle the southern frontier.

While nominally loyal to the powerless remnants of the Le dynasty, the Nguyen fought endlessly with the Trinh, a rival group of northern aristocrats, across a border not too far from the later line of demarcation between North and South Vietnam. The Tay Son routed the Nguyen from Hue in 1775, but by 1802, following retaliation by Nguyen Anh (later King Gia Long), the Nguyens unified the country and estab-lished their capital at Hue.

Hue's imperial monuments comprise one of five sites in Vietnam inscribed on UNESCO's World Heritage List. Quang Nam is home to a pair of World Heritage sites—the antique Southeast Asian port of Hoi An and the Cham ruins at My Son.

International tourists tend to make less of Hue than they should. Partly, the fault lies with the weather. From October to January, cloudy skies and rain can plague the city for weeks at a stretch. But the problem, too, is an absence of vision. The city's tombs, palaces, museums, pagodas, garden homes, colonial French villas, and municipal buildings, coupled with a poetic landscape, are the richest vein for cultural exploration in Vietnam. But historically, Hue's hotels and restaurants have lacked the ambience and nightlife to keep people coming back for more. That should change now as two new five-star hotels and one historic four-star option provide a much-needed upgrade to the city's infrastructure.

Farther south, Danang is more of a springboard to local attractions—Hoi An, the Marble Mountains, My Son, China Beach—than an attraction in its own right. In the 19th century, the city's reputation as a port and a commercial center was brightening as nearby Hoi An's was dimming. But its reputation is also sullied by its situation as a beachhead for the great foreign incursions of the 19th and 20th centuries. The French established their first toehold in Vietnam at Danang in 1858; and in 1965, the first U.S. ground troops waded ashore at My Khe Beach, where local girls in *ao dai* dresses greeted them with leis.

Today, Danang is setting itself up as a jaunty commercial center, with international flights landing at its airport and a busy seaport. Hoi An, by contrast, is all about tourism, nostalgia, and the beach.

Many come to Vietnam thrilled by the prospect of a north-south train journey on the Reunification Express. The trip gets old faster than you might think, but its most beautiful stretch winds through the rugged Hai Van headlands between Danang and Hue. ■

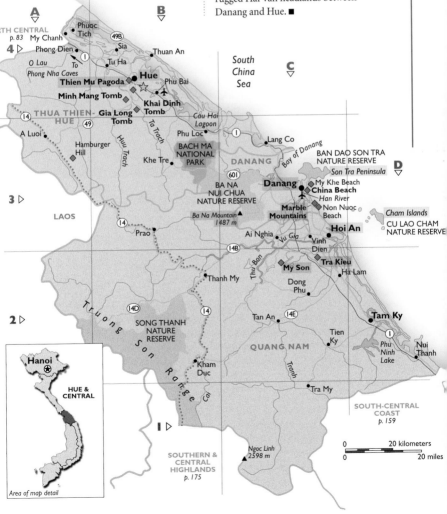

Hue

Though Ho Chi Minh's government extinguished Hue's glory days as the imperial capital of Vietnam in 1945, many architectural and cultural relics of the imperial era have been assiduously preserved. The dervishes of urban renewal have largely ignored the city, leaving its centuries-old pagodas, villas, garden homes, and river with an enduring aesthetic hegemony.

All of Vietnam prides itself on Hue, as a languorously genteel place whose singularly accented people are not merely behind the times but lost in time. The city is spliced, not divided, by the Perfume River. Life is as vital on the north bank, where the Nguyen kings reigned from within the Forbidden Purple City, as it is on the south bank, where the French laid out their sprawling new district in the late 19th century.

The Forbbiden Purple City is contained by the walled Imperial City, where the most resplendent structures and relics—the Palace of Supreme Harmony, Noon Gate, Mieu Temple, and Nine Dynastic Urns—survived both the French War and, to a lesser extent, the Vietnam War. Breached by a complement of ten Oriental gates, the fortresslike walls of the citadel encompass both walled cities, as well as expansive neighborhoods of leafy streets, parks, museums, markets, and bistros.

The French bequeathed a graceful European counterpoint on the south bank, with several marvelous art deco buildings and a broad range of villas, churches, and

Hue
▲ 129 B4
Visitor information
✉ Hue Tourist, 5 Ly Thuong Kiet
☎ (054) 823-577
✉ Mandarin Café, 3 Hung Vuong
☎ (054) 821-281

municipal buildings. From any of the three bridges that span the river, the upstream vistas of mountains and sunsets provide a natural complement to the city's chiseled charm.

Upstream from the citadel, the tower of Thien Mu Pagoda looms over the Perfume River as the city's most prominent landmark. The nearby garden district of Kim Long basks in a timeworn ambience emanating from its houses of columns and panels.

Out along Dien Bien Phu, the level urban terrain rumples into picturesque hills sown by the tombs of the Nguyen kings and lesser royalty and nourished by countless pagodas—perhaps one for every thousand residents. ■

Left: Biking along the Perfume River past Thien Mu Pagoda
Below: Docents in traditional garb at the Imperial City's Mieu Temple

A walk along Le Loi

After taking control of Hue in 1885, the French ceded the Imperial City to the Vietnamese and made over the south bank as a European enclave. Along the Perfume River, they improved an avenue that King Gia Long blazed in the early 1800s and named the street after French Prime Minister Jules Ferry. Today, the avenue, now called Le Loi, tunnels beneath the bowers of towering tamarinds and flame trees from the railway station to the Trang Tien Bridge. Its old colonial buildings have borne witness to personages and events that loom large in the history of Vietnam.

Hue is renowned for its music, poetry, cuisine, and residents' distinct accent.

In 1906, the raspberry red **Hue railway station** ❶ *(2 Bui Thi Xuan)* opened as the northern terminal of the Danang-Hue leg of the Transindochinois line. Construction on the railway began in 1899, though the 1,072 miles (1,715 km) between Saigon and Hanoi would not link up until the mid-1930s. Gustave Eiffel's firm designed the White Tiger Bridge north of the station.

Across the Phu Cam River, **La Residence Hotel** *(5 Le Loi)* was built in 1930 as the colonial government's guesthouse. Its bowed front, long horizontal lines, porthole windows, and nautical accents are hallmarks of the streamline moderne branch of art deco architecture.

Next door is Hue's **Ho Chi Minh Museum** ❷ *(7 Le Loi, closed Mon., $)*. Its prized relics are trifles—a radio, a pair of watches, cotton shirts—that Ho gave to local supporters. The museum keeps a bronze bust cast by an American in 1967 and Ho's autograph among a catalog of 1,300 pieces.

Slightly more profound Ho memorials include the reconstructed house in nearby Duong No *(5 miles/8 km NE of Hue)*, where Ho (then Nguyen Sinh Cung) lived as a boy from 1898 to 1900, and the house at 112 Mai Thuc Loan, where he lived in 1901.

In 1908, Ho attended the prestigious **Quoc Hoc High School** *(10 Le Loi)*, a national school founded by King Thanh Thai in 1896. A statue of the boy-student stands in the school's main avenue, though access is restricted. Pham Van Dong and Vo Nguyen Giap also studied here. The school's first headmaster, Ngo Dinh Kha, was Thanh Thai's minister of rites and the father of South Vietnam's President Ngo Dinh Diem.

Opposite the school gate is an **imperial monument,** erected in 1920 to commemorate colonial French and Vietnamese soldiers who died in France during World War I. Evidence of its original purpose is etched on the riverside face, where the names of Vietnamese soldiers remain visible. Until recently, the streetside face of the monument was a billboard for Ho Chi Minh's most famous maxim: "Nothing is more precious than independence and freedom."

Continuing along Le Loi, **Hai Ba Trung Secondary School** ❸ *(12 Le Loi)* opened in 1917 as a girls' school complement to Quoc Hoc. Its raspberry red facade, like Quoc Hoc's, is a legacy of Ngo Dinh Kha's tastes.

Farther along, you'll pass the magisterial new **People's Committee Building** on your right. Across the street, the streetside ward of Hue's **General Hospital** was built after the Battle of Hue in 1968.

Across the Hanoi intersection, the **Cercle Sportif** is another streamline moderne design. From **Phu Xuan Bridge,** note the building's pronounced veranda, porthole windows, and bridge-like penthouse on the upper deck. During the colonial era, the Cercle was a leisure club.

Farther east, stretching for an entire city block along Le Loi, the 1901 **Saigon Morin Hotel** ❹ *(30 Le Loi)* was an unfortunate casualty of a Saigon Tourist restoration in the 1990s. Charlie Chaplin honeymooned here with Paulette Goddard in 1936, and writers André Malraux and Somerset Maugham also checked into the Morin brothers' hotel.

Across the street, a **marble obelisk** topped by the Buddhist wheel of law commemorates eight protesters who died on May 8, 1963, during a rally against anti-Buddhist measures enacted by Ngo Dinh Diem. The protests escalated here in Hue and ultimately brought down the Diem regime.

The French-built **Trang Tien Bridge** *(at Hung Vuong)* is mentioned in more than a few melancholy songs about lost love and dreary weather in Hue. The seven trestles of the quarter-mile (400 m) bridge opened to great fanfare in 1900, with King Thanh Thai himself cutting the ribbon. ∎

🗺 See area map p. 129
▶ Hue railway station
↔ 1.1 miles (1.8 km)
⏱ 1 hour
▶ Trang Tien Bridge

NOT TO BE MISSED
- Quoc Hoc High School
- Imperial monument
- Cercle Sportif

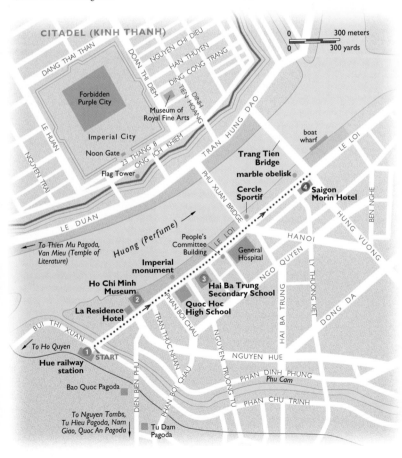

Hue Citadel

Hue Citadel

- ⬛ Map p. 133
- ✉ N bank of Perfume River, via Phu Xuan & Trang Tien Bridges. Enter at Ngan Gate.

Imperial City

- ✉ Enter at Ngo Mon ("noon") Gate, 23 Thang 8, within the citadel
- ☎ (054) 523-058
- 💲 $

THE MASSIVE HUE CITADEL, WHICH ENCOMPASSES THE grandiose Imperial City and fabled Forbidden Purple City, is an Asian wonderland of palaces, pavilions, temples, ponds, gardens, gates, and halls. Capital of the Nguyen dynasty from 1802 until the abdication of the last emperor, Bao Dai, in 1945, the Imperial City is a sublime interpretation of the larger, more austere dynastic capital at Beijing. Though a catastrophic 1947 fire destroyed many of the 150 royal structures built during the Nguyen's 143-year reign, the most magnificent structures survived and have been restored with such meticulous fidelity to the past that it's hard to tell what's old and what's new.

Gia Long, first emperor of the Nguyen dynasty, broke ground on the colossal imperial complex in 1804, conscripting 30,000 subjects to toil on his architectural fantasy. He soon boosted the daily workforce to as many as 80,000 unhappy laborers, prompting European observers to condemn his despotism.

Bounding the complex is the **citadel** *(kinh thanh),* a 1.5-square-mile (4 sq km) fortification of 22-foot (6.5 m) walls, ramparts, parapets, and bastions, with a commanding flag tower that fronts the Perfume River. Designed on designs by pioneering 17th-century French military architect Sébastien de Vauban, the sheer walls rise from a 13-foot-deep (4 m) stone-lined moat between 130 and 165 feet (40–50 m) wide.

Impregnable as it may seem, the citadel was militarily obsolete even at the time of its construction. Still, Viet Cong and North Vietnamese troops managed to hold out inside the citadel for 25 days in a pitched battle against U.S. Marines during the 1968 Tet Offensive. Battle scars remain, though the rubble is fast disappearing as preservationists gradually restore monuments that UNESCO identified in 1992 as a World Heritage site.

INTO THE IMPERIAL CITY

The Imperial City, a second walled and moated city with a 6,700-square-foot (603 sq m) perimeter, follows the same layout at Beijing's Forbidden City. Tree-shaded paths, crumbling palaces, and flowering gardens make for a pleasant stroll.

Enter through the **Ngo Mon** ("noon") **Gate,** the 190-foot-wide (57 m), U-shaped entrance once reserved for the sole use of the emperor. Atop the gate's 15-foot (4.5 m) brick foundation is the **Belvedere of Five Phoenixes,** from which the emperor presided over state ceremonies. Between the flag tower and the gate are the **Nine Holy Cannon.** Gia Long had these forged from captured Tay Son weapons in 1803.

Cross the **Trung Dao Bridge,** spanning lotus-dotted Thai Dich Lake, and enter into the **Esplanade of Great Salutations,** where mandarins stood in ranks of nine during court ceremonies. The emperor, who declared himself the Son of Heaven, ruled from the **Thai Hoa Palace** (Palace of Supreme Harmony) beyond the courtyard. The sole furnishing in this tiled expanse of lacquered vermilion columns and gilded wood carvings remains the throne, elevated on terraces beneath a canopy representing the heavens.

Behind the palace, the wartime toll is made painfully obvious by huge swards of green space where other royal structures once stood, including 21 acres (8 ha) of the

For nearly 150 years, Nguyen kings reigned from the Palace of Supreme Harmony within the Hue Citadel.

One of the Imperial City's regal gates. The middle portal of a triple gate was reserved for the king, while mandarins used the doorways on either side.

Court music performances

✉ Royal Theater, Imperial City

🕐 Daily performances, 8 a.m. & 2 p.m.

💲 $

Forbidden Purple City, a third walled enclosure that was off-limits to all but the emperor, his wives, concubines, and eunuchs.

The extant **Left** and **Right Mandarin Halls** once flanked the now vanished Can Chanh Palace, a second throne room where the emperor conducted daily business. The mandarins wore court dress when meeting with the emperor. Now, tourists don mandarin attire for photo ops in the left hall; the right hall displays works from the Hue Museum of Royal Fine Arts (see p. 143).

Behind and to the left of the Palace of Supreme Harmony, a leafy avenue leads toward the restored **Chuong Duc Gate.** To the left before you reach the gate is **The Mieu,** a temple Minh Mang built in 1821 to worship his father, Gia Long. Last restored in the 1990s, the interior is a stunning indulgence of vermilion columns and gilded wood carvings. Its ten bays are dedicated to the veneration of the Nguyen emperors. Although the French overlords first balked at the inclusion of emperors Ham Nghi, Thanh Thai,

and Duy Tan, each of whom had been deposed by the colonial masters, the three rebels were duly accorded their bays in 1959.

Across the courtyard, the **Nine Dynastic Urns** stand before the **Hien Lam Pavilion,** the tallest and, to some Vietnamese, most beautiful structure in the city. The pavilion memorializes those who've helped perpetuate the dynasty. Still more intriguing are the urns. Cast between 1835 and 1837, these 2-ton (1.8 metric ton) vessels served both to collect heaven's mandate and to celebrate the country's beauty and dynastic stability. The hips of each urn are embossed with 17 separate depictions of plants, landscapes, animals, boats, and weapons that, taken together, form a lexicon of Vietnamese culture. Each is dedicated to one of the Nguyen emperors and stands opposite his bay in The Mieu.

If possible, cap your visit to the Imperial City by attending a concert of court music (*nha nhac;* see p. 56), a ritual genre once performed at coronations, funerals, and other royal events. ■

Thien Mu Pagoda

THE SEVEN-STORY TOWER OF THIEN MU ("HEAVENLY LADY") Pagoda is Hue's defining landmark, as you'll clearly see from the plethora of images on postcards, T-shirts, paintings, and other souvenirs. Thankfully, the pagoda's setting, storied history, and relics make good on its promise as a precious place.

Thien Mu Pagoda
🅐 Map p. 133
✉ From the citadel, follow Kim Long SW beyond railroad bridge

In 1601, a female mystic decreed that whoever founded a pagoda on this bluff above the Perfume River would also found a great dynasty. Nguyen Hoang gambled on the mystic's prophecy, and his lineage, all the way down to Vietnam's last emperor, Bao Dai, stood as a testament to her wisdom.

From Kim Long, a stairway climbs to four pillars inscribed with Chinese characters that praise Buddhism and the pagoda. The **Phuoc Duyen** ("source of happiness") **tower** stands 70 feet (21 m) over the pagoda's trapezoidal terrace. A stela to the right details the tower's construction in 1844, while a stela to the left is inscribed with Thieu Tri's poetry.

In 1710, Lord Nguyen Phuc Chu ordered casting of the 8-foot (2.5 m) bronze bell framed within a six-sided pavilion to the left of the tower. Then, in 1715, Chu engraved a hymn to himself and Buddhism on a stela perched atop the sculpted marble tortoise in the pavilion to the right of the tower.

Buddhist guardians flank each portal in the triple-gate entrance to the courtyard. Once through, look back up to see helmeted Ho Phap, guardian of the law, standing above the Taoist Jade Emperor.

Beyond, the **Temple of the Great Hero** shelters a gallery of statues. In the vestibule, a glass case holds a smiling bronze Di Lac Buddha, while farther in you'll find the ten netherworld kings and a fine collection of 18 clay brown arhats in ceramic robes with gray

tracery. Above one threshold, a bronze, black-haired Sakyamuni sits before another iteration of Di Lac and a sanctuary of Buddhas of the past, present, and future.

However superb the statuary, though, there's no relic at Thien Mu more emotive than the one garaged in the monk's apartment building. This robin's egg–blue Austin sedan ferried Thien Mu's Thich Quang Duc to the Saigon intersection where he set himself ablaze in 1963 (see p. 45). ■

Thien Mu's tower is as much a landmark to Hue as the Eiffel Tower is to Paris or the Empire State Building is to New York City.

Hue's other pagodas

**Hue's other
pagodas**
Map p. 133

MORE THAN 300 PAGODAS SOW THE SEEDS OF BUDDHISM in and around Hue, enlightening the city's reputation as the soul of Vietnam. While their statues and wood carvings do not rival those of the finest northern pagodas, their pleasant settings and feng shui channel *chi* like nowhere else in the country.

A Chinese monk, Giac Phong, founded **Bao Quoc Pagoda** *(off N end of Dien Bien Phu)* at the end of the 17th century. In 1747, Lord Nguyen Phu Khoat chartered the pagoda with a royal decree and inscribed the name board that hangs in the main sanctuary. Later in the 18th century, the Tay Son king Quang Trung stored arms and gunpowder in the pagoda. Beyond the name board and a bronze bell cast during Gia Long's reign in 1808, few of the pagoda's relics survived a fire that broke out during fighting at Tet in 1968. But do check out Giac Phong's three-story pink stupa beyond the main hall. At the bottom of the steep stairway is the 15-foot (4.5 m) **Ham Long** ("dragon's jaw") **well.** Though murky these days, its water was once famed for its freshness and clarity and was reserved for the king.

About a half mile (1 km) south on Dien Bien Phu, **Tu Dam Pagoda** has served as a rallying point for Buddhist causes nationwide since the 1930s. Inside the triple gate, a two-story conference hall stands to the right of an expansive courtyard, designed to accommodate throngs of people. The bodhi tree inside the gate grew from a sprig cut in the 1930s from the bodhi tree under which the historical Buddha is said to have received his enlightenment. Following Thich Quang Duc's example in Saigon, a monk immolated himself in this courtyard in 1963.

At the south end of Dien Bien Phu, turn right on Le Ngo Cat. About a half mile (1 km) from the turn are the gates to picturesque **Tu Hieu Pagoda.** Tu Hieu owes its present stature to imperial eunuchs who, fearing oblivion after death, offered money and land to the pagoda in 1848. In return, the monks allotted a graveyard to the eunuchs and pledged to honor their souls. Inside the triple gate, the crescent lotus pond dates from an 1894 restoration. Beyond the main sanctuary, Quang Hieu Duong Hall honors Le Van Duyet (see p. 209) and Quan Kong. This pagoda is also renowned as the "root pagoda" of Thich Nhat Hanh, who lived here as a novice and later rose to prominence as the most celebrated teacher of Buddhism in the West after the Dalai Lama.

Turn left at the end of Dien Bien Phu and then left again at Dao Tan to reach **Quoc An Pagoda.** Like Bao Quoc and Tu Hieu, Quoc An was laid out in the square shape of the Chinese character for mouth *(khau).* Four buildings surround an interior courtyard of potted bonsai, with the main sanctuary at front, a hall to worship the pagoda's benefactors at rear, and a reception hall and monks' quarters to either side. Quoc An is one of Hue's oldest pagodas, founded in 1684 by the monk Nguyen Thieu from Guangdong, China. ■

Nguyen tombs

THE TOMBS OF THE NGUYEN DYNASTY KINGS ARE IN FACT grandiose temple complexes, anchored by burial sites and complemented by palaces, pavilions, stela houses, courtyards, gates, ponds, and gardens. Built between 1814 and 1931, the seven tombs were laid out south of the citadel according to the ancient Oriental art of *phong thuy,* known in the West as feng shui.

At King Tu Duc's tomb, all named structures contain the word *khiem* (modesty).

Nguyen tombs

▲ Map p. 133
$ Minh Mang, Tu Duc, or Khai Dinh: $

Most visitors to Hue confine their explorations to the tombs of Minh Mang and Tu Duc, which are the most majestic and best preserved. The other tombs would rate as major tourist attractions were it not for the proximity of these grand neighbors. Unbound by walls, the monuments to Gia Long, Thieu Tri, and Dong Khanh sprawl across open landscapes, inspiring intimate links with the natural environment. Khai Dinh is a fusion of Oriental and Occidental styles. Duc Duc was buried closer to town, on the spot where his corpse accidentally fell in transit.

The Nguyen, who often succumbed to Chinese influence, modeled their eternal cities on the Ming dynasty tombs. Their geomancers strived to nestle the structures within the protective confines of hills, with a dominant elevation in the near-distance to serve as a hedge against ill winds and a lower hill at the rear to cushion the complex. To the extent possible, they laid out the major monuments—triple gate, court of honor, stela house, temple, and burial site—along a common axis, known as the Way of the Spirit. The statues of mandarins, horses, and elephants that flank the court of honor stand in service to the king after death. Not every tomb subscribes exactly to the model, though Minh Mang's does so with remarkable fidelity.

MINH MANG (*R.*1820–1841)
From the **Great Red Gate,** shut since Minh Mang's corpse passed through in 1841, the Way of the Spirit channels through the

Minh Manh's tomb

Thong Minh Chinh Truc Bridge

Ton Nguyet Lake

Minh Lau Pavilion

Trung Dao Bridge

Trung Minh Lake

Getting there

To reach every tomb but Duc Duc's, which lies closer in on Duy Tan, you'll turn right at the south end of Dien Bien Phu. Turn left on Minh Mang to reach Thieu Tri's and Khai Dinh's tombs. Stay straight and take Le Ngo Cat to its end, then turn left on Huyen Tran Cong Chua to reach Tu Duc's and Dong Khanh's tombs. Both Minh Mang's and Gia Long's tombs are accessible via sampan ferries across the Perfume River or via the bridge that crosses the river along Minh Mang. The entrance to Minh Mang's tomb lies a couple hundred yards from the bridge. The route to Gia Long's is more complicated and follows an unmarked path along the river.

Court of Honor, ascends a stela house raised on three terraces, then ambles across another courtyard, past two more gates and bridges, and through a temple and a pavilion to its terminus at Minh Mang's tumulus, almost a half mile (700 m) later. A wall, 10 feet (3 m) high and more than a mile (1,750 m) long, encircles 40 structures and a parkscape.

The emperor dragooned 3,000 soldiers and laborers into work on the tomb in 1840. From the **Pavilion of Light** (Minh Lau), Minh Mang watched the tomb take shape. After he died, his son Thieu Tri enlisted 9,000 soldiers and workers to finish the job, which they did in 1843. Until French soldiers plundered this tomb and others in 1885, the **Temple of Infinite Grace** (Dien Sung An) held the emperor's most prized personal possessions. Written by Thieu Tri, the Chinese inscriptions on the **stela** detail

Minh Mang's merits and accomplishments, including a reference to the king's 142 offspring.

TU DUC (R.1848–1883)

Tu Duc sired no children, despite having 103 concubines. He nevertheless begot a fairyland for his eternal rest before succumbing to smallpox. His tomb caught the eye of French filmmakers, who used the **Xung Khiem Pavilion**, where Tu Duc wrote poetry, in the 1992 epic *Indochine*.

A 4,950-foot (1,500 m) wall encloses 50 distinct elements, including a theater and lake. Following its construction in 1867, the king used the compound

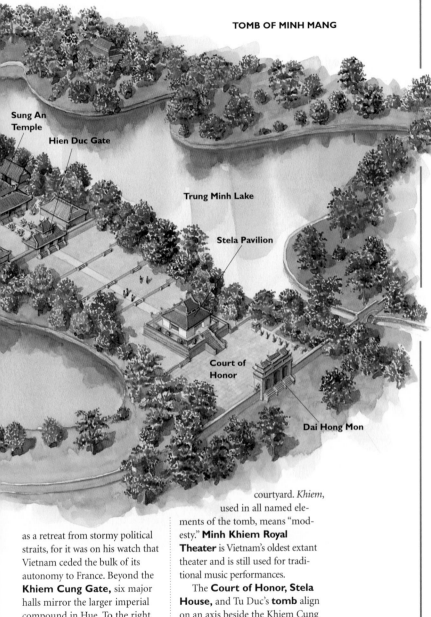

TOMB OF MINH MANG

Sung An Temple

Hien Duc Gate

Trung Minh Lake

Stela Pavilion

Court of Honor

Dai Hong Mon

courtyard. *Khiem,* used in all named elements of the tomb, means "modesty." **Minh Khiem Royal Theater** is Vietnam's oldest extant theater and is still used for traditional music performances.

as a retreat from stormy political straits, for it was on his watch that Vietnam ceded the bulk of its autonomy to France. Beyond the **Khiem Cung Gate,** six major halls mirror the larger imperial compound in Hue. To the right and left are houses for the military and civil mandarins. Tu Duc lodged in both **Hoa Khiem Palace,** where his cult is most active today, and **Luong Khiem Palace,** on the other side of the

The **Court of Honor, Stela House,** and Tu Duc's **tomb** align on an axis beside the Khiem Cung compound. Stroll around the finger of **Luu Khiem Lake,** and you'll pass the tomb of Tu Duc's queen and arrive at the tomb of Kien Phuc, an obscure Nguyen emperor who ruled from 1883 to 1884.

GIA LONG (*R.*1802–1819)

Gia Long incorporated far fewer man-made structures in the design of his eternal city. The grace notes here are mostly natural. A constellation of 42 hills, big and small, surrounds his tomb.

Beyond **Minh Thanh Temple,** dedicated to the memory of

Stone mandarins stand eternally at attention in the Court of Honor at Khai Dinh's mausoleum, a familiar sight at most of the Nguyen kings' burial sites.

Gia Long and his wife, the first Nguyen emperor and his wife lie side by side in mausoleums of dark blue stone, riddled with scars from wartime fighting. Statues of mandarins in the **Court of Honor** were also damaged, though they, as well as some of the animal appendages, have been restored. Twin obelisks across Long Lake herald **Thien Tho Mount,** the tomb's screen.

KHAI DINH (*R.*1916–1925)

Khai Dinh's tomb mounts a steep hillside in terraces of cement, concrete, slate, and marble. Such austerity was at odds with the lavish personality of the king, but consistent with his embrace of the trappings of Western civilization.

Inside **Thien Dinh Palace,** the walls of the first room are bedecked in mosaics of ceramic and glass. Panels of the four seasons depict bamboo for winter, the plum blossom for spring, the lily for summer, and the chrysanthemum for fall, while panels in a two-tiered frieze contain the eight precious objects (scroll, lute, wine gourd, etc.), complemented by such modern motifs as a tennis racket and alarm clock. The king's remains are entombed in a vault 30 feet (9 m) beneath this statue.

DONG KHANH (*R.*1885–1888)

After Dong Khanh's death, King Thanh Thai rehabbed a temple the previous king had built to worship his father's memory. Inside, much of the temple's decor are gifts from the French and carry a subtext of supremacy, from the tricolor stained-glass windows to a lithograph of a Napoleonic battle scene and a pillow used when smoking opium.

THIEU TRI (*R.*1841–1847)

As at the tombs of Gia Long and Dong Khanh, this complex lacks a surrounding wall. From its wide **Court of Honor,** the axis mounts a second terrace where Thieu Tri's accomplishments, written by his son Tu Duc, occupy a timeworn shelter. Beyond the commanding stone obelisks, three bridges span **Ngung Hy Lake** to Thieu Tri's tumulus.

DUC DUC (*R.*1883)

Duc Duc, his son Thanh Thai, and his grandson Duy Tan are all revered in **Long An Temple,** a complex that's fallen on hard times. Duc Duc's altar occupies the central bay, flanked by altars and bronze busts of his son and grandson. The French used the compound as a garrison during their war, and at least one of the bunkers remains. Duc Duc is buried in a detached compound behind the palace, without attendant statues or a stela. His son and grandson are interred nearby in simpler tombs. ■

More places to visit in & around Hue

HON CHEN TEMPLE

A collection of shrines, stelae, altars, and spirit houses cling to the side of a picturesque bluff above the Perfume River at Hon Chen Temple. The Cham worshipped Po Nagar (see p. 164) on this site a thousand years ago. The Viets absorbed the goddess into their own tradition and continue to worship her under the name Thien Y A Na. During the third and seventh lunar months, the goddess' cult throngs the temple grounds to perform sacred rituals. King Dong Khanh embraced the goddess as a patron saint, referring to her as "older sister," and enlarged the temple in 1886. Dong Khanh himself is also worshipped at the temple.
⊠ Six miles (9 km) west of Hue, accessible only via river; join a boat tour or hire a sampan ($)

MUSEUM OF ROYAL FINE ARTS

Widely considered Vietnam's most elegant palace, **Long An Palace** also rates as one of the country's finest museums and houses the grandest collection of Nguyen dynasty relics. Its two-tiered roof, buffered by inscribed wooden panels, is a hallmark of Hue architecture. Inside, 128 ironwood pillars partition the gallery into seven bays, with wings at either end. Glass paintings lean off the capitals of six columns in the vestibule, each inspired by a poem King Thieu Tri wrote and sent to China for illustration. Exhibits include imperial robes, porcelain, furnishings, screens, coins, gongs, and ceremonial weapons.
⊠ 3 Le Truc ☎ (054) 524-429 (no English spoken) ⊕ Closed Mon. 🅂 $

NAM GIAO ESPLANADE

The Nguyen kings prayed for the stability of their dynasty and welfare of the country in a ceremony of great ritual and sacrifice at this open-air monument, laid out in 1806. The esplanade comprises three superimposed terraces. The lowest represents man; the square middle terrace represents Earth; and the circular terrace 15 steps above represents heaven. Until 1942, the kings paraded to this site annually (after 1890, every three years)

in a procession of great fanfare, with sumptuously attired court musicians, mandarins, soldiers, elephants, horses, and dancers. Before making sacrifices, the king fasted for three days in the **Fasting Palace,** which still stands in a walled enclosure adjacent to the esplanade. Planted by mandarins and royal family members, pines stand as emblems of eternity and nobility.
⊠ From 5 Le Loi, follow Dien Bien Phu south a little over a mile (2 km) to its end.

TEMPLE OF LITERATURE

After Gia Long assumed the throne in 1802 and moved the capital to Hue, he ordered construction of another temple of literature to complement Hanoi's venerable Van Mieu (see pp. 72–75). The wars demolished the temple's seven ironwood structures, but the triple gate remains, as do 32 stone stelae, borne by tortoises and inscribed with the names of 293 successful candidates. Two additional stelae stand under separate covers.
🄰 Map p. 133 ⊠ Follow Kim Long along river from White Tiger railroad bridge, past Thien Mu Pagoda. Temple is on right, just over 2 miles (3.7 km) from bridge.

TIGER'S ARENA (HO QUYEN)

Between 1830 and 1904, the Nguyen kings pitted elephants and tigers in mortal combat in this arena on the Perfume River's south bank. The arena is in remarkably good condition, ringed by two concentric brick walls with an interior diameter of 144 feet (44 m). Two stairways climb to the tribune where the king and his retinue enjoyed the spectacles. Opposite, five doors at the base of the arena wall open onto pens for tigers and panthers. Elephants paraded in through a 13-foot (4 m) door beside the tribune. Before combat, tenders declawed the tigers, sewed their mouths shut, and weakened them through starvation so that the elephant, a symbol of royal prestige, invariably prevailed over the wild threats to order.
⊠ From train station, turn right and follow Ben Ngu Canal to Bui Thi Xuan, which runs along river. Arena is off left side of road, about 1.5 miles (2.5 km) from train station. ∎

Garden homes

While the Nguyen kings indulged their architectural fantasies in the Forbidden Purple City and the sumptuous mausoleums south of the Perfume River, the aristocrats of Hue cultivated the urban landscape with hundreds of garden homes. Hunkered behind tall hedges and minded by a serried rank of areca palms, these homes are a pure expression of the Vietnamese sensibility of living space.

Their roofs are vast, hipped realms of flat terra-cotta tiles, four insulating layers deep. Suites of doors stretch across the facade. Inside, ironwood and jackfruit pillars do the work of walls, partitioning the living space into bays. Timberwork tenons often include elaborately carved dragons, waves, flowers, and other traditional motifs. The Vietnamese refer to such a home as a *nha ruong* (house

of panels), for the squares and oblongs of exquisite wood carvings and mother-of-pearl inlay that hang from the truss.

The charm of a garden home lies not merely in its physical appearance but in its metaphysical accord. Builders invariably summoned masters of feng shui (known in Vietnam as *phong thuy*—wind and water) to position the structure with regard to the ancient art of placement. Ideally, a garden home should face south, the most auspicious direction for living. In front of the principal entrance, the owners erect a *binh phong* screen as a hedge to thwart the entry of malevolent spirits. Some nha ruong are so naturally ensconced in their surroundings, it's tempting to believe that they've always been there and that the earth has simply eroded around them.

homes, selling off the timbers for as little as $2,000. One developer swooped in and bought 17 nha ruong, which he dismantled and rebuilt as the Nha Trang Sailing Club. The nouveau and nostalgic riche from Saigon are buying and rebuilding in the south.

A French organization has identified more than 800 nha ruong in the province—more than 200 in the city of Hue. One hundred of these are viable candidates for preservation, not as fusty relics inhabited by otherwise bereft families but as living and breathing opportunities. "B&Bs," suggested Antoine Erout, director of the program run by Nord Pasde Calais. "Restaurants. Cafés. Galleries." ∎

Unlike the venerable merchants' homes of Hoi An (see pp. 154–155), which stand in a frozen parade of architecture along a cluster of downtown streets, the garden homes are less visible. They're clustered in a number of Hue neighborhoods, particularly the Kim Long and Vi Da districts, crouched behind hedges and within garden foliage.

These homes once stood as the centerpiece of modest urban estates of 1 or 2 acres (half a hectare). However, land reform measures after 1975 divvied up many of the properties. The privations of the late 1970s and the early 1980s forced many homeowners to sell chunks of land. The homes have persevered, a bit worse for the wear, but now they're more threatened than ever.

As Vietnam's economy booms, people naturally want something modern, clean, and utilitarian. So, the descendants of the aristocrats are cashing in on their storied

Hoi An's preeminence as a trading port diminished after its river silted up in the 19th century.

Central Vietnam

The triangle formed by Hoi An, Danang, and My Son yields myriad charms for tourists, from the museum-like ambience of Hoi An's Old Town to the tropical pleasures of the beach at Danang and the ruins of a legendary kingdom at My Son. The region's pagodas and villages layer on additional diversions, as do the Truong Son mountains, which plunge into the ocean along the border between Quang Nam and Thua Thien Provinces.

Just north of this border lies Bach Ma National Park, famous for its ruinous colonial villas, spectacular forests, and 25 feet (7.5 m) of annual rain. Nearby is Phuoc Tich, one of Vietnam's ethnic Viet villages. There are no sights here, per se, just a naturally pretty village with foliage-draped pathways and good examples of domestic architecture.

Danang's urban charms are few, but the Cham Museum is the best place to view the art of this vanished kingdom. Though the beaches at My Khe and Non Nuoc regularly make various Top 10 lists, that has more to do with savvy marketing than reality, as the beaches throughout Vietnam rival or surpass those here. The Bay of Danang, on the other hand, is truly one of a kind.

South of Danang, on the way to Hoi An, a unique pagoda experience awaits at the Marble Mountains, where a combination of hilltops vistas, grottoes, and shrines rewards anyone willing to undertake the climb.

In Hoi An, the old trading port's merchants houses, assembly halls, and museums collectively exude a magnetism that's more powerful than any individual site. The city is also making a name for itself in its tailor shops, as well as for cooking classes that go easy on the teaching and heavy on the fun.

From either Danang or Hoi An, the Cham ruins of My Son are an easy day trip. The ruins themselves might disappoint, but the towers nestling in the jungly setting make for a singular Cham experience. ∎

Phuoc Tich

PHUOC TICH IS A PRISTINE VIETNAMESE VILLAGE OF traditional garden homes *(nha ruong)*, family temples, and pagodas, embraced by a loop of the lovely green O Lau River. This village is to the countryside what Hoi An is to the urban landscape—inimitable and seductive. Much is made of hill-tribe villages throughout the highlands, but none can compare to the serene splendor of this ethnic Vietnamese (Kinh) village.

In the week before Tet, an elderly Phuoc Tich resident cuts banana leaves in which to wrap rice cakes.

Phuoc Tich was founded in 1470 by a group of settlers from Nghe An Province. In the 19th century, pottery kilns fired up an era of wealth that made the construction of its many garden houses possible. The war spared these old homes, according to villagers, because their inherent feng shui kept the destruction at bay.

Cultural historians stumbled upon Phuoc Tich in 2003, and plans are afoot to recognize it as the country's first Heritage Village. Meantime, little has been done to accommodate tourists, though the mostly elderly residents are hospitable and tend to fawn over the odd foreigner who pays a visit.

Today, 31 of Phuoc Tich's 117 homes are classified as garden homes. You'll find neither a tourist trail nor a navigable road. Instead, park at the village gate and stroll the rutted dirt tracks, keeping the O Lau to your left. The hedged pathways, groves of bamboo and bananas, and gardens evoke the timeless grandeur of the Vietnamese village like few places you're likely to encounter.

Past the ruined pottery works stands the 200-year-old home of **Truong Cong Thanh,** possibly the village's oldest. As such, it may also serve as something of an architectural template, as most of the village's nha ruong, which date from the 1870s, share structural similarities. Here, the typical nha ruong centers on a colonnade

of jackfruit pillars that divide the interior space into three bays beneath a sloping roof, with wings on either end. Eighteen wooden doors swing through nine doorways across the home's facade.

At the home of **Le Tran Phu,** floral designs trace across many panels, while mother-of-pearl inlay adorns others. At the home of **Ho Dinh Lan,** a deceased mandarin who ruled this village and others in the early 1900s, the fan-shaped name board over the central bay was a gift of King Duy Tan. The carved wooden side panels have depictions of writing brushes and lutes.

In the home of **Ho Van Te** and others, the most intricate wood carvings cover the joints in the first compartment. The common *ba thuy* wave motif is often accompanied by a dragon's head. Also look amid the rafters for *Tho,* the Chinese character for longevity. ∎

Phuoc Tich
🅰 129 A4
Visitor information
✉ Hue Tourist, 5 Ly Thuong Kiet
☎ (054) 823-577

A DRIVE DOWN THE MANDARIN ROAD

The stretch of Highway 1 between Hue and Danang is one of Vietnam's most scenic drives.

A drive down the Mandarin Road

Between Hue and Danang, the legendary Mandarin Road negotiates a series of three mountainous spurs that peak at Hai Van, the 1,637-foot (496 m) Pass of the Clouds by the Sea. The road's misty origins are rooted in the Ho dynasty of the early 15th century and the necessity of a way for scholars to journey to the capital for the mandarin exams. In the early 19th century, Gia Long upgraded the route as a unifying artery between Gia Dinh (Saigon) and Thang Long (Hanoi).

South of Hue's **An Cuu Market,** a hodge-podge of houses-cum-shops cling to the edges of the heavily trafficked Mandarin Road, more commonly known as Highway 1. Once the congestion eases, you'll pass French pillboxes adrift in the rice fields, followed by Phu Bai Airport, a former U.S. Marine base.

Across the Truoi River, an old French railway station marks the center of **Loc Dien ❶,** a collection of hamlets 16 miles (25 km) south of An Cuu that had its 15 minutes of fame in September 1965 when *Life* ran a 10,000-word feature about eight men from this village who'd been "marked for death" by the Viet Cong.

Beyond Loc Dien, the Truong Son mountains skew east toward the coast, and Cau Hai Lagoon opens up views to the east. Three miles (5 km) along, a pink marble marker memorializes a branch of the **Ho Chi Minh Trail ❷** (see pp. 120–121), down which men and matériel traveled in 1975 to sever the supply line between Hue and Danang.

South of Phuoc Tuong Pass, turn right at Thuy Ta hamlet (32 miles/51 km south of An Cuu) for a 2.5-mile (4 km) run to the **elephant pools ❸** (*$*). A boulder decorated with a curved cement trunk and broken tusks minds a series of cascades and swimming pools in this steep-sided ravine.

Heading farther south on Highway 1, threading Phu Gia Pass, the reward is a vista of **An Cu Lagoon,** crowded by mountains and sown with fishing weirs. The road swings down onto a long, narrow spit at **Lang Co ❹,** whose true glory only reveals itself once you've zipped through and looked back from the headlands. In the meantime, park at one of the resorts and visit the beach, among Vietnam's most spectacular.

Unless you *want* to plow through the new 4-mile (6 km) tunnel, thus missing the best part of the drive, stay to the right as you leave Lang Co and start up into the headlands. Arcades of trees and brows of shrubbery lean over the road as it billows up toward **Hai Van Pass** ❺. At an elevation of 1,627 feet (496 m), the road crests amid a cluster of French forts and two imperial gates, the latter built during the reign of Minh Mang and inscribed with Chinese characters that read, "gate of the clouds by the sea" and "most grandiose gate in the world."

Two miles (3 km) beyond the pass, the tantalizing crescent of beach below serves a **leper colony** that still shelters dozens of families. Once ministered to by the Sisters of St. Paul, the families are now mostly cured though still subject to quarantine. Rumor has it the colony is destined for relocation as developers froth over the obvious possibilities.

Across the Cu De River Bridge, turn left and merge onto the 7-mile (11 km) boulevard that borders the **Bay of Danang.** Stop

at the new rest room facility to check out this stretch of **Xuan Thieu-Nam O Beach** ❻, where the first contingent of U.S. combat troops came ashore in March 1965. The Marine base sprawled all along this beach, though few traces remain, other than a collapsed bunker near the facility. A mile (1.6 km) farther, stop at Xuan Thieu Restaurant. North of the restaurant is a concrete slab Marines poured as the foundation of a service club. The graffiti signature of American soldier Ortiz Vasquez remains legible along the edge of the upper concrete terrace. ∎

🅼 See area map p. 129
▶ An Cuu Market, Hue
🔁 56 miles (91 km)
🕓 3 hours
▶ Bay of Danang

NOT TO BE MISSED
- Lang Co
- Hai Van Pass
- Leper colony beach
- Bay of Danang

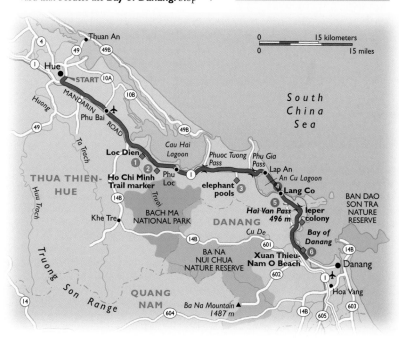

Danang

Danang
🄰 129 C3

Visitor information
✉ Danang Tourism, 118 Le Loi
☎ (0511) 896-138

Cham Museum
✉ 2 9 Thang 2
☎ (0511) 821-961
💲 $

VIETNAM'S FOURTH LARGEST CITY, WITH A POPULATION of 800,000, Danang primarily serves travelers as a gateway to Hoi An, My Son, and the Marble Mountains. Its Cham Museum houses the country's best sculpture, and its egg-shaped bay, bracketed by the Hai Van headlands and Monkey Mountain on the Son Tra Peninsula, yields a spectacular seascape.

CHAM MUSEUM

Built in 1915, the palatial Cham Museum displays some 300 terra-cotta, sandstone, and bronze sculptures from that kingdom's capitals and temples. Most famous is the **Tra Kieu Dancer,** a lithe *apsara* draped in hallmark loose belts and bead necklaces. Attendant musicians strum the vina, an ancient Indian instrument.

dancer at center. Also in this gallery, see the seventh-century statue of **Ganesha** dipping his trunk in a bowl of sweets—the oldest complete Cham sculpture.

VISITING THE TOWN

From the museum, a walking tour follows the **Han River** along Bach Dang, past colonial buildings, as far as the new

China Beach

The U.S. Marines built an R&R center on a fine stretch of sand that Americans know as China Beach. There are no longer any readily accessible vestiges of that R&R center; in other words, there's nothing to see. A new road was built along the beach in 2003 and is now lined with hotels and restaurants that cater mostly to a local crowd. To see this place and listen for ghosts, turn left just before the Furama Resort and drive about a mile (2 km). That's China Beach. ∎

China Beach was a popular R&R spot for American soldiers during the 1960s and 1970s.

In the same gallery is the tenth-century **Tra Kieu Pedestal,** wrapped in a frieze with figures that detail scenes from the life of Krishna.

In the left wing, three steps climb the **Pedestal from My Son E1,** whose niches hold a popular turbaned flute player and a harpist with a distinctive chignon. Note the apsaras who serve as telamones on the risers, especially the spread-eagled

cable-stay bridge. Turn left, then left again, and return to the museum along Tran Phu, passing a 1923 Gothic cathedral with a Gallic cock atop its 230-foot (70 m) steeple.

If you follow Bach Dang to 3 Thang 2, you'll reach Nguyen Tat Thanh and one end of a 7-mile (12 km), four-lane boulevard that skirts the **Bay of Danang,** the city's most beautiful attraction. ∎

Bach Ma National Park

THE RUINS OF A THRIVING FRENCH RESORT FROM THE 1930s and '40s form the architectural centerpiece of 85-square-mile (220 sq km) Bach Ma National Park, adding a haunting, ghost-town atmosphere to this area of stunning natural beauty. With an average annual rainfall of 25 feet (7.5 m), Bach Ma is Vietnam's rainiest place. But during the drier spring and summer months *(Feb.–Aug.)*, the lush tropical forest is a first-rate destination for day hikes, birding, and swimming in cascade pools.

In 1932, the French broke ground on the upper flanks of 4,800-foot (1,440 m) Bach Ma as a refuge from the sweltering weather in Hue, 34 miles (54 km) northwest. By 1942, they'd clustered 139 villas, a hospital, a market, parks, a swimming pool, tennis courts, and two hotels on the hill. During the Vietnam War, the villas were largely destroyed in heavy fighting between U.S. soldiers and the Viet Cong.

Check in at the visitor center, from which rangers ferry *($$)* vanloads of tourists 10 miles (16 km) up a narrow, winding road to the ruins and back. From the summit parking area, a paved stone pathway climbs a third of a mile (0.5 km) to an octagonal summit house. Off one side of the path, steep stone steps lead to a onetime American helicopter base. Not far from the bottom step, an unmarked cave entrance marks a Viet Cong hideout.

If the clouds aren't roosting about the summit, which they often are, the views are long and inspiring. Below the summit, a trail drops 1.25 miles (2 km) through evergreen monsoon forest to an orchid nursery. The trails are fairly well marked, and it's best not to stray too far. Not all the wartime ordnance blew during the war, as evidenced by an exhibit in the visitor center.

Bach Ma is renowned for its wildlife, though the grandest fauna is all but gone. Elephants last trod this region in 1995, and rangers last spotted tiger tracks here in 2001. The park's deeper recesses still shelter Asiatic black bears, leopards, and saola, a deer species first discovered in 1992. ∎

The backcountry is home to Asiatic black bears, leopards, and the recently discovered saola.

Bach Ma National Park

🔺 129 B3

www.bachma.vnn.vn

☎ (054) 871-330

💲 $

Getting there
No regular buses run to Bach Ma, and there's only occasional demand for a traveler's café bus from Danang or Hue. By private vehicle, travel S from Hue along Hwy. 1 for 25 miles (40 km) to Phu Loc and turn right for the 2-mile (3 km) ride up Rte. 6 to park reception. You can take your own car but not a motorbike into the park.

Marble Mountains

🗺 129 C3

✉ Take coastal road 5 miles (8 km) S of Danang, turn left on Huyen Tran Cong Chua. Entrance is on left a bit farther along.

💲 $

Visitor information

✉ Danang Tourism, 118 Le Loi, Danang

☎ (0511) 896-138

Visitors read a Chinese tablet at a Marble Mountains pagoda.

Marble Mountains

SOUTH OF DANANG, THE MARBLE MOUNTAINS COMPRISE a cluster of five limestone and marble outcrops, famous for their grottoes, their pagodas, and their role as a Viet Cong redoubt during the Vietnam War. The peaks yield sweeping views of the strand American soldiers dubbed China Beach. At the base of one mount is a 500-year-old stonecutters' handicraft village known to locals as Lang Da ("stone village").

The first emperor of the Nguyen dynasty named these outcrops the Ngu Hanh ("five elements"), after the essential elements of water, wood, earth, metal, and fire. **Thuy Son** ("water mountain") is the most rewarding. Start at the base of the 156-step stairway King Minh Mang ordered built in the 1820s.

Before beginning your climb, stop in at **Tam Son Pagoda,** to the left of the stairs. Atop the stairs, at the triple gate to **Tam Thai Pagoda,** turn left for a short climb to **Vong Giang** ("river watchtower"), which offers views south to the sister peaks, Danang's Han River, and the Quang Nam rice fields.

Behind Tam Thai, a path leads through a stone gate to a two-level cave the Viet Cong used as an operations center and first-aid station. The upper level, **Hoa Nghiem,** includes an altar and adjacent stela that dates from 1640. In the more compelling lower level, **Huyen Khong,** where sunlight streams down from gaps in the ceiling, is a large seated Buddha.

From Huyen Khong, head back through the gate to the circular entrance to **Van Thong.** From this cave a muddy climb through a steep, narrow slot emerges atop one of Thuy Son's multiple peaks.

Another stone gate leads down to the more interesting **Linh Ung Pagoda** and the seven-story tower at **Xa Loi Temple.** Climb the tower's interior stairway, not so much for the views but because it's among the few accessible pagoda towers in Vietnam. ∎

Hoi An

HOI AN IS A DREAMY OLD SOUTHEAST ASIAN TRADING port, renowned for its timeworn merchants' homes, grid of riverfront streets, and Chinese assembly halls. While the rival 17th-century ports of Malacca and Penang evolved into modern cities, Hoi An lost its raison d'être in the late 19th century after the silting of its river shunted commercial activity to nearby Tourane, now Danang. The town consequently ossified and now ranks as the best preserved port of a bygone era in Southeast Asia, prompting UNESCO in 1999 to inscribe the site on its World Heritage List.

Hoi An
🅰 129 C3
Visitor information
✉ Hoi An Tourist, 12 Phan Chu Trinh
☎ (0510) 861-276
✉ Sinh Café, 18B Hai Ba Trung
☎ (0510) 863-948

Though its Old Town dates largely from the late 16th to early 18th centuries, Hoi An's otherwise dubious claim as an ancient town is partly justified by archaeology that proves the Sa Huynh people used it as a port as early as the second century B.C. Before the Vietnamese gained control of the area in the 14th century, Cham merchants had developed the port into the kingdom's primary trading center, though no extant structures date from that era. With an invitation from the Nguyen lords, the Japanese and Chinese settled on either side of a waterway spanned by the Japanese Bridge (see p. 156),

which remains a central landmark. Portuguese merchants came calling in 1535; the Dutch, English, and French followed suit in the 17th century. While the Europeans left little trace of their tenure, the Japanese and Chinese played fundamental roles in the development of the port then and the town's enduring appeal today.

From five stalls in Old Town, the tourist office sells tickets *($)* that are good for admission to any five attractions, including one old home, one assembly hall, one temple, one museum, and one other attraction, but not two of any one category. To see more

Worshippers revere second-century Chinese general Quan Kong at the Cantonese Assembly Hall.

A wood-carver applies finishing touches to his version of the happy Buddha.

than one, you must buy an additional ticket. All attractions center on one of the town's three main streets. Tran Phu, the oldest and best known, historically linked the Japanese Bridge and Quan Kong Temple, across from the market. The route along Nguyen Thai Hoc opened in 1841, and the riverfront Bach Dang in 1886.

MERCHANTS' HOUSES

Along Tran Phu and south toward the river, the Chinese merchants' homes are the single most potent ingredient in the spell cast by Hoi An. Nearly all claim 17th- or 18th-century pedigrees, which may be so, though the present structures date from 19th-century reconstructions. It may seem odd that most of these old Chinese homes are in the half of town settled by the Japanese. But after a shogun issued a decree in 1635 restricting overseas maritime activities, the Japanese community died off. None of their houses survive, though the floor plans of later homes built by Chinese merchants do resemble those of older homes in Kyoto, Japan. The

Japanese influence also endures in woodwork trusses, which include Chinese and Vietnamese aesthetics in a fusion fundamental to Hoi An's fame.

The tourist bureau has placed the following three homes on its register, so they're the most heavily visited. But Old Town is a trove of similar homes, now tricked out as restaurants, hotels, and shops.

On Nguyen Thai Hoc, the sixth generation of a Vietnamese family lives in **Tan Ky House,** a home their ancestors acquired from Chinese merchants out of Fujian province. Like most homes in Old Town, this is a corridor house, not unlike the tube houses of Hanoi's Old Quarter (see pp. 62–64). At 10 to 12 feet (3–3.5 m), these houses are typically wider than Hanoi's, but the run of rooms from front to back is similar—shop, living room, open courtyard, sleeping quarters, and kitchen. The shop is raised slightly higher than succeeding rooms, a good omen, as income is more likely to run downhill. *Tan Ky,* as it's embossed in Chinese characters on the name board in the living room, means "progress." The triple-beam construction of the living room ceiling is distinctly Japanese, while crab motifs in the woodwork are Chinese. The flooring is Vietnamese, made from Bat Trang bricks and stone slabs from Thanh Hoa.

Across the Japanese Bridge is the 1780 **Phung Hung House** (*4 Nguyen Thi Minh Khai*), whose balconies evoke China, four-sided roof Japan, and three bays Vietnam. Eight generations of the same Vietnamese family have occupied the house, selling medicine, silk, and porcelain from their shop. During a 1999 flood, water rose 5 feet (1.5 m) in the house. In 1964, the floodwaters climbed 8 feet (2.5 m), and the family hosted one hundred stricken neighbors on the second floor. The same Chinese family has occupied the **Quan Thang House** (*77 Tran Phu*) since the 18th century.

ASSEMBLY HALLS

Hoi An's Chinese settlers predominantly came from five of China's southern provinces, and each rallied in their own assembly hall, which served as both temple and guesthouse to transient Chinese merchants. These halls are sometimes referred to as pagodas, but are not temples to Buddha.

The red-faced Quan Kong takes center stage at the **Cantonese Assembly Hall,** (aka Quang Trieu Pagoda; *176 Tran Phu*). Kong was a second-century Chinese general revered in temples throughout Vietnam and East Asia. His telltale red face symbolizes loyalty and righteousness. The goddess of the sea, Thien Hau, occupies the bay to Quan Kong's left, accompanied by two grotesque assistants, one of whom points at his eyes, the other at his ears, underscoring their ability to see and hear across the waters for a thousand miles.

Down the street, the **Chinese Assembly Hall** (*62 Tran Phu*) still serves as a language school for the local Chinese population.

The most opulent hall is the **Fujian Temple** (aka Phuoc Kien; *46 Tran Phu*), which is set far from the street, through a single-door gate and a lower courtyard, then a garishly modern triple gate. The principal deity here is Thien Hau, a wise choice for a seafaring people. She sits in the

Calligraphy and silk art lure shoppers to Hoi An's centuries-old storefronts.

central altar at back, in garments that are changed annually. To the right of the rear temple is a model junk of the type sailed by Chinese traders.

Built in 1875, the **Hainan Assembly Hall** *(10 Tran Phu)* honors 108 Chinese merchants murdered in 1851 by a rogue skipper in King Tu Duc's navy, a massacre detailed in Chinese characters on the entry hall storyboard. Next door is the largely unrestored, somewhat impover-

Historically, the Japanese Bridge linked Hoi An's ethnic Chinese and Japanese communities.

ished **Minh Huong Temple.**

Phuc Ba is the principal deity at the **Trieu Chau Assembly Hall** *(157 Tran Phu)*. More compelling, however, is the intricately carved woodwork that frames the altar, with crab and woman motifs that clearly speak to the work's Chinese origins, if not its antiquity, which stretches back 250 years.

OTHER SIGHTS

Unless you're an archaeology buff, Hoi An's museums will likely disappoint. Your best bet is the **Museum of History and Culture** *(7 Nguyen Hue)*, whose collection includes bronze bells, Sa Huynh ossuaries, Cham artifacts, and a pair of wooden shutters from a wine house at 46 Nguyen Thi Hoc.

At the **Museum of Trade Ceramics** *(80 Tran Phu)*, artifacts from shipwrecks and old pottery fragments anchor the contents. The house itself, particularly the balcony doors and woodwork panels, is a prime example of a traditional wood house. So is the **Museum of Sa Huynh Culture** *(149 Tran Phu),* whose building is a fusion of corridor-house and French architecture. Downstairs, you'll find Sa Huynh burial jars and other artifacts unearthed in nearby sand dunes. Upstairs, the streetside room highlights artifacts from the French War, while the back room exhibits Vietnam War paraphernalia, including a hand-drawn map of Hoi An used in a 1969 attack on the town.

Past the museums, at the end of Tran Phu, the **Japanese Bridge** spans a stream that flows into the Thu Bon. Historically, the stream divided the Japanese district, which stretched down present-day Tran Phu, from the Chinese district. The bridge was built in the middle of the 17th century, as was an adjacent **Taoist temple.** The latter was dedicated to a god who the bridge builders hoped might exorcise a subterranean beast whose thrashing tail was believed to be the cause of earthquakes in Japan. The beast's head was beneath India, but its heart was beneath Hoi An, hence the temple. At either end of the wood-planked bridge is a pair of statues, monkeys on one end and dogs on the other, which are believed to represent the years construction was started and finished. The name board of Chinese characters on the bridge was hoisted by one of the Nguyen lords in 1791. The characters denote the span as the "faraway people's" bridge. ■

My Son

LIKE CAMBODIA'S ANGKOR WAT, THAILAND'S AYUTTHAYA, and Myanmar's Pagan, My Son is Vietnam's opus in the canon of ancient Southeast Asian holy lands. Standing in a lush valley 28 miles (45 km) west of Hoi An, the 1,500-year-old brick-built temple complex lay forgotten for centuries until rediscovery by the French in 1898. Archaeologists stripped the temples of their most valuable sculptures, which are now on display in Danang's Cham Museum and in the history museums in Hanoi and Ho Chi Minh City. But this UNESCO World Heritage site retains an incomparable ancient resonance.

My Son

⚑ 129 C2

✉ 28 miles (45 km) SW of Hoi An via Hwy. 1 to Duy Xuyen; turn left and go last 12 miles (20 km) to the site.

💲 $ (includes transportation from booking office to towers)

Visitor information

✉ My Son Sanctuary Management Board, Duy Xuyen District, Quang Nam

☎ (0510) 731-757

My Son served as the heart and soul of its culture for a thousand years. Cham king Bhadravarman founded the first temple here late in the fourth century, and except for a 200-year gap between the eighth and tenth centuries, My Son was the holy epicenter of the Cham world. Every Cham king built at least one edifice here. After a Cham king married a Vietnamese princess in the 14th century and ceded a huge chunk of his kingdom for the privilege, My Son drifted into obscurity and the ruinous grip of jungle growth. After rediscovery, a French archaeologist identified 14 groups of 71 ancient relics, using a system of nomenclature still in use today.

Through 1945, the French exhumed, studied, catalogued, and, on several occasions, restored these ancient monuments. Twenty years later, the Viet Cong moved into My Son as a base, and the United States launched a bombing campaign that ruined many structures, including two magnificent *kalans,* or temples, in the designated A and E complexes. Today, 20 of the 71 Cham relics are more than less intact, most clustered in the B, C, and D groupings, where the visit begins. While most visitors take guided tours from Hoi An ($), you can also hire a car. Go early to avoid crowds and the heat.

At the **BCD cluster,** note how seamlessly the Cham put together these temples. An enduring mystery of Cham architecture is how they managed to construct brick towers with seeming disregard for mortar. Some have suggested that the Cham may have baked one 100-foot (30 m) tower in situ, while others reason the bricks are fastened by vegetal resin and a mortar derived either from powdered lime and brick or from clay.

In all, Cham builders employed seven distinct architectural styles, all of which are represented at My Son. In the **C group,** the intact **C1 kalan** tower was built toward the end of the tenth century in a style now dubbed the A1 My Son style. Its roof is saddle-shaped, a departure from the classical norm, which rose in a three-story steeple. The hollowed-out interior leaves little room to maneuver, but these interior spaces were the province of Brahmans, not worshippers. The Cham believed their deities actually dwelled within the statues sheltered by these temples. The statue of Siva from this tower is now on display at Danang's Cham Museum (see p. 150).

In the neighboring **B group,** the **B5 koshaghara** (storehouse) tower mirrors C1's saddle-shaped roof and exhibits many features

of the A1 My Son style, notably in the elegant pairs of pilasters. Between the pilasters, note how the figures stand on a lotus balanced on an elephant's head. The Cham carved this art directly onto the spongy brick after construction, except for the heads, which are sandstone and were obviously attached later. B5 also features a pair of elephants in bas-relief, their trunks wrapped around a coconut tree.

French archaeologists believed that the two long *mandapas,* or assembly halls, belonged to a distinct group they labeled

D group, east of the B and C groups. But later studies showed that these mandapas, D1 and D2, were actually built for pilgrims who used the halls to prepare offerings for temple visits. The mandapas' tile roofs long ago collapsed, and their interiors today serve as crude museums for statuary that hasn't been carted off to other museums.

From the D temples, cross the Suoi The stream and turn right to reach the largely ruined **A group** temples. The commanding peak before you is 2,460-foot (750 m) Rang Meo ("cat's teeth").

The most heartbreaking loss at My Son is the **A1 kalan tower,** which stood 79 feet (24 m) high and 32 feet (10 m) wide. It was the masterpiece of the complex and stood for nearly a thousand years until a U.S. bombardment in late 1969. A photo of the ruined tower is on display in the museum near the lower 4WD terminal. The 13 heaps of ruins are otherwise overgrown with vegetation, which is how the French first encountered these monuments at the end of the 19th century.

Outside the BCD cluster, the path winds to the left past the **G group,** now undergoing extensive restoration and reconstruction. A few minutes farther along the path is the **E group,** the oldest complex at My Son. The **E1 kalan** was also a casualty of the 1969 bombing. Between E1 and the also damaged E4 are the two offending bomb craters. Luckily, E1's magnificent pedestal and pediment had been removed long before the war and are on exhibit at Danang's Cham Museum. **E7,** used as a library during My Son's heyday, is the most intact structure in this cluster. Before it stands one of the site's 31 stelae. ■

The Bay of Danang is gaining popularity as one of the world's most beautiful waterways.

More places to visit in central Vietnam

BA NA MOUNTAIN
In 1919, the French founded a hill station atop 4,879-foot (1,487 m) Ba Na to escape Danang's sweltering climate. Attractions include a half-mile (800 m) cable car route, hiking paths, the colonial villa ruins, and a handful of waterfalls. The view from the summit takes in Danang, the Han River, the ocean, and expansive rice fields.
🏔 129 C3 **Visitor information**
✉ Danang Tourism, 118 Le Loi, Danang
☎ (0511) 896-138

CHAM ISLANDS
Nine miles (15 km) off Hoi An are seven lightly touristed islets. Coral abounds in the crystalline waters off **Lao** ("pear"), the largest islet. Each spring, islanders harvest birds' nests, used in soups and medicine. The slow boat from Hoi An takes 2.5 hours, while a speedboat makes the trip in 30 minutes.
🏔 129 D3 **Visitor information**
✉ Hoi An Tourist, 12 Phan Chu Trinh, Hoi An ☎ (0510) 861-276

SON TRA PENINSULA
This mountainous peninsula brackets the Bay of Danang to the west and China Beach to the south, its bights rapidly filling with resorts anxious to replicate the success of nearby Furama. Dominating the headland is 2,274-foot (693 m) **Monkey Mountain,** the centerpiece of a reserve that shelters endangered Javan silvery gibbons. Son Tra is also home to the forlorn **Spanish Tomb,** a 40-foot (12 m) ossuary containing the remains of Spanish and French soldiers who died during the 1858–1860 campaign against Danang.
🏔 129 C3 ✉ Spanish Tomb: From Han River Bridge, follow Ngo Quyen, turn onto Yet Kieu, then drive 5 miles (8 km) to Tien Sa

TRA KIEU
From the 4th to 11th centuries, the Cham capital was at Simhapura ("lion citadel"), on the site of modern-day Tra Kieu, about 10 miles (16 km) northeast of My Son; visitors from Danang can stop here on the return trip. All that remains of the citadel are some ramparts, banisters, and traces of the wall, but the main gallery at Danang's Cham Museum (see p. 150) is filled with sculptures unearthed here, including the Tra Kieu Dancer and the Tra Kieu Pedestal.
🏔 129 C2 **Visitor information**
✉ Hoi An Tourist, 12 Phan Chu Trinh, Hoi An ☎ (0510) 861-276 ∎

Vietnam's fledgling resort scene has staked claims to the alluring golden sands of the south-central coast. Beyond the beaches and turquoise water, the region resonates with echoes of the kingdom of Champa, whose towers stand in ruins on forlorn knolls.

South-central coast

Sea stars cluster on a beach at Phan Thiet.

Traditional boats, their latticework sealed with tree pitch, anchor near Mui Ne.

South-central coast

THE SOUTH-CENTRAL COAST IS AN ARC OF SIX SEASIDE PROVINCES, FROM Quang Ngai in the north to Binh Thuan in the south, whose sandy shores, coastal waters, and scenic promontories are doing much to redefine the face of Vietnam to the rest of the world. Until the 14th century, this balcony on the Pacific was the domain of the Cham people, whose magnificent towers command knolls up and down the littoral. Most of the region's attractions, like the population itself, hug the shore.

Don't look for azure waters or placid bays here. Unlike the islands and bays of Thailand and Indonesia, the south-central coast fronts a long fetch of the Pacific where the surf is more dramatic than sublime. Do look for coconut palms that crane over dazzling white sand, for freshets that burst from the flanks of riotously verdant headlands, and for coastal roads that course through fishing harbors jostling with fancifully painted boats.

Nha Trang is the crown jewel in Vietnam's constellation of beach resorts and the only city along the coast with a nightlife to complement its sunny appeal. Its municipal beach is internationally renowned, its islands kissed by some of the country's most beautiful coral reefs.

As beautiful as the south-central coast is, it was also a frightening battleground, particularly during the Vietnam War. The Americans built an air base at Phan Rang; a combat base at Chu Lai, north of Quang

Ngai; and a massive logistical base at Cam Ranh Bay. At My Lai in Quang Ngai Province, the war reached its nadir in two little hamlets where a powerful memorial now commemorates the notorious 1968 massacre.

North of Nha Trang, the Khanh Hoa coast gradually fades in popularity, as most travelers vault over the country's great underbelly. To do so means forfeiting the white sands of Doc Let and Van Phong Bay, the bay that intrigued Jacques Cousteau, as well as disregarding the horrors of My Lai.

The surviving Cham towers are nowhere more collectively appealing than they are at Po Klong Garai, near Phan Rang, which remains home to half of Vietnam's ethnically identifiable Hindu Cham people. Phan Rang also boasts Ninh Chu, one of Vietnam's finest and less touristed beaches.

Farther south, the beaches of Binh Thuan Province, especially Mui Ne, are the new kids on the block. Starting in the mid-1990s, this rain-shy seaboard has surfed a tidal wave of mostly tasteful development. Just north of the provincial capital of Phan Thiet, the Po Shanu towers herald the former kingdom of Champa, whose land eroded under the relentless Vietnamese march to the south.

Though geographically more southern than south central, Vung Tau is where the beach party really kicks off. Known as Cap St.-Jacques to the French, who popularized its coastal charms in the late 19th century, Vung Tau is now at the dawn of a third act, in which the players are mostly Vietnamese. Its beaches lack the appeal of gems farther north, but at a stone's throw from Ho Chi Minh City, it makes a fine diversion and great starting point for a coastal tour. ■

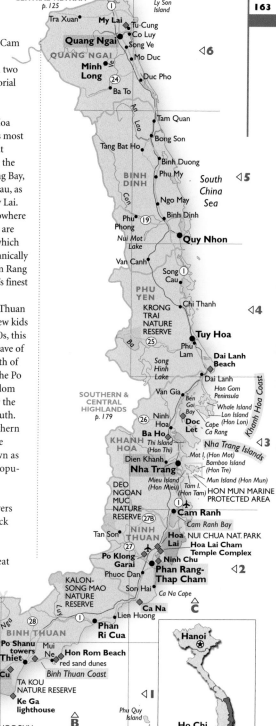

Nha Trang

NHA TRANG IS THE DEAN OF VIETNAMESE BEACH TOWNS
and a great place to kick back. Its gorgeous strand, happening
nightlife, and indolent ambience are an antidote to the freneticism
of Saigon and the cerebral demands of pagoda-hopping. Still, with its
grand complex of Cham towers and two fine museums, the city can
toss a few cultural curveballs beyond the beach.

Nha Trang

🗺 163 C3

**Visitor
information**

www.nhatrangtourist.com.vn

✉ Khanh Hoa Tourism,
1 Tran Hung Dao

☎ (058) 822-753

**Po Nagar
Cham towers**

✉ 2 Thang 4, near
Xom Bong Bridge

First and foremost is the beach,
a 4-mile (7 km) crescent of lightly
toasted sand and turquoise water,
flanked by a pair of promontories.
Tran Phu skirts its length, dividing
an ever expanding wall of hotels
from palm-happy esplanades that
overlook the shore.

On the southern promontory,
five of **Bao Dai's villas** (see p.
253) once served Vietnam's fun-
loving final emperor as a getaway.
Today, the French colonial buildings are guesthouses. To the north,
on **Hon Chong** promontory,
stone steps descend to a jumble
of rocks where fabled fairies once
frolicked and played chess. The
seaside of one boulder bears the
"handprint" of a voyeuristic male

fairy who lost his balance while
spying on naked female fairies.

PO NAGAR CHAM TOWERS

Inland from Hon Chong, on a
bluff above the Cai River, stand the
Po Nagar Cham towers ($), the
city's most august attraction. The
site is named for the ten-armed
mother goddess who taught the
Cham how to plant rice and weave.
Javanese raiders sacked the original
wooden structures in A.D. 774.
Within a decade, however, the
Cham had built their first stone
structure and a *mandapa* (assembly hall) whose saddle-shaped roof
rested atop 24 columns. The roof is
gone, but 14 columns remain.

The most impressive of four

extant towers is a 74-foot (22.5 m) 11th-century *kalan* (temple) known as **Thap Ba** ("tower of the lady"). Draped in yellow robes, Po Nagar reigns from within its sooty black interior. The statue, its pedestal, and its stela were sculpted from a monolith in 965, though Po Nagar's head was lopped off by the French in 1946 and replaced by a Vietnamese-looking surrogate. As you enter, note inscriptions on the lintel and jambs in Sanskrit-style Cham lettering, as well as the graceful *apsara* dancer above the lintel.

On the back of the saddle-roofed **northwestern tower,** a cross-legged figure rides the back of an elephant, holding a spearhead and a weapon thought to symbolize the god Indra. Though a statue of a robed Po Nagar now sits in this tenth-century tower, as well as a *linga-yoni,* historically this space venerated Sandhaka. The **south temple,** with its saddle-shaped roof, exalted Ganesha.

MORE SIGHTS

Across the Cai River, a gleaming white Buddha presides over the city from his perch above **Long Son Pagoda.** From the sanctuary, stone steps climbs to the 80-foot (24 m) landmark, erected in 1964 to protest South Vietnam President Ngo Dinh Diem's repression of Buddhism. Its octagonal base holds bronze busts of eight monks who immolated themselves in 1963, each framed in a halo of flames. Below reclines a massive Buddha cut from local stone.

Nearby, the **Alexandre Yersin Museum** (*Tran Phu, closed weekends, $*) honors the doctor (1863–1943) who spent the better part of his life in Nha Trang and discovered the pathogen that sparked the 1896 bubonic plague. The museum offers a surprisingly compelling narrative, well-written

captions, and top-notch exhibits, such as Yersin's library, furnishings, and instruments, including the microscope he used to isolate the notorious pathogen. Hand-drawn maps detail Yersin's 1892–1894 explorations, including his 1893 discovery of the site that later blossomed into Dalat.

Across town, a 1923 French colonial building anchors the

Oceanographic Institute. The museum's central attraction is a humpback whale skeleton, unearthed by northern villagers in 1994. One gallery of floor-to-ceiling shelves holds 8,000 pickled sea creatures, while a second-floor gallery in the old building displays antique maps, a globe, and a collection of 18th-century seafaring books, presumably left behind by the French. ∎

Oceanographic Institute

✉ Tran Phu, near Bao Dai's villas at S end of beach

💲 $

Topped with its landmark white Buddha, the Long Son Pagoda presides over the Cai River.

Heading out to the Nha Trang islands

Nha Trang islands

IN PLEASANT WEATHER, A FLEET OF BEAMY WOODEN BOATS casts off from a pier south of Bao Dai's villas and motors out to this cluster of largely deserted, rock-rimmed islands off Nha Trang. The boats moor among splendid coral reefs for snorkeling and tie up at a fishing village, an aquarium, and an activity-packed island. These day trips are the city's most popular pastime and tend to reach a feverish, party pitch by midday.

Nha Trang islands

🗺 163 C3

Visitor information

www.nhatrangtourist.com.vn

✉ Khanh Hoa Tourism, I Tran Hung Dao, Nha Trang

☎ (058) 822-753

Boat tour operators

All tours cost $$ for an all-day trip.

✉ Con Se Tre, 100 Tran Phu St.

☎ (058) 527-522

✉ Glass Bottom Boat, Tran Phu St.

☎ (058) 527-522

✉ Mama Linh Café, 2A Hung Vuong

☎ (058) 522-844

✉ Hanh Café, 10 Hung Vuong

☎ (058) 527-466

✉ Number 4 Boat Trip, 6 Tran Phu St.

☎ (058) 816-097

Five tour operators run boats out into the bay, each with a band, a buffet lunch, and buckets of beer. These fun-loving party boys will grudgingly answer questions about flora or fauna but much prefer to whoop it up with passengers. Hiring your own boat is another affordable option; ask for info at one of the tour shops on Biet Thu.

The largest and least visited island is **Hon Tre,** which rises 600 feet (180 m) above the bay. The posh Sofitel Vinpearl resort claims the best strand at **Tru Beach,** though a portion remains open to the public.

Four miles (6 km) southeast of the pier, **Hon Mun** is the premier snorkeling venue. A garland of buoys protects the island's 350 coral species from boat anchors, while an attractive array of some thousand fish species flits to and fro over the fantastic formations. In the distance, **Hon Yen** ("swal-low island") is a source of salan-gane nests, the principal ingredient of bird's nest soup.

At noon, the tour boats bunch together off **Hon Mat** for lunch and happy hour partying. While the island's shingle beach doesn't make for great sunbathing, there's decent snorkeling offshore.

Billed as a "tourist island," **Hon Tam** attracts vacationers and day-trippers with a pebbly swimming beach, parasailing, waterskiing, Jet Skis, and other watersports. You can rent a shady cabana behind the shoreline.

Closest to shore is **Hon Mieu,** where fishermen in colorful boats deposit their catch in pontoon pens. Several restaurants tempt the hungry with fresh fish and terraces that jut over the water. On the far side of the island, **Tri Nguyen** is home to an aquarium, worth visiting if your boat calls at the pier. ∎

Khanh Hoa coast

NORTH OF NHA TRANG, THE SEABOARD OF KHANH HOA Province is a largely undeveloped region of white-sand beaches, rustic peninsulas, rocky promontories, and streams that gush from the coastal mountains. Accommodations cater to domestic tourists, foreign pioneers, and the escape-minded. The region is also accessible to day-trippers from Nha Trang.

At the province's northern border, 50 miles (80 km) from Nha Trang, **Dai Lanh** is a half-mile (1 km) swath of powdery white sand between a crystal-clear bay and a range of low, green mountains. This much beloved beach is even embossed on one of the Nguyens' Nine Dynastic Urns at The Mieu in Hue (see p. 136).

Just south of Dai Lanh, a new paved road shoots across long, sandy **Hon Gom Peninsula** as far as the fishing village of Dam Mon. Beyond the coast guard station, 11 miles (18 km) from Highway 1, the peninsula bulks up into roadless, thicket-covered headlands.

Offshore, a French ecotourism company has built a clutch of quaint bamboo bungalows around the small beach at **Whale Island** (see p. 255) and has blazed a 3-mile (5 km) loop trail through bushy wilds inhabited by barking deer and parrots. The resort welcomes day-trippers to relax on the beach, hike the trail, or eat at its on-site restaurant.

Farther south, casuarinas and coconut palms lean over the white sands of **Doc Let,** Khanh Hoa's grandest peninsula. The 4-mile (7 km) strand is bracketed by a shipyard to the south and Cape Ca Rang to the north. Offshore to the northeast is **Hon Lon,** the province's largest island.

Inland from the peninsula, 10 miles (16 km) south of Ninh Hoa, a stream cascades into a series of

Jacques Cousteau

The world-renowned marine biologist explored the under-sea realm of the Khanh Hoa coast and Van Phong Bay in 1933 as a sailor in the French navy. The French were mapping the bay, known then as Port Dayot, in preparation for a naval base that was never built. But the area's coral and marine life fired Cousteau's imagination and led him toward his lifework. ∎

three small swimming holes at **Ba Ho** ("three lakes"). The first pool is 700 yards (700 m) from the trailhead, while the others lie several hundred yards upstream.

Near Ba Ho, boats ferry day-trippers from Da Chong Pier to **Hon Thi,** an island populated by ostriches and deer, while nearby **Orchid Stream Island** offers more swimming holes. On **Monkey Island,** monkeys, dogs, and bears frolic in circus acts popular with domestic tourists. ∎

Khanh Hoa coast

◪ 163 C3–C4

Visitor information

www.nhatrangtourist.com.vn

✉ Khanh Hoa Tourism, 1 Tran Hung Dao, Nha Trang

☎ (058) 822-753

Whale Island

www.whaleislandresort.com

✉ 2 Me Linh, Nha Trang

☎ (058) 513-871

Kingdom of Champa

The Indian-influenced kingdom of Champa flourished along the south-central coast from the 600s until the destruction of its capital by the Vietnamese in 1471. The Cham artistic and archaeological legacy perseveres today in its sandstone sculptures and the powerful stone temple towers at Phan Rang, Nha Trang, My Son, and scattered sites along the country's littoral. Their descendants are physically indistinguishable from the Vietnamese, though many wear a telltale headdress or the trappings of Islam.

Unlike the Viets, who struggled within China's mighty orbit, the Cham took their cultural cues from India. Their gods were the Hindu gods Siva, Brahma, and Vishnu. Their script was Sanskrit. They adopted the caste system as a social infrastructure. But they were not immune to the osmotic influence of other cultures. By the 800s and 900s, the influence of Buddhism began to pepper Cham art, and later, many migrated to Islam.

The Cham warred on and off with the Chinese, who first sacked the fledgling Cham capital in 446 and made off with tons of gold. The Javanese destroyed the Po Nagar temples near present-day Nha Trang in the 700s. Yet the Cham thrived, expanding north and south from central Vietnam. By the 900s, the Cham ranked with the Khmer as the leading regional powers after China.

Most research into Cham culture centers on art, thanks largely to a bounty of extant sculpture. Little is known about their society, religion, or language. Marco Polo mentions them in his travels, as did Arab traders, who prized Cham sandalwood, cinnamon, ivory, rhinoceros horn, and glazed ceramics.

As the newly independent Vietnam matured, the Cham exerted tremendous influence, particularly among the educated elite between the 11th and 15th centuries. However, the kingdom's loose confederation of principalities would ultimately prove no match for the Vietnamese, who, bucking their Chinese overlords in the tenth century, set their sights on Cham territory.

In response, the Cham moved their capital south from Indrapura to Vijaya, in today's Binh Dinh Province. While they gave up lands around present-day Hue for the hand of a Vietnamese princess in 1306, they also scored victories against their looming neighbor to the north, killing a Tran king in 1377 and winning the riches of various Vietnamese cities throughout the 1300s.

Retribution was harsh. The greatest of all Vietnamese emperors, Le Thanh Tong, razed Vijaya in 1471, decapitated 40,000 Cham people, and deported another 30,000, thus ending 1,100 years of Hindu primacy on the eastern edge of Southeast Asia.

The Cham limped on with nominal autonomy for several hundred years, but the great age of temple building was over. By 1653, the Vietnamese were ensconced as far south as Cam Ranh, leaving the Cham to make do with just two provinces. King Minh Mang extinguished the last flickerings of the Cham state in the 1832. ■

Cham towers such as Thap Poshaknu (above left) are the grandest legacy of a subsumed people. While artwork still adorns some towers (at My Son, above right), archaeologists sent their best pieces, like this seated goddess (left), to Danang's Cham Museum (below) and museums in Hanoi, Saigon, and France.

My Lai

EIGHT MILES (13 KM) NORTHEAST OF QUANG NGAI ARE THE hamlets of Tu Cung and Co Luy, better known worldwide as My Lai. In four hours on March 16, 1968, a U.S. Army unit raped, tortured, and murdered 504 Vietnamese civilians, the majority of whom were women, children, and the elderly. The site of the My Lai massacre is now a memorial to the dead and presents the most emotionally charged couple of hours you're likely to spend in the country.

Cement figures memorialize the 504 villagers massacred at Tu Cung and Co Luy hamlets, known collectively as My Lai.

My Lai
🅰 163 B6

Son My Memorial
✉ Tu Cung hamlet
💲 $

The massacre erupted as a perfect storm, fueled by tin-pot leadership, frustrated GIs, and a U.S. military policy that condoned free-fire zones. My Lai was not the only American atrocity of the war, but it was the most horrific, the most exposed, and the most thoroughly documented. That documentation forms the core of a memorial museum that opened in the village of **Son My,** at Tu Cung hamlet, in November 2005, replacing a smaller, older, less affecting memorial.

The powerful new hall is an austere, square edifice of dark stone blocks, as windowless and dour as a mausoleum and thus perfectly suited to its contents. It sits on the edge of the Thuan Yen sub-hamlet of Tu Cung, overlooking a 5-foot-wide (1.5 m) irrigation ditch where rogue American soldiers gunned down 170 people. Up a dark flight of exterior stairs, an interior stairway brings you to the upper-level gallery and a black granite wall that lists the names, ages, and genders of the dead.

Moving clockwise around the hall, a diorama gives a bird's-eye view of Tu Cung hamlet, which the GIs knew as My Lai 4. The most arresting display begins on the wall to the left of the inscribed names, where a collection of 51 enlarged photos graphically detail that day's events, from the arrival of the helicopter-borne troops to the V-for-victory sign flashed by Lt. William Calley in the wake of the operation. These color photos shocked the world after they ran in *Life* magazine in 1970. Prodded by British documentary makers, the U.S. Army released the black-and-white photos in 1988. Here are the notorious images—the huddled group of 15 women and children just prior to execution, the two boys cowering in the road moments before they were shot dead, and the many corpses strewn across the road. Beyond the photos is a heartbreaking diorama of soldiers shooting civilians at the irrigation ditch.

Unlike the previous memorial, which was compromised by its heavy-handed good-versus-evil interpretation of the warring parties, this memorial lets the images and story speak for themselves. Since 2000, the museum's guide has been a passionate young woman named Kieu, whose mother survived the onslaught at Co Luy by hiding in a bunker with her sister and mother.

Other exhibits include yellowed clippings of worldwide newspaper coverage of the atrocity, including photos of a girl, Vo Thi Lien, who survived the massacre and became a key subject of subsequent propaganda tours. Lien died at age 43 in 1995 while giving birth to her third child. Look as well for the small red slipper worn by a four-year-old

girl named Truong Thi Khai, killed at Thuan Yen.

OUTDOOR MEMORIAL

Outside, cement footpaths wind among the reconstructed foundations of Thuan Yen's **19 destroyed homes.** The paths are textured with boot treads, villagers' footprints, and bicycle tire tracks, as the muddy paths probably looked that morning. A metal placard beside each foundation lists the names, ages, and genders of the people who lived there and died nearby.

As you wander these paths, look for bullet scars in the coconut palms, a flourishing bodhi tree that survived the torching of the village, and two plots of 21 graves. The irrigation ditch has been encased in cement in order to maintain its 1968 proportions. At the center of the outdoor memorial is a concrete statue, erected in 1982, of a woman holding a dead baby in one arm while lifting the other arm in defiance. This figure, as well as the figures of two cowering boys at her feet, was based on the photos.

Beyond the compound, a narrow track runs behind the former memorial hall and curves left across the rice fields to **Tu Cung.** Most of the massacre's survivors still live in this sub-hamlet. Fewer than 100 yards (90 m) from the far edge of the rice field is a collection of stone markers. Off the right side of the path is the foundation of a watchtower where GIs positioned machine guns and shot 102 people. Farther down this path on the right is the infamous silk-cotton tree where 15 women and children were shot after a photo was snapped. In the courtyard of the house across from the tree is the well into which a 72-year-old man was thrown and then shot. ■

Phan Rang

M 163 C2

Visitor information

✉ Ninh Thuan Tourist, 626 Thong Nhat, Phan Rang

☎ (068) 822-719

Phan Rang & around

SOUTH OF NHA TRANG, PHAN RANG IS HOME TO THE country's greatest concentration of Hindu Cham people, a wonderfully preserved cluster of 13th-century towers, and the Kate New Year Festival. The region's arid climate rivals Phan Thiet's sunny appeal, although the great crescent of beach at Ninh Chu attracts mostly domestic vacationers. Most travelers breeze through Phan Rang, headed north or south along Highway 1, or turn here for the 87-mile (140 km) overland trip up Highway 26 to Dalat.

Vietnam's finest extant Cham towers stand at Phan Rang.

Nine miles (14 km) north of town, the one collapsed and two standing towers of the **Hoa Lai** Cham temple *(tel 068-822-719)* rise alongside Highway 1. While the roofs of these ninth-century towers have crumbled, the pilasters retain fine decorative details, including images of Garuda and a deity riding atop a tiger.

In Thap Cham, 6 miles (9 km) west of Phan Rang, the **Po Klong Garai** temple *($)* features Vietnam's most impressive cluster of towers. Dedicated to a 12th-century king who engineered an effective irrigation system, the 13th-century towers include a 70-foot (21 m) *kalan* with an intact roof and original bas-relief statues, a gate tower, and a saddle-roofed *mandapa* with buffalo horn accents.

The provincial capital, **Phan Rang,** boasts an attractive market building on Thong Nhat and a grand boulevard that leads to the beach. April 16th Boulevard was named for the day in 1975 that North Vietnam won control of the city from South Vietnam.

At the end of the boulevard, Yen Ninh parallels **Ninh Chu,** a 6-mile (10 km) beach of steeply pitched brown sand, once the favorite of Phan Rang native and South Vietnamese president Nguyen Van Thieu and now a draw for domestic travelers, with amusement park–themed resorts.

Over the door of the three-story kalan is a bas-relief of the temple guardian, Po Klaun Tri, a six-armed dancing Siva, while superimposed on the vestibule gable are four arcatures with flame-shaped flourishes, hallmarks of 13th- and 14th-century architecture. Each roof corner supports smaller towers capped with lotus buds. Inside, the superimposed statue of a local king stares from the *linga.*

Every year during the popular Kate New Year Festival in October, a procession of worshippers carries King Po Klong Garai's garments to the temple complex. ∎

Binh Thuan coast

UNTIL THE MID-1990s, THE BINH THUAN COAST BARELY blipped on anybody's radar screen as a destination. Now, thanks to the most dependably sunny weather in Vietnam and its proximity to Ho Chi Minh City, the booming beachfront between Mui Ne and Ke Ga has emerged as Nha Trang's archrival for sunseekers. Famous as well for dragon fruit *(thanh long),* fish sauce *(nuoc mam),* and sand dunes, the arid region packs a clutch of interesting relics from the Cham and French colonial eras.

Sledding the red sand dunes just north of Mui Ne is a popular pastime.

Binh Thuan coast

🗺 163 B1

Visitor information

✉ Binh Thuan Tourist, 82 Trung Trac, Phan Thiet

☎ (062) 816-821

NORTH OF PHAN THIET

It took a 1995 solar eclipse to draw tourists to **Mui Ne's** 12-mile (19 km) swath of plush sand and prize open the eyes and wallets of developers. Thankfully, the latter eschewed sterile high-rises in favor of low-rise garden resorts, which run chockablock between the water and a palm-shaded shoreline road. Nearly every resort cultivates its own beach along Mui Ne and the rockier coast south of Phan Thiet. Breaking waves thump a shore primed for bodysurfing, while steady winds lure boardsailors.

On the cusp of Vietnam's richest fishing grounds, Mui Ne itself is a fishing village devoid of any real attractions but for its spectacular fleet of sky-blue boats, moored off the town's crescent beach. (Similarly attractive are views of Phan Thiet's fleet from the Tran Hung Dao Bridge.)

Just north of the village, red sand dunes rise like a misplaced patch of Arabian landscape. The dunes are a mecca for ski buffs, who coast the furrowed slopes on plastic sleds rented by local kids.

Farther north, *so do* bushes speckle the savannas beyond the beach at **Hon Rom,** and 175-acre (70 ha) **Bau Trang** ("white lake") offers a fetch of clear waters amid a sea of white dunes. Locals refer to the highest dune as **Bui Trinh Nu** ("virgin hill"), a dubious moniker now that 4WD tours comb the area. Lotuses bloom along the lakeshore in April, yielding seeds for sweetmeats and soups.

Eleven miles (18 km) south of Mui Ne, closer to Phan Thiet, the

garrison. A war monument memorializes the capture of 35 French soldiers by a Viet Minh squad in December 1947.

PHAN THIET

In Phan Thiet proper, **Van Thuy Tu Temple** shelters the 72-foot (22 m) skeleton of a fin whale that washed up nearby in 1893. With great reverence, the villagers buried the whale along the shore, exhuming the skeleton three years later. Though the Vietnamese reject few creatures as a food source, they won't dabble in whale, believing they protect fishermen at sea.

The Ca Ty River flows through Phan Thiet, passing a landmark water tower with Chinese motifs built during the colonial era. An eighth of a mile (200 m) upstream of the bridge at Le Hong Phong is the **Duc Thanh School.** As a fledgling nationalist in 1911, Ho Chi Minh taught Chinese and *quoc ngu* (see p. 48) to students at this select private school. Today, the varnished benches and sloped desktops fitted with inkwells evoke a bygone era. Across the street, a 1986-built **Ho Chi Minh Museum** holds a hodgepodge of memorabilia. ■

Phan Thiet's boat-filled harbor

Po Shanu towers
🅰 163 B1
✉ Ba Nai Hill, Phu Hai
💲 $

Van Thuy Tu Temple
✉ 54 Ngu Ong, Phong Thiet
💲 $

Duc Thanh School
✉ 41 Trung Nhi, Phong Thiet
💲 $

three towers of **Po Shanu** stand atop Ba Nai Hill, at the southern border of the vanished kingdom of Champa. Built in the eighth century, they're among the oldest surviving Cham towers and are notable as an architectural bridge between Cham and Khmer styles. The 50-foot (15 m) kalan to the south is dedicated to a son of Po Nagar (see pp. 164–165), while the whole complex pays homage to Po Shanu, a Cham queen famed for her talent, virtue, and tact.

Near the towers are the foundational remains of a 13-room villa built by a French prince in 1911. The prince turned over the villa to King Bao Dai, and the structure later served as a colonial

Bamboo coracles

The bamboo basket coracle is a familiar sight along Vietnam's south-central coast. Fishermen propel these boats by churning a single oar. It takes a week to weave the strands of a basket boat and seal the bamboo lattice with a pitch derived from the *dau trai* tree. The boats sell for about 400,000 dong, or $27 each. Boatbuilders frequently make boats on the grounds of the Van Thuy Tu Temple and in surrounding streets in Phan Thiet. ■

Vung Tau

The statue of Giant Jesus has drawn visitors to Vung Tau since the early 1970s.

VUNG TAU IS TO VIETNAM WHAT ATLANTIC CITY IS TO THE United States—a coastal resort with proximity to a metropolis, whose beach is less appealing than its history and whose aura is more festive than sublime. The town crouches between Nui Nho ("small hill") and Nui Lon ("big hill"), which hold the area's two big cultural attractions—a giant statue of Jesus and the White Palace. Vung Tau itself is borne up by a clutch of noble colonial buildings and a pleasant seaside ambience.

Vung Tau
🅰 163 A1
Visitor information
✉ Ba Ria–Vung Tau Tourist, 33–35 Tran Hung Dao, Vung Tau City
☎ (064) 857-527

The French colonials popularized Vung Tau as Cap St.-Jacques in the late 19th century and built the **Bach Dinh** (White Palace) on the site of a demolished imperial fort, renowned for firing the first shot of the resistance against the French in 1859. Built in 1898 as a resort for the French governor-general, the palace later served as a cushy jail for the deposed emperor, Thanh Thai. Set amid a frangipani grove, the palace is now a **museum** *(Tran Phu, $)* whose main galleries display blue-and-white porcelain pottery salvaged from a ship that wrecked nearby in 1690.

In town, stroll **Tran Hung Dao** past two-story French colonial buildings, built between 1911 and 1915. Turn left on Ha Long for St. Jacques Church, designed by a French architect and built in 1942

with Indochinese flourishes. Next door is a onetime opera house, now an English language training center, crowned by two turreted pavilions.

Heading south out of town on Ha Long, you'll hug the hills past the rocky beach of **Bai Dua,** a colonial-era lighthouse, and a succession of pagodas and temples. Standing at the tip of the promontory, 92-foot (28 m) **Giant Jesus** implores the sea with outstretched arms. This landmark statue was raised in the early 1970s. An interior stairway climbs to an observation deck on Jesus' shoulders for fantastic views.

Development is mushrooming along **Bai Sau** ("back beach"), a 3-mile (5 km) swath of brown sand and decent surf. Farther north along the coast, the beaches of **Long Hai** are less crowded and offer greater water clarity. ■

More places to visit along the south-central coast

CA NA

Ca Na is a bay of startling clarity, jumbled boulders, and white sand that most travelers catch as a lunch break on the Highway 1 run up the coast from Ho Chi Minh City to Nha Trang. The offshore waters boast some of the best diving and snorkeling opportunities in Vietnam, and a dive shop now operates from the small balcony of level ground that skirts a spur of the southern highlands. You'll find few budget hotels amid this arid landscape of rocks and cactuses, and the barreling traffic along Highway 1 saps much of the charm of its natural beauty.

⚠ 163 C2

CAM RANH BAY

At Cam Ranh, two sandy peninsulas embrace 23 square miles (60 sq km) of water in a harbor frequently hailed as the best in the world after Sydney, Australia. The United States built a massive supply depot on the larger peninsula during the war, though scant evidence remains of this sprawling complex but for the old airfield, now revamped to handle Nha Trang's tourist traffic. In April 1975, some 100,000 refugees converged on the largely abandoned base ahead of the southward marching communists. Beyond its historical relevance, the bay's principal attraction is its natural splendor.

⚠ 163 C2

DIEN KHANH

After the Hue Citadel, the four gates of Dien Khanh, 5 miles (8 km) west of Nha Trang, are the best preserved remnants of a feudal fortress in the country. Prince Nguyen Anh (later King Gia Long) built the walled city in 1793 as a Vauban-style citadel, a form later employed with greater majesty at Hue. Short segments of the original earthworks stretch away from either side of the restored gates, gradually petering out up against modern developments, but the moat,

royal palace, mandarin houses, and jail of this once thriving 9-acre (36,000 sq m) city no longer exist.

⚠ 163 C3 **Visitor information**
✉ Khanh Hoa Tourism, 1 Tran Hung Dao, Nha Trang ☎ (058) 526-753, www.nhatrangtourist.com.vn

LONG PHUOC

Though they hardly compare to the tunnels of Cu Chi (see pp. 214–215), neither in size nor in strategic importance, the tunnels of Long Phuoc open yet another hatch on Viet Cong tenacity. These tunnels burrow 2 miles (2.5 km) beneath ground once patrolled by U.S. soldiers and Australians, who operated from a base at Nui Dat, 1,000 feet (300 m) from the present museum. In 1993, the original tunnels were cased in cement and opened to the public. A quarter-mile (400 m) tour of the works takes you past underground cells and, close to the surface, gun slits from which the Viet Cong would ambush passing patrols. The first of Long Phuoc's three tunnels was dug in 1948, while the longest stretch (1.25 miles/2 km) was started in 1963.

⚠ 163 A1 ✉ 16 miles (26 km) north of Long Hai ☎ (064) 827-033 ⑤ $

TA CU

One of Southeast Asia's two largest recumbent Buddhas—160 feet (49 m) long and 33 feet (10 m) high—reclines against an upper flank of Ta Cu Mountain, off Highway 1, 19 miles (30 km) south of Phan Thiet. To reach the statue, you can either hike two hours—a 1,500-foot (475 m) climb through the 60,000-acre (25,000 ha) **Ta Cu Nature Reserve**— or spend eight minutes on an Austrian cable car (*$*). The tram docks below the 19th-century **Ta Cu Mount Pagoda** and three towering Buddhist deities dressed in flowing robes. While the pagoda itself is only so-so, the view of the Binh Thuan countryside, **Ke Ga lighthouse,** and the coast are worth the trip.

⚠ 163 B1 ☎ (062) 867-484 ■

The ethnically diverse southern and central highlands
boast evocative hill-tribe architecture, timeless landscapes, and
wildlife sanctuaries, while Dalat
offers colonial ambience and a climate of eternal spring.

Southern & central highlands

Elephant ride at Yok Don National Park

Southern & central highlands

ALONG VIETNAM'S WESTERN BORDER WITH CAMBODIA AND LAOS, THE
Truong Son mountains dominate the rugged topography of the central highlands' four
provinces. Waterfalls plunge through evergreen forests. In timeless hill-tribe villages,
matriarchal ethnic minorities preserve age-old traditions in longhouses and blade-roofed
communal houses that soar for the sky. Coffee is the king cash crop. But nature reigns
supreme at ten reserves and national parks.

Vegetables suited to the temperate climate thrive in the mile-high fields around Dalat.

The old French hill station of Dalat is all
most travelers see of these highlands. You
have to approach this city with discretion,
however. If your first impression is made by
the market, or the town center, or the gaudy
attractions that have turned Dalat into the
honeymoon capital of Vietnam, there's a
tendency to wonder what all the fuss is about.
But as soon as you start to wander the streets
lined by old colonial villas and take in the
hilly vistas and steep ravines cultivated with
vegetables, its charms can captivate.

Outside Dalat and throughout the highlands, waterfalls command attention. Too few
are left to their pristine charms and instead

are "enhanced" with ferroconcrete flourishes,
tourist elevators, and the proximity of karaoke
culture. Fortunately, the natural majesty of
some cascades, like Dambri Falls near Bao Loc,
retain the ability to impress.

In the national parks at Yok Don, Chu
Mom Ray, and Cat Tien, Vietnam's most
emblematic fauna—the Indochinese tiger,
Javan rhinoceros, and Asian elephant—are
making a last stand in a country that has no
room for them. The animals prove elusive,
but the scenery and sublime silence, in a
country that does not place a premium
on quietude, are invigorating. The central
highlands' tallest peak, Ngoc Linh, tops out

at 8,523 feet (2,598 m) in the Ngoc Linh Nature Reserve north of Kon Tum.

Farther south in Buon Ma Thuot, the capital of Vietnam's coffee industry, cafés and wholesalers peddle countless brands of Robusta, Arabica, and Culi bean coffee. The premium brands retail at about $2 per pound.

Until the early 20th century, the modern world had hardly intruded upon the primitive peoples who inhabited the highlands. Stimulated by the region's rich red earth, the French cultivated the plateaus with coffee plantations, forcing the natives into the first of a long string of losing propositions. During the war, the United States garrisoned the highlands in a futile attempt to stem the tide of matériel flowing down the Ho Chi Minh Trail.

Highland place-names still call to mind momentous wartime events—Ia Drang, Pleiku, Buon Ma Thuot. But today the area is winning more welcome notice as one of Vietnam's most naturally enticing and least plumbed regions. Unlike the highly touristed northern highlands near Sa Pa, few Western tourists trek to the hinterland homes of Bahnar (Ba Na), Giarai, and E De (Ede) highlanders near Kon Tum, Pleiku, and Buon Ma Thuot. Though these groups lack the compelling wardrobes of their northern cousins, the architecture of their villages is unrivaled among Vietnam's ethnic minorities. ■

Dalat

Dalat
🅰 179 D2
Visitor information
✉ Dalat Travel Service, 7 3 Thang 2
☎ (063) 822-125

PERCHED ON A PLATEAU 5,000 FEET (1,500 M) ABOVE sea level, the old French hill station of Dalat was and remains the geographic antidote to the swelter and smog of Ho Chi Minh City, 190 miles (300 km) to the southeast. Its fresh air, pine-clad hills, and mild temperatures—from an average daily high of 59°F (15°C) in winter to 80°F (27°C) in summer—have earned Dalat the moniker "City of Eternal Spring." Beyond its delightful weather, Dalat's treasury of colonial French villas and châteaus is unrivaled in Vietnam.

The last king of Vietnam vacationed in this art deco villa, now the Dalat Palace Hotel, during the 1930s and '40s.

During an 1893 exploration, Alexandre Yersin, the doctor who discovered the plague pathogen, also identified the plateau as an ideal location for a health resort. After an initial burst of enthusiasm, interest in Dalat waned, until the 1920s when the colonial government opened the sumptuous Lang Bian (now the Dalat) Palace Hotel and a golf course and dammed the Cam Ly River to create the Grand Lac (now Xuan Hong Lake). In 1932, a cog railway conquered the steep pitches between the coast and the hill station, and from the mid-'30s through World War II, a building boom speckled the hillsides with hundreds of villas inspired by architecture in Normandy, Brittany, and other French provinces.

FRENCH LEGACY

The villas and an abundance of colonial structures are the essence of Dalat's charm and its least exploited resource. Begin at the lavishly restored **Dalat Palace Hotel** (*12 Tran Phu, S of Xuan Hong Lake; see p. 255*). In 1942, a Vichy French governor stripped the architectural confections from the hotel's opulent exterior and made it over with the art deco facade that endures today. Inside, however, Victorian grandeur still reigns, in the heavy drapery, chandeliers, monumental lobby fireplace, and reproductions of European masterpieces.

Traveling east on Tran Phu, continue along Tran Hung Dao, where the richest vein of villas fans away from the colonial governor's château atop the hill.

The last king

Though frequently cited as Vietnam's last emperor, King Bao Dai (1913–1997) never ruled any state but Vietnam, and there only as a puppet. History remembers him as a playboy who indulged in women, sports cars, speedboats, airplanes, hunting, golf, and a sumptuous suite of villas in the mountains and along the south-central coast. His mother was a peasant who became a concubine, and his alleged father was King Khai Dinh, who preferred to keep his distance from women. As a sovereign, Dai meant well, but he lacked the wherewithal to wrest control from his French overseers or the resolve of his revolutionary peers. After he abdicated in 1945 to Ho's government, he led an affluent life near Cannes, France. He married a French woman and converted from Buddhism to Catholicism. He is buried in the Passy Cemetery west of Paris. ∎

Norman villas include Tudor-like wood detailing on the facade, while heavy, ground-floor stonework characterizes Breton villas. **16 Tran Hung Dao** is the former home of Paul Veyesseyre, Dalat's most prominent colonial architect. The restored Landaise-style villa with one distinctively long roof slope at **27 Tran Hung Dao** is the former home of a Michelin rubber plantation director. As you continue up Tran Hung Dao, Lang Bian mountain dominates the northern horizon.

At 4 Hung Vuong, the **Lam Dong Museum** features a collection of archaeological exhibits from the seventh- to tenth-

Photos of Bao Dai—as head of state and as rich playboy—adorn his summer villa in Dalat.

Lam Dong Museum

✉ 4 Hung Vuong
☎ (063) 822-339
🕐 Closed Sun. & 11:30 a.m.–1:30 p.m.
💲 $

Benedictine monastery

✉ 20 Hung Vuong

☎ (063) 830-825

Dalat Railway Station

✉ 1 Quang Trung

☎ (063) 834-409

century Funan culture, as well as ethnic minority exhibits, including photos of a buffalo sacrifice and a skewer used in such a ceremony. This 1935 villa was built for Bao Dai's father-in-law. The marble hearths in each room were imported from Italy.

Follow the signs to Dinh 1, another of Bao Dai's residences. This villa is closed to visitors, but 200 yards (180 m) before its gate

cog stretch supposedly remains operative in Switzerland today. The Japanese engine on the tracks is for show, but a Russian diesel does ferry passengers 10 miles (16 km) to and from the village of **Trai Mat** (*$$*).

From the station, follow Nguyen Trai to Yersin and look up to the right for the château built as a **maternity clinic** for French and high-society Vietnamese

The three gables of the Dalat Railway Station echo the triple summit of nearby Lang Bian mountain.

Crazy house

✉ 3 Huynh Thuc Khang

☎ (063) 822-070

is a **Benedictine monastery** designed by Veyesseyre. Note the empty belfry and square block towers that flank its maw of a door—telltale art deco details.

Loop back toward town along Quang Trung and check out the **Corsican villa** across from No. 4. This villa's turreted wings flank a gallery punctuated by three stone arches. On the left turret, a Cham *apsara*, or Khmer dancer, struts her stuff in bas-relief.

Farther along Quang Trung on the left is the 1938 **Dalat Railway Station,** inspired by the *gare* in Deauville, Normandy. Its two marquees jut from either end of a triptych of gables. Bombing during the Vietnam War closed the line in the '60s, though the engine from its 10-mile (16 km)

women who wanted to give birth in a temperate climate.

Heading west on Tran Phu, look for the 155-foot (47 m) steeple atop the **Dalat Cathedral** (*15 Tran Phu*), built between 1931 and 1942. Manufactured in Grenoble around the same period, its stained-glass windows filter the late afternoon sun into bursts of lush color against the salmon-pink interior walls.

WEST OF THE LAKE

Follow Tran Phu west to Pasteur Street and loop up around Le Hong Phong to another clutch of French villas. Before road's end, turn left on Huynh Thuc Khang and stop at the Hang Nga Guesthouse and Gallery, or **crazy house,** a fantasy of a guesthouse/art gallery conjured up by a Moscow-trained Vietnamese architect named Hang Nga. The house is actually a compound of ferroconcrete villas shaped like molten tree trunks, entwined by giraffes and bridged by concrete spans. Writhing stairways of fabricated stumps climb the insides of these villas to rooms with jigsaw puzzle–piece beds and grotesque artwork—bears, eagles perched on giant eggs and acorns. Open to visitors ($), this apogee of kitsch is a must-see.

Less surprising is **Bao Dai's villa,** a museum near the end of Trieu Viet Vuong. From 1938 until the end of World War II, the last emperor vacationed in this nautical moderne villa. The flat-roofed château is incised with a grid of coping, a hallmark of the style. Inside the 26-room villa, wander from the reception room to the festivities room, with its 30-foot (9 m) banquet table, then upstairs to the roped-off private chambers of the royal family, all with original furnishings.

Down Pasteur, a dirt track on the left takes you to **Lam Ty Ni Pagoda** (2 Thien My) to meet Dalat's most eccentric personality, a monk/artist named Vien Thuc. The pagoda's sole occupant, Thuc moved here in 1964 as a 19-year-old. Today, larger-than-life cement busts watch over the garden, each a representation of Thuc in the trademark knitted cap he wears like an open hood. In a studio out back, thousands of his paintings, calligraphy, and Zen poems lean framed and stacked against the walls or draped from hooks. The pagoda is named for the garden where the Buddha was born.

CITY CENTER
Across the Cam Ly River dam is

the less lovely heart of town. The facade of the main **market,** built in the 1960s, describes a short arc before a run-of-the mill victory monument in Hoa Binh Square. Atop the stairs to Khu Hoan Binh, the long, rectangular building to the right was the city's first market, now a movie cinema.

Below the market, follow Xuan Hong Lake's north shore and turn left on Tran Nha Tong to the **Dalat Palace Country Club,** the only bent-grass venue in Southeast Asia. First laid down in 1922, it was upgraded to an 18-hole championship course in the 1990s.

Past the steepled tower of the Teachers' Training College, Bui Thi Xuan leads to **Linh Son Pagoda.** Completed in 1941, the pagoda once sheltered an offbeat, ascetic monk named Vien Ngo, who cloistered himself in the log cabin behind the main hall for five years. The bell tower no longer houses the bell, as its walls would crack whenever the bell was rung. In the main hall, an enormous bronze of Sakyamuni is framed by an ornate wood carving of dragons and bats. ∎

The crazy house is part hotel, part gallery, and altogether hallucinatory.

Bao Dai's villa
- ✉ Off Trieu Viet Vuong
- ☎ (063) 826-858
- 💲 $

Dalat Palace Golf Club
- ✉ Phu Dong Thien Vuong
- ☎ (063) 823-507

Linh Son Pagoda
- ✉ 120 Nguyen Van Troi
- ☎ (063) 822-893

Around Dalat
🖼 179 D2

Visitor information
✉ Dalat Travel Service, 7 3 Thang 2
☎ (063) 822-125

Cable car to Truc Lam Pagoda
✉ Robin Hill
☎ (063) 837-938
🕐 Closed 1st Mon. of the month & 11:30 a.m.–1:30 p.m.
💲 $

A textile weaver in Lat Village, near Dalat

Around Dalat

WHILE INTERNATIONAL TRAVELERS EXTOL THE DELIGHTS of Dalat proper, domestic tourists fancy the region's sylvan charms. Honeymooning couples throng viewing sites below a half dozen nationally renowned waterfalls and dress up for pony rides and pictures at the Valley of Love. Kitsch and crowds notwithstanding, several of the waterfalls merit attention, as does a popular Zen monastery.

Just south of town, Highway 20 tops Robin Hill, where you can ride a cable car down to **Truc Lam Pagoda,** a Zen monastery built in 1993 on Tuyen Lam Lake. The flying eaves of its two-tiered roof echo the aesthetics of Zen temples in Japan. Inside, a bronze-painted Sakyamuni holds a single lotus flower beneath a cement frieze that details the

story of his life. The 80 monks and 60 nuns rise at 3:15 a.m. for meditation followed by three hours of daily chores.

You can also approach the pagoda and lake by road; it's 3 miles (5 km) south of Dalat via Highway 20. A couple hundred yards farther south, a long stairway leads to **Datanla Waterfall** (Thac Datanla; *tel 063-831-804, $),* which tumbles down rock chutes lined by a path. More impressive is 30-foot (9 m) **Prenn Waterfall** *($),* another 3 miles (5 km) south, though its appeal is marred by a crocodile pool and couples dressed up like bunny rabbits.

Just over a mile (2 km) from downtown Dalat is **Cam Ly Waterfall** *(36 Hoang Van Thu, tel 063-824-145, $),* whose name pops up in a treacly song that goes, "Oh, Dalat. Can you hear Cam Ly sobbing for its first broken love?"

The treacle reaches a fever pitch at the **Valle d'Amour** *(Dap 3 Da Thien, tel 063-821-448, $),* 4 miles (7 km) north of town, where young couples ride ponies, play dress-up, and race toy speedboats on the Da Thien reservoir.

A little farther north, the **Lang Bian mountain** *(tel 063-839-088, $)* peaks in three summits, the tallest of which is 7,109 feet (2,167 m). You can walk or drive to the top. At the massif's southern foot, the K'Ho ethnic minority of **Lat village** sound ceremonial gongs for tourists. ■

Cat Tien National Park

Cat Tien's thitpok trees tower more than 200 feet (60 m) above the forest floor.

THIS 179,000-ACRE (72,000 HA) PRESERVE OF WETLANDS, grasslands, evergreens, and bamboo forest lies off Highway 20, 105 miles (170 km) southwest of Dalat. The restricted northern tract harbors the critically endangered Javan rhinoceros and perhaps a small population of Indochinese tigers, while Asian elephants, gaur, civets, muntjacs, and Siamese crocodiles dwell in the park's southern reaches. The fauna may elude you, but trails probe engaging wetlands and forests of magnificent trees.

Visitors usually overnight in plain but comfortable guesthouses near park headquarters on the Dong Nai River. Branching off a sealed road that leads from headquarters are the park's dozen trails, each less than 6 miles (10 km) round-trip. Rangers ask visitors to refrain from entering the forest unguided, though the reasons may have more to do with revenue than safety.

From headquarters, tour boats (*$$$$/hour*) ply the river, which winds through the park for 56 miles (90 km). On night safaris (*$$*), jeep lights scour the forest for muntjacs, porcupines, and wild boars. At the **Crocodile Lake** ranger station, a 3-mile (5 km) hike from the park road, lucky guests sometimes spot gaur (a type of wild ox) and crocodiles. Towers here and at **Bird Lake** enable birders to spot standouts among the park's 348 bird species.

The fauna may be hit or miss, but the park's majestic trees are accessible. Near headquarters, the **Lagerstroemia Trail** winds amid these speckle-trunked trees, which tower as much as 230 feet (70 m). One thitpok tree (*Tetrameles nudiflora*) on this trail is 500 years old, its buttressed roots sprawling far out across the forest floor. Another featured specimen is the **Uncle Dong tree,** an *Afzelia xylocarpa* named for celebrated Vietnamese leader Pham Van Dong, who visited the park in 1987 and advised locals to care for the forest.

Cinder cones and steep-sided conical hills evince the region's volcanic origins. In the dry season, a Dong Nai tributary tumbles through porous volcanic rocks at the **Ben Cu Rapids,** among three accessible sets in the park. Locals use these rocks to build farmyard walls. ∎

Cat Tien National Park
🅰 179 B2–B3
Visitor information
✉ Cat Tien Ecotourism Center
☎ (061) 669-228
💲 Entrance: $
  Half-day guide: $

A last stand for elephants, tigers, and rhinos

The knell is tolling for Vietnam's three best known wild animals—the Javan rhinoceros, Asian elephant, and Indochinese tiger. Conservationists in the region concede these species are biologically doomed here and hope the requiem will serve as a clarion call to conservationists in neighboring Laos and Cambodia, where populations of tigers and elephants remain viable. At the same time, researchers have discovered a spate of new species of large mammals in the remote forests of central and northern Vietnam, including the giant muntjac (a barking deer) and the saola.

As exciting as these discoveries are, the loss of Vietnam's wild elephants and tigers is heartbreaking. At the end of the Vietnam War in 1975, approximately 2,000 Asian elephants roamed Vietnam's highlands and central plateaus. Today, fewer than 135 animals survive.

The reasons for the elephants' near-extirpation from Vietnam are many, and

it's the same sad story across Asia: Poaching. A burgeoning human population. Habitat degradation. Logging. In Vietnam, one of 13 Asian countries that still harbor wild pachyderms, coffee, pepper, and tobacco plantations have backed the animals into increasingly smaller islands of forest. While more than 50 percent of neighboring Cambodia remains forested, the percentage is half that in Vietnam.

The elephants, for one, are not going down without a fight. In the 1990s, rampaging herds and the odd rogue trampled dozens of villagers to death in a series of isolated incidents throughout the highland provinces. In 2005, the government heralded a plan to administer a trio of conservation zones for the elephants, an announcement many conservationists greeted as too little too late.

Tigers and rhinos face similar challenges in Vietnam, particularly from poaching. Nearly three-quarters of the poached tigers wind up at pharmacies in China, where the flesh, bones, and skin are coveted for medicinal qualities and command a $10,000 price tag. Fewer than 50 Indochinese tigers stalk the hinterlands of Vietnam. The news is even grimmer for the country's subspecies of Javan rhinoceros, one of only two surviving populations in the world. (The other is in Indonesia.) Conservationists estimate that only between two and seven individuals remain in Cat Tien National Park. No one has spotted the animals since 1999, when wildlife biologists rigged an automatic camera near a wallow and shot a series of pictures on infrared film.

Culturally, elephants and tigers have loomed large in Vietnam's history. In the 15th century, King Le Loi's elephant cavalry stunned the horse cavalry of their Ming antagonists and won the country's independence after a 20-year occupation by the Chinese. In the 19th century, the Nguyen emperors pitted elephants and tigers in deadly combat in an arena in Hue (see p. 143) and worshipped the majestic elephant at a nearby temple. Vietnam's ethnic minorities built their houses on stilts to guard against attack by tigers and other wild animals.

While the country's elephant, tiger, and rhino numbers dwindle, wildlife biologists have been thrilled by the spectacular discoveries of giant muntjac, a species of barking deer, and the saola, a species of long-horned rain forest animal that's as big as a sheep and sometimes described as a kind of cow and sometimes as an antelope. Discovered in 1993, the saola is likely to be the last new species of large mammal brought to the world's attention. Scientists believe that 500 to 1,500 of these animals live in the forests of Vietnam and Laos. ■

Fewer than 50 Indochinese tigers remain in Vietnam's highlands, as poaching and other infringements continue to exact a heavy toll.

Buon Ma Thuot & around

Buon Ma Thuot & around

🗺 179 C3

Visitor information

✉ Dak Lak Tourist, 3 Phan Chu Trinh

☎ (050) 852-108

Ethnography museum

✉ Entrance on Nguyen Du, near intersection with Le Duan

☎ (050) 850-426

🕐 Closed Mon.–Tues. & 11:30 a.m.–2 p.m.

💲 $

Waterfalls

✉ Dray Sap: 17 miles (28 km) SW of Buon Ma Thuot via Ho Chi Minh Hwy.; go to MM 739 and turn right. Gia Long: 4 miles (7 km) beyond Dray Sap along same secondary road.

💲 Dray Sap: $

ON THE NORTHERN EDGE OF THE SOUTHERN HIGHLANDS, Buon Ma Thuot is the capital of Dak Lak Province and the hub of Vietnam's booming coffee industry. The café-rich town is a connoisseur's delight, especially if you're partial to the Robusta bean, though you'll also find Arabica and Culi. Most visitors use the town as a base for excursions to waterfalls southwest of the city, Lak Lake, and villages of the E De (Ede) ethnic minority. A couple of spare hours in the city can yield mildly interesting returns at an intown E De village, a somewhat eccentric pagoda, and a botanical garden.

At the heart of town is the **Victory Monument,** a bland war memorial of a tank, an arch, and a column at the intersection of Le Duan and Phan Chu Trinh. From the monument, head a mile (2 km) north on Phan Chu Trinh and turn left on Tran Nhat Duat to reach the small E De settlement of **Ako Dhong,** which includes one notable street of longhouses in hedged, rectangular plots. After the ethnic Vietnamese (Kinh), the E De are the most populous group in Dak Lak Province, comprising about 14 percent of the population.

Back toward town, turn right

on Phan Boi Chau to the intersection with Nguyen Trai to reach **Khai Doan Pagoda,** built in 1952 to memorialize Bao Dai's mother. Inside, a sprawling bodhi tree shelters a pure white statue of the Buddha. To the right is a library and Buddhist school. The pagoda itself marries E De longhouse architecture with such imperial hallmarks as the two-tiered roof and dragon balustrades on either side the central stairway.

The botanical garden is home to an **ethnography museum.** Housed in a 1921 French villa, it features a gallery of Sedang, Giarai, and E De costumes worn at festivals, judicial proceedings, weddings, and other rituals.

Twenty miles (30 km) south of town, several waterfalls jockey for attention in the wet season, including **Gia Long** and **Dray Sap,** the most scenic. ∎

Vietnamese coffee

With nearly 500,000 acres (200,000 ha) under cultivation, Dak Lak alone harvests 70 percent of Vietnam's annual coffee output. Swiss-owned Nestlé buys 20 to 30 percent of the crop, which amounted to 834,000 tons (750,000 metric tons) valued at $612 million in the 2004–2005 season. Vietnam is now the world's second largest coffee exporter after Brazil. Production surged in the last decade of the 20th century when farmers planted the lion's share of its acreage. French missionaries planted the first bean plants here in 1857. ∎

Coffee blossoms near Buon Ma Thuot

Yok Don National Park

The Serepok River sustains resident wildlife at Yok Don, Vietnam's largest national park.

YOK DON NATIONAL PARK BORDERS CAMBODIA IN LUSH plateau country that once nurtured sizable herds of wild elephants. While the wild herds have dwindled to a few dozen animals at best, elephants remain the draw here, either for treks in Yok Don or kitschy rides in the nearby Mnong village of Ban Don. Though the park is Vietnam's largest, at 115,450 acres (46,180 ha), its attractions are slight unless you hire guides and elephants for a safari into the bush.

Hire a guide to explore the dry deciduous forest and 1,581-foot (482 m) **Yok Don Mountain** by elephant, foot, or even motorbike. Sightings of wild boars, deer, and monkeys are rare, while even veteran guides have yet to spot the park's half dozen tigers or several dozen wild elephants.

Across the Serepok River, a 2-mile (3 km) upstream trek from the park's botanical garden leads to the **Seven Branches Rapids.** In the dry season, one can rock-hop to one of the midstream monkey-inhabited islands. Downstream, guided hikes lead to white water at the **Buddhist Rapids,** named for a vanished pagoda.

Just outside the park is **Ban Don,** a Mnong Bubong village of Laotian people that until recently housed the region's legendary elephant hunters. The main attraction in the now touristy village is the **home of Y Thu Knul** *($),* an elephant hunter and trainer who netted 444 pachyderms before he died at age 89 in 1924. In 1883, for the equivalent cost of 12 elephants, he built the gabled wooden home that now houses his great-great-great-grandson's family. Hanging from the walls are chains and other elephant-hunting equipment.

About a mile (1.5 km) from the house, **Knul's tomb** stands amid others trimmed with elephant motifs, including the tomb of his daughter and son-in-law, Ma Krong, another renowned *"chasseur des éléphants,"* as is written on his tomb.

If you're up for some kitsch, you can tramp the cable-stayed bamboo bridge on the Serepok's east bank or parade down the main street atop a trained elephant. ∎

Yok Don National Park
179 C3–C4

Visitor information

✉ 25 miles (40 km) NW of Buon Ma Thuot via Rte. 681

☎ (050) 783-049

💲 Half-day trekking tour: \$\$\$\$\$. Elephant trek: \$\$\$/hour

Ban Don Tourist Center
☎ (050) 783-020

Kom Tum Province

179 C5–C6

Visitor information

Kon Tum Travel Service Center, 2 Phan Dinh Phung

(060) 861-626

Kon Tum Province

THE PROVINCE OF KON TUM IS PEPPERED WITH 635 ETHNIC minority villages and 200 alluring *nha ruong* (communal houses), whose blade-shaped thatch roofs soar as high as 56 feet (17 m). Most visitors venture into this accessible highlands region from the provincial capital of Kon Tum, on the Dak Bla River.

Above: Rice matures outside Kon Tum. Below: Kon Tum's missionary church.

Eight ethnic minority groups live in Kon Tum Province, including the Sedang (the most populous contingent), the Giarai, the Rongao, and the Bahnar (Ba Na).

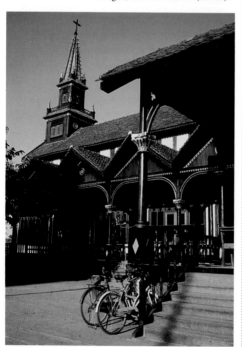

French missionaries began converting highlanders to Catholicism in the 19th century, wooing them all the harder in 1913 with construction of a large **wooden church** in town at the east end of Nguyen Hue. In deference to, or perhaps to entice, the Bahnar, the French lofted the church on a familiar footing of short stilts. Inside, Bahnar textiles drape the sanctum, and prayerful mottoes are written in the Bahnar language. Behind the church, nuns tend to local orphans.

Two blocks north on Tran Hung Dao, a bishop and two dozen priests live in a defunct **Catholic seminary.** Built in 1935, the structure calls to mind an alpine hotel. On the second floor is a museum devoted to the region's ethnic minorities.

KON TUM VILLAGE

Within Kon Tum township, eight nha ruong continue to play a central role in community dealings. West of Phan Dinh Phung, along Ba Trieu, is **Plei To Nghia,** a village that moved its 1968-built nha ruong to its present location in 2003. As with every ruong, the crest of this 52-foot (16 m) structure is rimmed with vertical stakes that symbolize the skewers used in buffalo sacrifices, a gruesome ritual Francis Ford Coppola filmed for a scene in the 1979 film *Apocalypse Now*. The roof's distinctive blade shape serves to protect occupants against supernatural harm.

Inside, the jaw and skull of a bull sacrificed during construction of the hall hang above the door. Many highland groups still sacrifice buffalo on auspicious occasions, believing that the screams of the buffalo, as it writhes in agony on a skewer, will wake the deities. The longer and harder the buffalo screams and suffers, the better.

On the eastern edge of town, two more nha ruong rise in the villages of **Kon Tum Kopong** and **Kon Tum Konam** ("upper" and "lower" Kon Tum). Five miles (8 km) southeast of Kon Tum, across the Kon Klor suspension bridge, is **Kon Kotu,** home to 60 families of 350 Bahnar and one of the loveliest nha ruong in the area. The thatch of this hall is matted in bamboo, which extends the life of the roof and guards against sparks from the frequent ceremonial fires in the adjacent courtyard. The tourist office can arrange an overnight stay in this ruong.

On the way back into town, turn left into **Kon Jri** ("apricot village"), where two stepped tree trunks climb to the terraced porch of another ruong. The men use the seven-stepped ladder on the right, while the women use the five-stepped ladder on the left. In this matriarchal society, the five steps signify quicker, preferential access for women.

Ten miles (16 km) west of Kon Tum, the Giarai village of **Ro Lay** also features a nha ruong, as well as a fascinating cemetery rife with animist traditions. Following a death, the Giarai will mind the staked burial mound every day for a period of three, five, or seven years. At the end of that time, they hold a ceremony to "aban-

don the grave." After sacrificing a water buffalo, villagers mount carved wooden figures of moping men and copulating couples atop the fence posts. Look for French berets on some of the primitive figures. Objects placed atop the mounds offer clues as to who is buried beneath—a jar for a single person, a canteen for a soldier, a teapot for a woman, and bicycle tires for a youth.

Farther west, Highway 24 winds toward a vast reservoir of the Dak Bla River. The lofty peak to the northwest is 5,816-foot (1,773m) **Chu Mom Ray.** ■

Kon Tum is a hub for the province's 635 villages of ethnic minority people.

Elephants ferry tourists across the shallows of increasingly popular Lak Lake.

More places to visit in the southern & central highlands

CHU MOM RAY NATIONAL PARK

Along the border with Cambodia, just south of Laos, Chu Mom Ray is the most remote of Vietnam's national parks, home to its largest population of Indochinese tigers, as well as the kouprey, a recently discovered wild ox. The park also shelters such precious timber as ironwood, margosa, and sindora. The government designated the 136,000-acre (55,000 ha) tract a national park in 2002. 179 C5 **Visitor information** Kon Tum Travel Service Center, 2 Phan Dinh Phung, Kon Tum (060) 861-626

DAMBRI FALLS

In the midst of a forest 11 miles (18 km) northwest of Bao Loc, Dambri drops more than 295 feet (90 m), including one superb cascade. A glass elevator shuttles tourists up and down 130 feet (40 m) of the falls, or you can climb the more than 245 stairs. In the ethnic Ma language, *dambri* means "cascade of the lion," while in Coho it means "the stream of hope." 179 C2 **Visitor information** Dalat Travel Service, 7 3 Thang 2, Dalat (063) 822-125

LAK LAKE

Thirty-two miles (52 km) southeast of Buon Ma Thuot, Lak Lake is the largest in Vietnam's central highlands. King Bao Dai, who had a sharp eye for prime real estate,

built a summer villa here in the 1930s. Tourism authorities have since turned the old place into a small hotel, still known as **Bao Dai's residence** *(tel (050) 586-184).* Most visitors ferry down to the lake in groups from Buon Ma Thuot for dugout boating, elephant trekking, and exploration of Mnong and E De villages. 179 C3 **Visitor information** Dak Lak Tourist, 3 Phan Chu Trinh, Buon Ma Thuot (050) 852-108

PLEIKU

The capital of Gia Lai Province, Pleiku is the municipal hub of a region laced with ethnic minority villages, populated mainly by the Jarai and Bahnar peoples. Provincial authorities have dampened the region's tourism potential with overly restrictive access privileges and an insistence on guides. Six miles (10 km) east of town, the 44-acre (8 ha) **Green Meadow Cultural Village** *(open at end of each month, $$)* holds traditional Bahnar and Giarai houses, sculptures, a garden, zoo, and water park. For a more authentic experience, head about 25 miles (40 km) east of Pleiku to the Bahnar villages of **De Ktu, De Cop, De Doa,** and **De Rol.** 179 C5 **Visitor information** Gia Lai Tourist, 205 Hung Vuong, Pleiku (059) 874-571 ■

Ho Chi Minh City (aka Saigon) retains the zest and charms that won over legions of French colonial and American devotees. Today, tourists linger for the region's vibrant nightlife, colonial and wartime vestiges, museums, temples, and heady pace of life.

Ho Chi Minh City

The motorbike: Ho Chi Minh City's popular form of transport

At the head of Nguyen Hue, the 1908 former city hall now houses the People's Committee.

Ho Chi Minh City

THE WEST'S LOVE AFFAIR WITH VIETNAM IS NOWHERE MORE PASSIONATE than it is in Saigon, District 1 of the larger municipality known as Ho Chi Minh City. This booming metropolis nets about 40 percent of the country's revenue from international travelers. Its heady growth rate and low cost of labor are as alluring to foreign businessmen as its legendary opium dens and taxi girls were to previous generations.

The city owes its origins to the Khmer, who'd dwelled here for centuries before the Viets developed an appetite for the fertile Mekong Delta. In 1698, the Nguyen lords established the prefecture of Gia Dinh, with mandarin Nguyen Huu Canh as founding father. After the French arrived in 1859 and founded the colony of Cochinchina, they adopted Saigon, a locally popular alternative to Gia Dinh, as the name of their capital.

In its first 20 years as a colonial capital, Saigon blossomed. The French laid out wide boulevards flanked by kapok and tamarind trees that now tower above the avenues. They built a monumental cathedral, an opera house, palaces, and villas, as if their tenure were to last a millennium.

By the 1870s, travelers had begun to wax lyrically about the city as the Pearl of the Orient, the Paris of the East.

Today, you'd be hard-pressed to refer to this urban frenzy in such genteel terms, but its former glories and architectural gems, many all but subsumed by agglomerations of shanty shops, can still dazzle.

Officially, six million people pack the city's 19 urban districts, five rural districts, and 770 square miles (2,000 sq km), though on-the-street estimates put that number closer to eight million. Its history is shallower than that of Hanoi or Hue. Its pagodas, temples, museums, and scenic beauty are wanting in comparison. But its café society, its nightlife, and the ambience stoked by its markets, hotels, and business climate are inimitable. As "mythalopolis," the city also doesn't disappoint, especially if you're attuned to the French or American legacy. It's not at all difficult to conjure the ghosts of French legionnaires, American GIs, or Saigon bar girls flooding old rue Catinat, since renamed Dong Khoi.

The grand monuments of Lam Son Square—the former opera

house, the Continental and Caravelle Hotels—evoke Saigon's legendary renown. Though it's far less common these days to spot a bulbous-fendered Citroën or a Peugeot 404 prowling these streets, the descendants of rickshaw coolies still spin down the city's byways on their cyclo pedicabs.

The echoes of war resonate profoundly at the city's top three tourist attractions— the War Remnants Museum, Reunification Palace, and Cu Chi Tunnels. The war may no longer be the big story in Saigon and across Vietnam, but it's certainly a dominant driver in the tourist trade. ∎

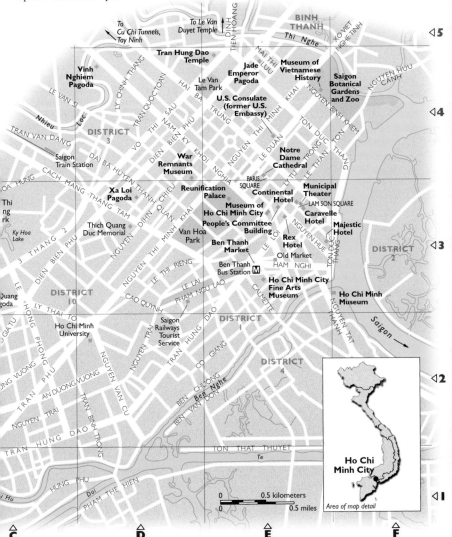

Lam Son Square

Lam Son Square

195 E3

Municipal Theater
✉ 7 Lam Son Square, District 1
☎ (08) 829-9976

THE SAIGON OF MYTH AND MEMORY TRULY RESONATES IN Lam Son Square, home to the city's storied hotels, a colonial French opera house, and the cinematic heart of the city. Though it's no longer possible to take its pulse from the terrace of the Continental Hotel, where the French colonials sipped their *citron pressé* and absinthe, the Givral Café is still open, and the tenth floor of the Caravelle Hotel remains the best perch for a late afternoon cocktail.

fanfare, Italian marble, and bullet-proof glass. The bomb didn't kill anyone, but it damaged nine rooms and blew out the windows of cars parked below. During the Vietnam War, CBS and ABC operated bureaus here.

The **Municipal Theater,** with its broken mansard roofs and arched facade, has reigned over the square since its debut as the Saigon Opera House on January 1, 1900. It once housed the legislature of South Vietnam. Restored for its 100th anniversary, the 800-seat hall again serves as a performing arts center. ■

A new addition to the Caravelle towers over the landmark 1900 Municipal Theater.

British writers Graham Greene and Somerset Maugham both stayed at the 1880-built **Continental** *(132–134 Dong Khoi;* see p. 257) and alluded to it in their writings. In Greene's *The Quiet American,* the two lead characters first meet in the Continental, and a bomb explodes in Lam Son Square.

In 1964, a real bomb exploded on the fifth floor of the **Caravelle** *(19 Lam Son Sq.;* see p. 256), a 10-story hotel that opened on Christmas Eve 1959 with great

To say or not to say

Go ahead and say it: Saigon. Wary travelers often stick to the politically correct Ho Chi Minh City—since 1976 the name of the vast municipality that encompasses Saigon. But the two lovely syllables of the old name are not verboten. Communist officials routinely use the name. The river remains the Saigon. Buses still flash SAIGON as their destination. The largest state-run tourist company is Saigon Tourist. The three-letter airport code is SGN. In fact, the city's District 1 officially remains Saigon. So go ahead and say it. ■

Notre Dame Cathedral

NOTRE DAME (DUC BA) CATHEDRAL, ON THE NORTH END OF Dong Khoi, is the grandest expression of French Catholic architecture in the country. Its facade boasts two matching bell towers that rise 187 feet (56 m) above Paris Square (Cong Xa Pari). Visible from afar, these landmarks have defined the skyline for decades.

Notre Dame Cathedral
🄰 195 E4
✉ Paris Square

French architect Jules Bourard designed the cathedral in the mid-1870s, and a French cleric laid the cornerstone in 1877. It opened to worshippers three years later, with bricks imported from Marseilles, granite from nearby Bien Hoa, and a construction tab of 2.5 million francs. Its six bells weigh nearly 30 tons (27 metric tons).

As in the Vatican's basilica, Notre Dame's nave is divided by a double colonnade and centered on a semicircular apse. The design departs from form with a vaulted Gothic ceiling. A series of niches along either side of the sanctuary houses the Stations of the Cross and statues of the patron saints. While the statuary is not especially satisfying, commemorative stones cemented to the walls are deeply evocative of the church's colonial past. Beginning around World War I, parishioners began placarding the walls around a favorite saint—Anthony in particular—with expressions of gratitude such as *Merci* and *Reconnaissance*. After the colonials departed and the Vietnamese assumed command of the congregation, the gesture continued, albeit in Vietnamese.

Stained glass from the Lorin Company of Chartres originally lit the niches. Replacement glass from Grenoble in the 1940s and '50s delivered such motifs as St. Theresa before a map of Indochina and St. George slaying the dragon.

The Vietnamese have gradually infused the staid Catholic decor with fanciful modern touches.

Blue neon halos one niched saint, white neon beyond the apse spells out *Ave Maria*, and fluorescent

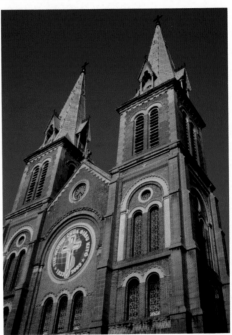

tubes hang vertically from columns in the nave.

In 1962, the Vatican elevated Notre Dame to basilica status, though its exalted designation didn't spare the structure from wartime scarring. Check the exterior walls for damaged bricks, splattered by bullets when the war came to downtown Saigon.

In late 2005, pilgrims flocked to the statue of the Virgin Mother in Paris Square, persuaded the statue was shedding miraculous tears. ∎

Six massive bells in Notre Dame's flanking towers have summoned Catholics to Mass since the 1880s.

A walk along Dong Khoi

If Lam Son Square is the heart of legendary Saigon, then Dong Khoi is its marrow. Here's the street that inspired the city's reputation as the Paris of the East. Here's where war-weary GIs whooped it up with the city's racy bar girls. The French knew the street as rue Catinat. The South Vietnamese called it Tu Do ("freedom"). Now it's called Dong Khoi ("general uprising") and is home to the city's most posh shops and profound echoes.

A portrait of Ho Chi Minh graces the colonial interior of the Main Post Office.

Start at the **Main Post Office** ❶ on Paris Square, across from **Notre Dame Cathedral** (see p. 197). Designed by Gustav Eiffel's firm and built between 1886 and 1891, the post office's vaulted interior and skylights echo the railway stations of 19th-century Europe. Symmetrical wings flank a grand pavilion and arched entryway with a marquee. The escutcheons on the first-floor piers bear the names of Franklin, Volta, Ampère, and other notables who made their mark in electricity. Inside, a map from 1892

depicts an era when marshland separated Saigon and Cholon. On the opposite wall, a 1936 map details the colonial telegraph lines.

Leaving the post office, turn left and start down Dong Khoi. The 100-yard-long (90 m), two-story building at **164 Dong Khoi** ❷ was built in 1917 to house the colonial Sureté, the national security arm of the French police. Its roll of inmates reads like a who's who of Vietnamese nationalists, including future prime minister Pham Van Dong.

Make your first left and stop outside the nine-story apartment building at **22 Ly Tu Trong** *(closed to the public)*, which housed CIA staff during the war. Retrace your steps to Dong Khoi, turn left, and stop at the stairway to **Ce Square**, a little park opened by the colonials in 1935. From here, gaze up toward the roof of the apartment building and the landmark penthouse elevator shaft famously pictured as a helicopter landing pad during the fall of Saigon (see p. 45).

A right on Le Thanh Ton brings you to the head of Nguyen Hue for a gander at the 1908 **People's Committee Building** ❸. Still referred to locally as the Hôtel de Ville, the ornate structure also served as the French colonial city hall. As at the former embassy apartments, the interior of this building is inaccessible to tourists.

Less than a block down Nguyen Hue stands the **Rex Hotel** *(141 Nguyen Hue, tel 08-829-2185; see p. 257)*. During the war, this former parking garage served as the American BOQ (Bachelor Officers' Quarters). Early in the war, on the ground floor of this building, the U.S. military held daily press briefings, known pejoratively among journalists as the "Five O'Clock Follies." Ride the elevator to the rooftop terrace for a drink or a meal and a great view of downtown.

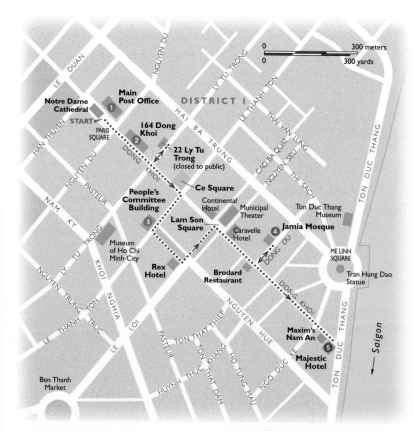

Turn left again at the fountain, stroll through **Lam Son Square** (see p. 196), then turn right on Dong Khoi. When the French decamped from the country in the mid-1950s, the legionnaires paraded up this street, singing *"Je ne regrette rien."* As Tu Do, this was the go-go girl bar district that figures into so many movies about wild, wartime Saigon. Today, the street brims with chic boutiques and older shops selling such wartime souvenirs as French piastres, dog tags, and U.S. government clocks made by the Chelsea Clock Company in Boston.

Turn left on Dong Du and walk half a block to the 1935 **Jamia Mosque** ➍ *(66 Dong Du)*, one of several active mosques in the city. Backtracking to Dong Khoi, check out the plate-glass facade of the **Brodard Restaurant** *(131 Dong Khoi, tel 848-822-3966)*, operating since 1950. Nearly 400 yards (365 m) farther, step inside

🅐 See area map p. 195
▶ Main Post Office
↔ 1.2 miles (1.75 km)
⏱ 1.5 hours
▶ Majestic Hotel

NOT TO BE MISSED

- Embassy apartments
- People's Committee Building
- Rex Hotel

Maxim's Nam An *(13-15-17 Dong Khoi)*. Opened in 1964, this place remains the archetypal nightclub.

At the foot of Dong Khoi, the signature arcade of the 1925 **Majestic Hotel** ➎ *(1 Dong Khoi; see p. 257)* sweeps up from the sidewalk to a facade of wrought-iron balconies. Photos in the lobby depict the hotel through the years. ■

Museum of Ho Chi Minh City

**Museum of
Ho Chi Minh
City**
🏛 195 E3
www.hcmc-museum.edu.vn
✉ 65 Ly Tu Trong,
District 1
☎ (08) 829-9741
$ $

THE COMPREHENSIVE MUSEUM OF HO CHI MINH CITY
takes a long, Michener-esque view of the settlement known first as
Gia Dinh, then Saigon, and now Ho Chi Minh City. Exhibits peer
back at prehistoric times, linger over the colonial era, and indulge
the city's ties to revolutionary activities against the French and resistance to the Americans.

The museum is housed in a
magnificent, pearl-gray French
imperial palace, designed by
architect Alfred Foulhoux in the
1880s. Foulhoux had designed
the palace as a museum, but
upon its completion in 1880, the
French governor of Indochina
retained it as his residence.

Today, brides and grooms
come to be photographed amid
the grandeur of the main foyer.
Pause as you enter, for it was here
on a November evening in 1963
that Ngo Dinh Diem, South Vietnam's prime minister, and his
brother, Nhu, descended into a
tunnel and the bowels of history,
pursued by generals on a coup
d'état who hours later would
execute the Ngos in Cholon.

The **first hall,** to the left, opens
a window on the area's past, from
the Precambrian through present
Cenozoic eras. More interesting
than references to the geologic
past is a diorama of stuffed animals—tigers, cobras, crocodiles,
several primates—indigenous to
the region. Toward the back of
this hall are pieced-together clay
ossuaries unearthed 2,500 years
after burial. All of the main
exhibits are tagged in English, as
well as Vietnamese, encouraging
all visitors to linger over this fascinating collection.

Beyond the first hall, a **second
hall** explores the city's primary
ethnic populations—the Khmer,
Vietnamese (Kinh), Chinese, and
Cham—who settled here in

roughly that order. Together,
according to one placard, they
"helped mutually to change wild
land into gardens and towns."

Four successive exhibits
display the traditional costumes
of women from a variety of
ethnic groups—a *tam pong*
(Khmer), a *tah* (Cham), a *ba ba*
(Vietnamese), and a *xa xau*
(Chinese), each culturally distinct but clearly similar. On
the opposite wall is a wonderful
display of photos that depict
city life in the early part of the
19th century, including a book-
mobile and a sidewalk dentist
from the 1920s.

The **third hall** traces the
city's transition from a Khmer
settlement into the colonial
capital later hyperbolized as
the Pearl of the Orient. Of all
the halls in the palace, this is
the one to linger over, both for
its focus and the variety and
quality of the exhibits.

Map aficionados can feast
on a series of charts that show
how the city progressed after
the Vietnamese subsumed its
Khmer inhabitants in the late
16th century and founded the
prefecture of Gia Dinh in 1698.
That name remained in place
until 1863, four years after a
French attack put Vietnamese
autonomy on long-term hold.

In the same room, an ex-
quisite diorama displays the
citadel of Gia Dinh, one of a
number of citadels constructed

in Vietnam in the 18th and 19th centuries. Today, Le Duan slices down the middle of the moated, polygonal citadel, though its remains are accessible only to archaeologists.

Here, too, stands Ho Chi Minh, in a muscular, socially realistic interpretation of a 21-year-old youth ready to embark from Saigon for the high seas and foreign countries to "learn from others and develop a path for national salvation."

SECOND FLOOR

The municipal journey continues upstairs from the foyer, where in the **fourth hall** you'll find the tools of Vietnamese trades, in agriculture, fishing, bronze casting, wood carving, weaving, lacquerware, pottery, and rubber tree harvesting. The **fifth** and **sixth halls** detail the revolution-

ary struggle against the French and subsequent reunification efforts. Though compelling to scholars, these exhibits will be of somewhat less interest to the average traveler. Most of the players are obscure, and any potential objectivity of the exhibits is compromised by references to "puppet regimes" and the heroism of certain participants.

One artful exhibit centers on an enlarged photograph of combat boots strewn across a South Vietnamese road in 1975—the flotsam of South Vietnamese soldiers who didn't want to be caught wearing the incriminating footwear. In a glass case beneath the photo is a mishmash of wartime booty picked up on "Liberation Day," including a billy club, mess kits, shoes, rifles, field telephones, gas masks, and plaques. ■

Patriotic art, like the museum's mural depicting the fall of Saigon, is de rigeur at most Vietnamese museums.

Reunification Palace

Reunification Palace

🏛 195 E3

✉ 106 Nguyen Du, District 3

☎ (08) 822-3652

$ $

ON APRIL 30, 1975, A RUSSIAN-BUILT TANK COMMANDED BY a North Vietnamese colonel bashed through the gates of South Vietnam's Independence Palace, delivering a dramatic coup de grâce to both a war and a nation. The victors renamed the building Dinh Thong Nhat (Reunification Palace) and left the structure and its contents intact as a time-warped memorial to the Great Spring Victory. Today, the palace is the city's dominant tourist attraction and a haunting relic of a vanished state.

A tank on the palace grounds symbolizes the April 1975 victory and war's end.

Though the current building dates from 1966, the site's relevance as a capitol winds back to 1868 when the French laid the cornerstone of a palace for the governor-general of Indochina. It was a romantic flight of Second Empire and Greek Revival fancy, with a pediment, a mansard roof, arched galleries, and jutting wings. In a failed 1962 coup d'état, two pilots bombed the renamed Independence Palace, dooming the fusty structure to the wrecking ball.

In his design of the new palace, a South Vietnamese architect worked the shapes of the Chinese characters for good fortune, education, and consistency into the building's floor plan and facade. The dominant exterior motif is a stone curtain of bamboo segments that shades floor-to-ceiling windows. Inside, a grand stairway rises through the five-story core of the 95-room palace.

The first resident was to have been Ngo Dinh Diem, who

ordered its construction, but South Vietnam's first president was assassinated in 1963 (see p. 42). At the building's completion in 1966, President Nguyen Van Thieu took up residence with his family. His thumbprints are all over the building today, from the parquet dance floor on the rooftop terrace to the back issues of *Tennis World* in the palace library.

TOURING THE PALACE

Visitors can roam the palace with remarkable leeway, but start with a free guided tour.

The cabinet room, dining room, and conference room on the **first floor** are worth a cursory peek. On the **second floor,** in the **president's office,** are framed seascapes of Ninh Thuan, the south-central province where Thieu was born. A now-closed passage leads from this room down a private stairway to the palace's underground bunkers. In the **lobby,** four dragons encircle a round red carpet that depicts the Chinese characters for longevity. In the grandest space, the **Credentials Presenting Room,** the president received foreign ambassadors before a gorgeous, 40-piece lacquer painting of 15th-century Vietnam.

On the **third floor** in the **casino,** the president gambled with cronies around a bar cut like a whiskey barrel. Nearby is a 42-seat cinema. From the rooftop **terrace,** you can look down on the helipad and two painted red circles that commemorate a pair of bombs dropped by a South Vietnamese pilot who showed his northern stripes in the closing days of the war. The view down Le Duan leads to the botanical garden and past the site of the former U.S. Embassy, which was destroyed in the mid-1990s

A landscape of Hue overlooks the banquet table in the first-floor dining room.

to make way for a more modern and less emblematic U.S. consulate.

The visit's highlight is the warren of concrete corridors and war rooms in the **basement,** an eerie time capsule of electronics, maps, and avocado-colored telephones. In the **radio room,** big black knobs and round meters trick out the industrial gray casings of equipment by GE and Motorola.

The ground-floor **kitchen** is filled with mixers, Zenith woks, and Electrolux dishwashers. A **photo gallery** on this level offers a snapshot of the war and history of the building, as does a worthwhile half-hour documentary.

Outside on the parklike grounds, neither of the tanks by the entrance is the one that smashed through the gates in 1975. (It rests in Hanoi.) The F-5E is the genuine article but not the one that bombed the palace on April 8, 1975. ∎

One gallery holds photos of those tortured and executed at Con Dao and Phu Quoc prisons.

War Remnants Museum

MANY PROVINCES AND CITIES THROUGHOUT VIETNAM memorialize the nation's struggle against the French and Americans with museums, but none speak with as much impact or devastation as this place, formerly known as the Museum of American and Chinese War Crimes. Despite its anti-American message, this museum is one of Vietnam's most popular among Western visitors.

War Remnants Museum
- 195 D4
- 28 Vo Van Tan, District 3
- (08) 930-5587
- Closed 12–1:30 p.m.
- $

The United States spent 130 billion dollars on the war and abandoned billions of dollars worth of equipment in Vietnam. Some of it stands on the museum grounds: a 175mm cannon able to hurl a projectile 20 miles (32 km); an M-48 tank, one of 370 in country at the war's height in 1969; and an emblematic Huey (UH-1 Bell helicopter).

The **main hall** is a monolith of granite-faced concrete suspended above an open floor. Inside you'll find photo after gruesome photo—some of them Pulitzer Prize-winning—depicting American brutality in the war. Among them are images of the My Lai massacre, and the deformative effects of Agent Orange, white phosphorous, and napalm.

Outside, other halls hold more photos, including the **Requiem exhibit.** All of the photos here are by correspondents who died during the conflict, including Larry Burrows, Henri Huet, Dana Stone, and Sean Flynn, the son of actor Errol.

The final gallery explores the worldwide protests against the war. The most touching exhibit is a collection of medals, including a Purple Heart donated to the museum by an American army sergeant with an inscribed brass plaque that reads: "To the people of a United Vietnam. I was wrong. I am sorry."

The museum is certainly not unbiased in its representation of events in Vietnam in the 1960s and '70s. Nonetheless, it drives home the fact that wars are devastating and that civilians are the biggest losers. ■

Ben Thanh Market

QUITE LITERALLY, THIS MARKET STANDS ATOP A MORASS, a swamp that was drained and filled in the early 20th century. The previous market sat on the banks of the Ben Nghe River near the old Gia Dinh citadel. The French destroyed that first Ben Thanh ("pier fort") during its assault on the city in 1859. Merchants rebuilt on the same site and traded there until the end of the century, when French authorities launched this new commercial center.

Opened in 1914 and capped by a landmark clock tower atop the south gate, the 3-acre (12,000 sq m) market is divided into quadrants by two main aisles crisscrossed by smaller aisles. Main gates front each quadrant, and 12 additional gates provide access.

Start beneath the **clock tower,** where a color-coded schematic details the market's wares. On the south side, the largest department peddles clothing. Footwear, handbags, and sundries claim the next largest share of space, followed by food counters frequented by shoppers and connoisseurs alike.

The 1,200 kiosks range from small cubbyholes to spreads along the main aisles. Buyer beware: Arabica coffee beans that sell for $2 per pound in Buon Ma Thuot are hawked here at five times that price, and the brand-name accessories are knockoffs.

On the north side, stroll from east to west and back again amid a cornucopia of vegetables, tubs of seafood, and busy butchers' chopping blocks. ■

Ben Thanh Market

🅰 195 E3

✉ Quach Thi Trang Square, District 1 (intersection of Le Loi, Ham Nghi, Tran Hung Dao, & Le Lai)

One of Ho Chi Minh City's liveliest indoor markets, Ben Thanh Market is a good place to find a conical hat, an *ao dai,* and other local goods.

Saigon Botanical Gardens & Zoo

Saigon Botanical Gardens & Zoo
- ▲ 195 F4
- ✉ 2 Nguyen Binh Khiem, District 1
- ☎ (08) 829-1425
- 💲 $

Museum of Vietnamese History
- ▲ 195 F4
- ✉ 2 Nguyen Binh Khiem, District 1
- 🕐 Closed 11 a.m.– 1:30 p.m. Mon.–Sat.
- ☎ (08) 829-8146
- 💲 $

THOUGH SOMEWHAT UNKEMPT, THE BOTANICAL GARDENS and adjacent zoo offer an oasis of green space in this vast cityscape, while the Museum of Vietnamese History and Temple to the Hung Kings, just inside the gardens' main gate, make for a fascinating introduction to Vietnam's past.

THE GARDENS

Under the auspices of French botanist J. B. Louis Pierre, the Saigon Botanical Gardens opened in 1865 as a proving ground for the imported plants—cocoa, coffee, vanilla, rubber—French colonists hoped to cultivate.

Beyond a pedestaled bust of Pierre, the **bonsai garden** boasts exquisite specimens of Far Eastern flora that have been under cultivation for as long as 50 years. But it's as an **arboretum** that the park achieves its real glory. Flanking the wide main avenue are rows of majestic African mahogany trees that top out at more than 100 feet (30 m). Other trees labeled in Latin and Vietnamese but not English include bodhi, flower, pagoda, plum, queen's, rain, skunk, tamarind, tea shade, thitpok, wild jackfruit, and yellowwood.

THE ZOO

The park also penned wild animals from tropical Vietnam for export to zoos in France. The zoo features the usual suspects—giraffes, elephants, hippos—and one rather glorious multidomed monkey cage that recalls the antiquated zoos often pictured in children's storybooks. The pens betray the poverty of their hosts. The zoo is a casualty of hard times that started during World War II when occupying Japanese forces used the park as a barracks. Still, conditions are far better today than they were ten years ago.

OTHER SIGHTS

Be sure not to miss either of the grand buildings just inside the main entrance. To the right is the 70-year-old **Temple to the Hung Kings,** built in homage to the 18 legendary lords who ruled Vietnam from 2879 to 258 B.C. Sitting before three altars holding replica ancient thrones is a fourth altar that contains two jars—one filled with earth and the other water from Nghia Linh Mountain, the ancestral seat of the Hung kings, which lies nearly 100 miles (160 km) north of Hanoi.

The dioramas are even more impressive across the avenue in the **Museum of Vietnamese History,** a light-filled, pleasantly arranged museum topped by a pagoda-style roof. In exhibits spanning 13 halls, the museum presents a collection of artifacts that detail Vietnam's history, from the discovery of 500,000-year-old teeth from *Homo erectus* to the Nguyen dynasty of the 20th century.

The journey dutifully begins in the Stone Age but doesn't hit its stride until the **second hall,** which features a bronze drum forged some 2,000 to 2,500 years ago during the Dong Son culture. (The best drums of this type are kept in Hanoi's museums.) In the next room, which spans the Chinese occupation from the first century B.C. to the tenth century A.D., the first in a series of exquisite dioramas depicts the legendary battle on the Bach Dang River in 938. In this battle, Ngo Quyen impaled the invading Chinese fleet on thick wooden of artifacts from the roll call of Vietnamese dynasties, the museum also houses worthy collections of Cham art, stone sculpture from Cambodia, and art made by Vietnam's ethnic minorities. In the **tenth hall,**

stakes planted in the river mud, a tactic used with similar success to repel Mongol invaders three centuries later. Three stakes from that later conflict are on display in the **fifth hall,** which showcases artifacts from the Tran dynasty.

Taken together, the meticulously arranged dioramas of legendary Vietnamese battles are worth a dedicated visit to the museum. So, too, are the mummified remains of a 60-year-old woman that are displayed with traditional Vietnamese burial garments and jewelry in their own alcove.

In addition to the march

look for the two 1,600-year-old wooden statues of the Buddha, carved by people of the Oc Eo culture. A Roman coin retrieved from an Oc Eo site demonstrates that these Mekong Delta denizens were trading with, and influenced by, cultures as far away as Rome.

The museum also hosts weekend performances by the **Saigon Water Puppet Theater** (*1 p.m.–4 p.m., on the hour*). These modest shows will either whet your appetite for, or encourage you to skip, the more grandiose production at Hanoi's Thang Long Theater (see p. 263). ■

An elephant gets up close and personal with a visitor at the Saigon zoo.

A statue of the jade emperor, Ngoc Hoang, presides over the main sanctuary of the splendidly colorful Chinese temple named in his honor.

Jade Emperor Pagoda

Jade Emperor Pagoda

📍 195 E4

✉ 73 Mai Thi Luu, District 3

BUILT BY SAIGON'S CANTONESE COMMUNITY IN 1909, THE Jade Emperor Pagoda is a surreal Taoist temple, populated by a singular collection of statuary and the best wood carvings in the city. On the outside, its signature mauve facade and jade green pantiles induce wild expectations that are fulfilled by the temple's equally fanciful contents. In a city bereft of really good temples and pagodas, it ranks among the best and is not to be missed.

As attractive as the temple is to tourists, it's even more so to devotees, who burn paper votives in an industrial-grade stove in the **courtyard** and sandalwood joss at an array of indoor altars. Don't miss the outdoor crescent pool, brimming with scores of turtles of various shapes and sizes.

Past the main doors is a secondary interior doorway flanked by a pair of parallel sentences that hang from the mouths of sculpted bats. The heavy wooden doors are carved with Taoist warriors who breathe fire from the mouth and nostrils.

Intricate carvings in ebony-stained hardwood frame the bays between columns throughout the **main hall.** A pageant of Oriental characters decks out the wide bay before the main altar, dedicated to Ngoc Hoang, the jade emperor. His towering, bearded attendants lean toward each other in textural detail made possible by their papier-mâché construction.

In an **annex temple** to the left of the main hall, women pray for fertility in a niche dedicated to Kinh Hoa, a deified maternity specialist, who's flanked by a host of husbands. On the left and right, a bumper crop of baby statues clamber in play about the laps, thighs, and sleeves of fruitful ceramic mothers.

Beyond this niche, Than Hoang lords over a **hall of tortures,** flanked by high-hatted papier-mâché guards painted black. In this chamber's middle hall, carved panels depict various means of retributive torture in the nether-world. While the ten kings of the netherworld write maxims above, devils feed onerous humans to flames, cut off their heads, and impale them on beds of spikes.

Back through the main hall, climb the stairs up the right side of the temple to a room dedicated to Quan Am. Here you'll find the best view of the chaotic pitches, crests, and flying eaves of the pantiled roofs. ∎

Le Van Duyet Temple

THIS TOMB AND TEMPLE COMPLEX HONORS A CHARISMAT-ic 19th-century eunuch whose cult throws an annual bash in his memory at the end of the seventh lunar month. The complex lies deep within a largely untouristed part of the city and attracts mostly a domestic following, who come to pray for luck, health, and myriad other desires.

Le Van Duyet Temple
🅰 195 E5
✉ 1 Phan Dang Luu, Binh Thanh District
☎ (08) 841-2517

Le Van Duyet (1764–1832) was a eunuch since birth, though it's unclear whether he was a hermaph-rodite or was castrated in prepara-tion for a life of royal service. In the early 19th century, he engineered a naval victory against the Tay Son and helped usher the deposed Prince Nguyen Anh to the throne as Emperor Gia Long. Later, Duyet ruled southern Vietnam as viceroy and defied King Minh Mang's order to persecute Christians.

Inside the mausoleum's triple-gate entrance, the viceroy and his wife lie buried under egg-shaped concrete mounds. Minh Mang ordered the desecration of the original graves to avenge Duyet's disobedience. The viceroy's loyal-ists then massacred Minh Mang's agents. Tit for tat, Minh Mang then razed the citadel of Gia Dinh, now Saigon. Perhaps as a gesture of penance, Minh Mang's successors restored the site in 1841 and 1847.

The temple comprises four main halls, built in 1925 to replace the previous bamboo structures.

In the **second hall,** massive whale jawbones arch from the mouth of a mythical beast, while beyond are elephant tusks. In a glass case to the left is the preserved carcass of a tiger that reputedly prowled the temple grounds during the colonial era. After a Frenchman killed the tiger, locals preserved it, believing the animal to be an agent of Duyet's security.

On a platform altar to the left is a black-and-white portrait of Phan Thanh Giang, one of Duyet's administrators, whom worshippers also honor here. Illustrations of a cheerfully optimistic Duyet stare from altars in the **third hall.** On your way to the rear hall, check out the fat, big-lipped fish in the concrete aquarium. It's said to be a manifestation of the viceroy.

In the **rear hall,** dragons spiral around tall cement columns that rise above sumptuous red Nguyen dynasty altars with gilt carvings. The glass cabinets are filled with robes, donated by local devotees, for Le Van Duyet, his wife, and Phan Thanh Giang. ∎

Cholon

The ethnic
Chinese heart
of the city pulses
with commercial
opportunities.

Cholon

 194 B1 & B2

✉ District 5, bounded
by Tau Hu Canal
to S, Nguyen Van
Cu to E, Nguyen
Chi Thanh to N,
and Nguyen Thi
Nho to W

CHOLON ("BIG MARKET") IS THE HYPERACTIVE, COMMER-
cial heart of Ho Chi Minh City and its Chinese population. Historically
notorious as a den of thieves, opium parlors, gambling halls, and
brothels, the district remains gritty, and cash is still king, though the
heavy hand of Hanoi stifled the obvious vice after 1975. However,
unless you're savvy in the ways and means of shopping Chinatown,
the most fulfilling dividends are to be found in the flamboyant
temples, wonton soup, and exposure to the feverish pitch of life on
the streets.

Cholon surged into prominence in
the late 18th century as a haven for
ethnic Chinese refugees from Bien
Hoa and the Mekong Delta, whose
loyalty to the Nguyen lords sparked
retaliation by Tay Son generals. The
Chinese named their settlement De
Ngan, after the embankments they

built as a hedge against flooding
along the Tau Hu Canal, which
feeds the Saigon River. In 1874,
Cholon merged with Saigon, and
today it comprises District 5.

On Thap Muoi, along the district's western border, **Binh Tay
Market** is a massive, two-story

Chinese market with pagoda-style roofs at the four corners and a clock tower above the main entrance. In the open courtyard, statues of dragons and lion-dogs spit continuous jets of water into goldfish ponds that surround a monument to the Chinese merchant who founded the market in 1930. The market stalls cluster by wares, with big departments for incense candles, bags, fabrics, household aluminum, and sealing wax. Most residents will steer you here for the best buys in the city.

CHOLON'S TEMPLES

The district's spiritual pulse beats loudest at a fairly dense cluster of temples between Nguyen Trai and Huong Vuong. These temples are not nearly as frequented by tourists as the temple-cum-assembly halls of Hoi An (see pp. 155–156), but they're equally picturesque and just as storied.

In the heart of the quarter at **Thien Hau Temple** (710 *Nguyen Trai*), devotees worship the eponymous goddess of the sea, whose robed statue in the temple's back compartment is flanked left and right by the goddess of fertility and the protector of fishermen. The temple's signature adornments are hundreds of exquisite ceramic puppets, congregated in 200-year-old friezes that crest the roofs of the entry hall and inner galleries.

Heading east on Nguyen Trai, as you cross **Trieu Quang Phuc,** make a quick detour south along this shop-filled road. The aromas of traditional Chinese medicine, drying in bushel baskets and brimming from bags plopped on the sidewalk, make for a wonderfully pungent experience. Inside the shops, look for the practitioners of traditional medicine as they diagnose the yin and yang imbalances of customers who

won't have far to go to fill their prescriptions. Some of the medicine is packaged, but much of it—the roots, bark, herbs, funguses, seeds, and other organic substances—is stored in voluminous wooden hutches that line the walls.

A little farther east on Nguyen Trai, the Taoist deity and Buddhist bodhisattva Quan Cong presides over **Nghia An and Quan De Temple** (676 *Nguyen Trai*) from a large glass display case in the temple's central compartment. Quang Binh, the pink-faced youth who symbolizes justice, and Chau Xuong, a warrior-saint, stand in glass-cased octagonal pavilions to the right and left, respectively.

Across the street is the **Jamia Mosque** (641 *Nguyen Trai*), built in 1932 by the district's Indian residents. While the mosque lacks a telltale dome or principal minaret, the four slender towers that rise from the building's corners are distinctively Middle Eastern, as are the ogee-style arches that frame the mosque's bi-level wraparound terrace. After the Indian population decamped during the war, the city's Cham Muslims appropriated the

Binh Tay Market's central courtyard features water-spitting statues and a goldfish pond, a peaceful retrieve from the hullabaloo of the indoor market stalls.

mosque for the 5,000 members of their community.

On the other side of Thien Hau Pagoda, off Lupong Nhu Hoc, the 1740 **Quan Am Temple** (*12 Lao Tu*) was dedicated to the eponymous goddess of mercy by the district's Fujian Chinese congregation. The colorful temple is most remarkable for its roof ornamentation. Quaint mosaic-faced Oriental gates and pagodas line the crests of the two-tiered entry hall. Inside, a gold-faced Thien Hau occupies the choice throne at back. On the other side of the wall, Quan Am faces a pantheon of Chinese deities, who dwell in seven separate bays.

Around the corner at 184

Fruit vendors at Binh Tay Market wind down after a long day of haggling.

here and at temples elsewhere in Cholon will burn for a month.

South on Chau Van Liem and west on Hai Thuong Lan Ong stands **Ong Bong Pagoda** (*264 Hai Thuong Lan Ong*). People from two districts of Fujian Province may have built the temple in 1765, as evidenced by a date scratched into a bronze bell at the site. Beneath a vast span of distinctive pink roofs, worshippers pay homage to both Ong Bong, the guardian of happiness and virtue, and the jade emperor.

For a religious counterpoint and a bit of history, stroll to the west end of Tran Hung Dao to **Cha Tam Church** (*25 Hoc Lac*). Father Tam is buried beneath a

Hong Bang, green-robed Quan Kong lords over the **Phuoc An Hoi Quan Temple.** Built in 1921, its roof crest sports an array of puppets. Inside, look up to spot the name boards of patronizing colonial French officials who, in mimicry of Vietnam's former kings, left behind these souvenirs in the 1920s. The long coils of sandalwood incense that hang

marble slab on the portico. More intriguing is the church's cameo in Vietnam's political past, for it was here, on November 2, 1963, that President Ngo Dinh Diem and his brother, Nhu, surrendered to troops loyal to a short-lived junta of South Vietnamese generals. The Ngos were executed soon after soldiers escorted them from the church grounds. ∎

Giac Lam Pagoda

FOUNDED IN 1744, GIAC LAM IS THE EXCEPTIONAL PAGODA in a cityscape that lacks venerable Buddhist sanctuaries. Its wealth of wood statuary, columns, parallel sentences, and intricately carved frames rival the appeal of northern pagodas.

Vietnamese Buddhists venerate spirits who dwell in the loftiest trees.

In 1799, Giac Lam's master launched a six-year restoration project that raised 98 columns of precious wood decked with 86 parallel sentences inscribed with gilded Chinese calligraphy. The enlarged pagoda diminished its contents' prestige, however, so the master also called for new jackwood statues.

Most of the 113 statues reign from terraced altars in the **main hall.** Along either wall, nine 32-inch (80 cm) wooden arhats, carved in the early 19th century, roost above older 20-inch (50 cm) versions of the same characters. Between the arhats, the ten kings of the netherworld (five to each side) stare at mirrored tablets to maintain solemn composure.

The Amitabha Buddha atop the **main terrace** dates from 1744. After carving, the statue was coated in clay paper, painted in vermilion (a brilliant red pigment made from mercury sulfide), then gilded. Below this statue is a 1757 bronze of the Nine Dragons, the most precious piece in the collection. On the **lowest terrace,** two bodhisattvas flank the Amitabha Buddha. They face the dharma guardian, who stands within the outer wall beside his grotesque companion, Tieu Dien. Armed with a sword, the guardian protects the Buddha, the dharma, and the monks.

Twenty-three name boards hang from the ceiling, and 28 chiseled screens frame the columns. Outside, the stupas nearest the sanctuary mark the graves of the pagoda's patriarchs, or abbots. The seven-story hexagonal tower near the entrance was completed in 1993. ∎

Giac Lam Pagoda
- 194 B2
- 118 Lac Long Quan, District 10
- Closed 12–2 p.m.
- (08) 840-4310

Cu Chi Tunnels

Cu Chi Tunnels
🗺 221 D4
www.cuchitunnel.org.vn
☎ (08) 794-8820 or
(08) 794-8823
(no English spoken)
💲 $

NO GROUND FROM THE VIETNAM WAR IS AS HALLOWED as the tunnel-ridden earth of Cu Chi, where 18,000 peasant guerrillas waged war from 125 miles (200 km) of hand-dug passageways and chambers. It was in Cu Chi that the Viet Cong (VC) planned their momentous assault on Saigon during the 1968 Tet New Year celebrations. In 1990, the government opened two tunnel sections to the public, including the command center at Ben Duoc, an area known to U.S. soldiers as the Ho Bo Wood, and Ben Dinh.

A tour guide demonstrates the fine art of concealment.

Getting there
Buses leave each morning from Pham Ngu Lao backpacker zone in Ho Chi Minh City, bound for Cu Chi and Tay Ninh. Alternatively, take local bus from Ho Chi Minh City 25 miles (40 km) up Hwy. 22 to Cu Chi, then rent motorbike and drive another 12 miles (20 km) to tunnels at Ben Duoc or Ben Dinh.

Cu Chi's peasant soldiers started burrowing into the district's clay ground in the late 1940s during the French War. By 1967, they'd excavated a network of tunnels, aid stations, kitchens, theaters, dormitories, weapons caches, wells, printing shops, and other chambers. So extensive was this three-tiered network, 10 to 30 feet (3–9 m) underground, that the 25th U.S. Infantry (aka Tropic Lightning) unwittingly situated its base partially above the tunnels just northeast of Cu Chi town.

The U.S. Army sent volunteers known as tunnel rats into this Viet Cong netherworld to root out intelligence and destroy the guerrillas' base. During Operation Cedar Falls in 1967, Army bulldozers razed more than 4 square miles (11 sq km) of neighboring forest to deprive the VC of cover. At the war's height, more than 200,000 shells rained down here each month, transforming Cu Chi into the "most bombed, shelled, gassed, defoliated, and generally devastated area in the history of warfare," according to British journalists Tom Mangold and John Penycate in their 1985 book *The Tunnels of Cu Chi*. Though bombing disabled some 70 percent of the tunnels, Cu Chi remained a staging area for VC operations throughout the war.

Visitors to Cu Chi's target range can fire wartime weapons at paper targets.

VISITING THE TUNNELS

Most day trips out of Ho Chi Minh City visit the reconstructed tunnels at **Ben Duoc** (formerly Phu My Hung), 37 miles (60 km) northwest of the city. The first stop on a guided tour is often at a camouflaged 10-by-12-inch (25 by 30 cm) hatch atop a **tunnel entrance.** A guide wearing fatigues and a floppy green bush hat will wriggle down the hole and then pop up, holding the hatch overhead for Cu Chi's signature photo op.

Nearby, a larger hatch covers a **booby trap** of bamboo spikes driven into the bottom of a pit. The VC cooked up grisly ways to kill and maim GIs, as an exhibit of eight booby traps makes painfully obvious. American GIs fell prey to traps both outside and within the tunnels.

Above ground, the tour winds past an American **M-41 tank,** disabled by a mine in 1970, as well as mannequins of VC cadres, resting in hammocks and working in excavated weapon-making shops. The guerrillas mined a good deal of gunpowder from duds dropped by American bombers and hurled from artillery cannon.

Though some **tunnels** have been enlarged to accommodate tourists, following in the footsteps of Cu Chi's guerrillas often means having to crouch or crawl through close, humid, bell-shaped corridors. The passages' many zigs and zags were designed to thwart weapons fire, while interior hatches served as a defense against flames, chemicals, and water blown through by the U.S. Army. The earthen walls retain the consistency of cement, a natural attribute that made the district particularly well suited for tunneling. As excavated earth was a dead giveaway of tunneling activity, the guerrillas would dispose of freshly dug dirt by raking it into rice fields and pouring it into streams and bomb craters.

The tunnels at **Ben Dinh,** 30 miles (50 km) northwest of Ho Chi Minh City, are also open to visitors. This small, renovated section of the real tunnels, unlit and cramped, are not for the claustrophobic.

Both Ben Dinh and Ben Duoc are known for their **target ranges,** where for a dollar a pop you can fire your wartime weapon of choice—an M-16, AK-47, Chinese carbine, shotgun, etc. ■

Cao Dai Great Temple

**Cao Dai
Great Temple**

✉ Long Hoa, 3 miles
(5 km) SE of Tay
Ninh

IN OCTOBER 1926, A CIVIL SERVANT AND MYSTIC NAMED Ngo Van Chieu settled near Tay Ninh with 300 followers and founded Cao Dai ("high palace"), a unique belief that elaborates on the traditional Vietnamese blend of Buddhism, Confucianism, Taoism, and ancestor worship with elements of Christianity and other religions. In the early 1930s, the new religion's high priests began channeling instructions via séance for construction of a stupendous temple that took two decades to complete.

**A Cao Dai
devotee arrives
for one of four
daily services.**

**Visitor
information**

✉ Tay Ninh Tourist,
210B Duong 30
Thang 4

☎ (066) 822-376

An architectural fusion of East and West, the temple is as long and lofty as a cathedral, with towers bracketing the facade, a domed tower over the sanctum, and a fourth tower in the rear. Staring from a third story mirador on the facade is the divine eye, which symbolizes both the spirit of God and the light of the heart. Above the eye, Buddha sits atop a tiger, recalling the year when construction began. The female statue on the left tower honors the first woman ordained into Cao Dai. The man to the right is Le Van Trung, the first Cao Dai pope, whose clerical hierarchy mirrors that of Catholicism.

Just inside, the patron saints—French writer Victor Hugo, Chinese revolutionary Sun Yat-sen, and 16th-century Vietnamese poet Nguyen Binh Khiem—are depicted as signatories to the Divine Contract of the Third Amnesty. The Cao Dai believe God revealed himself to mankind in three great revelations. Moses was a witness to the first; Christ, Sakyamuni, and Muhammad to the second; and Cao Dai to the third.

In the nave, sacred dragons swirl around pink Corinthian columns, while the holy lion-dog, tortoise, and phoenix dwell in bas-relief on ceiling medallions. Overhead are sky blue vaults puffed with clouds and speckled with stars. Before the sanctum are six gilded red chairs for the cardinals and a throne for the pope. Framing the sanctum is a screen populated by statues of eight Cao Dai deities, including Sakyamuni in the most prominent position, Jesus Christ, and the red-faced Quan Kong.

Ranks of costumed devotees pray here four times daily. From the galleries above the nave, visitors can observe and listen to the choir of mostly teenage girls. ∎

At Dam Sen Park, visitors escape the daily grind with Vietnamese-style amusements.

More places to visit in & around Ho Chi Minh City

DAM SEN PARK

Vietnam's answer to Disneyland, Dam Sen is jam-packed with kiddie and adult attractions. A monorail circuits a large, central lake from which recreational fishers haul catch to local grills for on-site consumption. The zoo features elephants, which double as amusement rides for tourists. On your way out, look for a remarkable, if kitschy, collection of oversize unicorns, dragons, and dinosaurs, made from ceramic soup spoons, tiny tea cups, and plates.

🅰 194 B2 ✉ 3 Hoa Binh, District 11 ☎ (08) 963-4963, www.damsenpark.com.vn

GIAC VIEN PAGODA

Weathering away on the edge of Dam Sen Park, Giac Vien is the city's second oldest pagoda and looks it, though it retains a woebegone appeal. The pagoda had an inauspicious start as a guard shack and meditation hut for the monk overseeing restoration at nearby Giac Lam (see p. 213) in 1799. By 1850, the hut had grown into a pavilion and then a pagoda in its own right, though its stepbrother standing is readily apparent. The courtyard is a mess of broken tiles, rainwater pools on its floors, and bats flit from the eaves, even in daylight. The sanctuary mirrors that of Giac Lam. Many of the same deities—the dharma guardian, Tieu Dien, the ten netherworld kings, the five personalities, the arhats, and others among the pagoda's 153 statues—pack the terraces and altars, all lacquered to a water puppet sheen. A multicolored disk halos Amitabha's head. Notice the carved wooden screens between the columns, including 18 arhats astride buffalos, pigs, cows, a dragon, and other mythical animals, as well as fruit widely cultivated in the south, such as coconut, mangosteen, durian, and rambutan.

🅰 194 B2 ✉ 247 Lac Long Quan, District 11

HO CHI MINH CITY FINE ARTS MUSEUM

The fine arts museum occupies a grand colonial building with stained-glass French doors and fanlights, a flared roof, and lots of balconies. Once home to a wealthy businessman, the foursquare palace opened as a museum in 1991. **First-floor exhibits** are largely given over to propaganda art. The **second floor** offers more lacquer and silk paintings of the requisite revolutionary relics, but includes a wonderfully redemptive gallery with a nine-panel lacquer masterpiece by Nguyen Gia Tri (1908–1993), a pioneering student of the Indochina School of Fine Arts. The **third floor** features bronze and wood statues of Buddhist deities and genii, 19th- and 20th-century ceramics, a fine wooden statue of Confucius, funereal statues from the central highlands, Cham sculpture, and Theravada art from the ethnic Khmers of the Mekong Delta. 🅰 195 E3 ✉ 97A Pho Duc Chinh, District 1 ☎ (08) 829-4441 🕐 Closed Mon. 🅂 $

HO CHI MINH MUSEUM

Unfortunately, this museum holds the same photos, yellowed newspaper clippings, and meager contents that plague every other Ho Chi Minh museum in the country. This one is mostly a photo gallery, with the odd trifle cased in glass—a radio that broadcast news of Ho Chi Minh's death in 1969 to a Saigon resident, carpenter tools that built a temple to Ho in Soc Trang. Known as the Dragon House for the two mythical beasts crawling along the roof crest, the building is a classic colonial structure with distinctive wrap-around verandas on the first two stories. In 1911, Ho embarked from this wharf to struggle for Vietnam's independence from abroad. 🅰 195 F3 ✉ 1 Nguyen Tat Thanh, District 4 ☎ (08) 940-2060 🕐 Closed Mon. 🅂 $

TRAN HUNG DAO TEMPLE

This tidy, well-heeled temple honors Hung Dao, the general who routed the Mongols from Vietnam in the 13th century. A suite of doors opens across the front of the brick-faced sanctuary. Inside, a pair of whale jawbones curve from the mouths of lion-dogs before the altar. A small statue of Tran Hung Dao stands on the middle altar, with a larger bronze to the rear. Paintings along the roof detail the general's triumphs. A neighboring museum, built in 1929, covers the history of the Tran dynasty. 🅰 195 E4 ✉ 36 Vo Thi Sau, District 1

U.S. CONSULATE

On Le Duan, the consulate occupies the site of the previous wartime American Embassy. That building, with its distinctive waffled sunshade and looming white walls, was a haunting reminder of U.S. involvement in Vietnam and was razed in 1998, some four years after the consulate opened. Today, a granite sidewalk marker memorializes an attack on the embassy during the 1968 Tet Offensive. 🅰 195 E4 ✉ 4 Le Duan, District 1 ☎ (08) 822-9433

VINH NGHIEM PAGODA

This pagoda's seven-story tower, dedicated to Quan Am, is the first landmark along the main route from the airport. The pagoda was built between 1964 and 1971 with assistance from the Japan-Vietnam Friendship Association, hence the telltale uplift to the tower's eaves. Despite its modernity and outsize proportions, the sanctuary is dazzling. A colossal trinity of Buddhas at the rear is painted a glossy gold. Vermilion panels on the many altars bear gilded images of famous pagodas and temples from around the world. In the vestibule, arhats save people from netherworld torments, teach devotees, and meditate in a wonderful series of color illustrations. 🅰 195 D4 ✉ 339 Nam Ky Khoi Nghia, District 3

XA LOI PAGODA

On June 11, 1963, Buddhist monk Thich Quang Duc immolated himself at the intersection of present-day Cach Mang Thang Tam and Nguyen Dinh Chieu. Today, the site bears a memorial to Duc's protest against the repressive South Vietnamese regime. Nearby is Xa Loi Pagoda, from which he set off that morning. The pagoda centers on an unattractive seven-story tower that was modern in Duc's day. Inside, a massive gold-painted Buddha presides over a largely empty hall. Near the ceiling, 14 illustrations depict landmark events in Sakyamuni's life. The panes of the pagoda's stained-glass windows are the colors of the Buddhist flag. 🅰 195 D3 ✉ 89 Ba Huyen Thanh Quan, District 3 ∎

Vast, watery, and timelessly grand, the Mekong Delta is the country's premier rice basket. Beyond My Tho, Can Tho, and Chau Doc, its towns and villages are lightly touristed. The beaches on Phu Quoc Island are the country's best.

Mekong Delta

Sheaves of rice wait on a thresher.

Produce distributors and retailers stock up by boat at the Cai Rang floating market.

Mekong Delta

AFTER ITS 3,000-MILE (4,800 KM) JOURNEY FROM THE TIBETAN PLATEAU, THE Mekong River splays across southern Vietnam in a web of waterways, exhausting itself at the South China Sea through nine branches known as the Cuu Long ("nine dragons"). Its rivers, channels, and canals irrigate a land as large as Holland, spreading alluvium over rice fields that yield three crops per year while the rest of the country's paddies muster only two. As with most breadbaskets, the landscape here is tiresomely uniform, though quietly impressive in places.

Until the 13th century, the 15,000-square-mile (44,000 sq km) tract was densely forested and barely populated. Chinese and Vietnamese pioneers stepped up settlement in the late 17th century, wrenching political control from the Khmer residents. The darker-skinned Khmer still inhabit the region. Their distinctive pagodas, with steeply pitched red roofs and horn-like finials, are the delta's signature architectural flourish.

To the northeast, the Mekong roils between My Tho and Ben Tre like a super-highway, churning with rice barges, ferries, and sampans. Its bountiful shorelines and islands teem with fruit orchards and cottage industry manufacturers of coconut candy and cane sugar. The attractions are tourist oriented and not very appealing. Unfortunately, My Tho provides most travelers' first impression of the delta—for some the only glimpse, since it's possible to visit the river town on day trips out of Ho Chi Minh City.

In Vinh Long, the waterways are less commercialized, and the floating market caters to local buyers, not tourists. These narrow channels bristle with verdant walls of water palms, banana plants, and other vegetation, while orchards and bonsai gardens flourish in the spongy alluvium.

The floating market is the delta's great attraction, though as a festival of vegetables, it's something of a one-trick pony. The one at Cai Rang, upstream from Can Tho, is the most colorful and bustling. As a city, Can Tho, with its hopping riverfront and clutch of good restaurants, offers a flavor and a charisma worth indulging for a few days. This is the delta's premier destination.

Chau Doc is next best place to uncork the region's possibilities. From the summit of Sam Mountain, the delta reveals itself as an amphibious marvel, part water and part land. From Chau Doc to Ha Tien, the scenic landscape, with its sugar palms, luminous paddies, and mountainous horizons, exudes a primeval majesty. At Ba Chuc, the beauty is marred by ten separate killing fields, where the Khmer Rouge massacred Vietnamese in 1978.

The quiet coastal cities of Ha Tien and Rach Gia, notable for history, peaceful pagodas, and beaches, front the placid Gulf of Thailand. They serve as gateways to Phu Quoc, a rugged island rimmed by white sand and clear waters. This idyllic island off Cambodia's southern shore is quickly becoming a favorite beach destination for Vietnamese and foreigners alike. ■

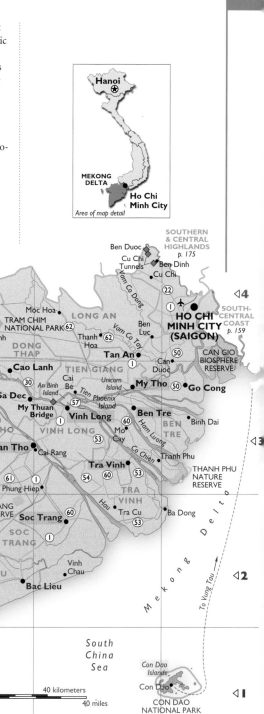

A Buddhist
devotee makes
an obeisance
at Vinh Trang
Pagoda in
My Tho.

My Tho & Ben Tre

THE TIEN BRANCH OF THE MEKONG RIVER DIVIDES THE
towns of My Tho and Ben Tre, 43 miles (70 km) southwest of Ho Chi
Minh City. Visitors hop aboard boats to explore narrow, mud brown
waterways and fertile islands and to call on cottage industry makers
of candy, honey, and sugar. In Ben Tre, the coconut monk's fantastic
pavilion of peace is singularly eccentric, while My Tho's Vinh Trang
Pagoda offers a fusion of Occidental and Oriental architecture.

**My Tho &
Ben Tre**
🅜 221 D3
**Visitor
information**
www.tiengtourist.com
✉ Tien Giang Tourist,
8 30 Thang 4,
My Tho
☎ (073) 873-184

As an entrée to the delta, this region
is thin gruel, but its proximity to
Ho Chi Minh City guarantees it
a steady stream of visitors. Most
arrive on tour boats from the city,
though it's possible to book your
own, more expensive trip through
the tourist offices on 30 Thang 4
in My Tho or with a private operator who has managed to dodge
the rigid licensing restrictions.

Tour boats call at **Unicorn,
Dragon,** and **Tortoise Islands,**
where the attractions are similar
(restaurants, orchards, coconut
candy) and proprietors are ready
at their cash registers. Whenever
possible, stay on the water in My
Tho. Better yet, opt instead for a
boat trip to Vinh Long (see p. 223)
or Can Tho (see pp. 224–225).

At **Phoenix Island,** the
so-called coconut monk struck a
blow for kitsch with construction
of his fanciful temple complex in
the 1960s. Multicolored cement
dragons spiral up nine open-air
columns, one for each branch of
the Mekong. A bridge spanning
two slender towers, one for Hanoi
and one for Saigon, represent the
monk's hopes for peace. A space
capsule on yet another kooky
tower served as an elevator to
the monk's meditation perch.
He attracted a host of young
American devotees in the 1960s,
including journalists Sean Flynn
and John Steinbeck, Jr.

Vinh Trang Pagoda (*60A
Nguyen Trung Truc, My Tho*) is
worth a detour from the river.
While the pagoda dates from
1850, its grandest flourishes date
from the early 1930s. The facade
is an amalgam of Roman arches,
French grills, Japanese tiles, and
Chinese and Gothic calligraphy.
Inside, the carved altar screen and
18 arhats all date from 1907. ∎

Vinh Long

IN THE HEART OF THE DELTA, VINH LONG OCCUPIES THE midsection on a long wedge of an island defined by the two main branches of the Mekong—the Tien and the Hau. While the town itself lacks appeal, it serves travelers as a decent launch for waterway exploration. The Cai Be floating market can be disappointing, but the channels themselves will fulfill your expectations of a delta trip.

Vinh Long
🔼 221 D3

From the pier beside the Cuu Long Tourist office, tour boats start out across the Co Chien arm of the Tien branch of the Mekong, which splits upstream beneath the **My Thuan Bridge.** (The 100-foot/30-m deck of the bridge offers stellar views of the vast delta.) Along the Dong Phu waterway, your boat will thread the upper end of **An Binh Island.** Nurseries and orchards thrive on its fecund banks, and feeder streams tempt detours from the usual route. This channel is thick with sampans and barges, which ferry mounds of unhusked rice between splints wedged in the hull to maximize the load. Glaring eyes are painted on either side of the boats' prows to deter malevolent water spirits.

Past the Dong Phu Market, you'll enter the main branch of the Tien and soon reach Cai Be village and its mundane **floating market.** Yams, onions, and other produce dangle from upright staffs lashed to the sides of the large sampans, signaling each boat's concealed payload to buyers, who paddle out in skiffs. The big boats peddle more than produce, as you'll see from the firewood and sculpted topiary perched on the cabin roofs.

Cai Be itself is a collection of sheds, shops, and houses, dominated by an august Catholic church. Onshore here and at a number of scripted stops, pathways parallel the riverbank and plunge at right angles through orchards of papayas, longans,

bananas, and pineapples.

Up the Cai Muoi channel on An Binh lies the quaint villa of a Vietnamese official in the colonial administration. A blend of French and Vietnamese architecture, this house marries the tall hardwood pillars, panels, and bay of a *nha ruong* (see pp. 144–145) inside with the arched gallery windows and pilasters of a French facade.

For mainland delights in Vinh Long, it's worth a short walk from the pier to check out the palatial villa at 2 Le Van. Note the colorful bas-relief wreaths above its massive wooden doors. A **military museum** on Phan Boi Chau has been closed for some time, though you can stroll out back to see several tanks, an F-5A, an A-37B, and a Huey helicopter. Just south of the tourist office along the river is a seldom visited temple of literature *(van mieu).* ∎

Watercraft still serve as the sole means of transport for many delta villagers.

Visitor information
✉ Cuu Long Tourist, 1 1 Thang 5
☎ (070) 823-616

Can Tho

Can Tho

🅰 221 C3

Visitor information

www.canthotourist.com.vn

✉ Can Tho Tourist, 20 Hai Ba Trung

☎ (071) 821-852

THE SEDUCTIVE RIVER CITY OF CAN THO NESTLES AGAINST its channel of the Mekong with an esplanade built for strolling, a restored French market, and a suite of restaurants with superb views. Down the channel, floating markets provide an alluring incentive to roll from bed at the crack of dawn and hit the water. An excellent in-town temple and one exquisite house just outside town offer opportunities to escape the riverbanks.

Merchants display the delta's bounty each morning at floating markets.

At the heart of town is **Ninh Kieu Park,** a riverfront esplanade that stretches along Hai Ba Trung between the wharf and the old city fish market, recently made over as a tourist market. Built by the French in the 1930s, the airy, attractive market houses kiosks of tourist trinkets and a very good café and restaurant on the water. That same progressive impulse razed the old riverside city market and opened up the space for pavilions, benches, and gardens. In the evening, neon bands light the rooflines of pavilions and markets, a gesture you could call hokey unless you let yourself be charmed by it.

Midway between the market and wharf, **Kuang-Tsao Temple** (aka Ong Temple) shelters a niche for Quan Kong and a rich collection of wood carvings. Prosperous Chinese immigrants imported columns, rafters, and ornaments from Guangdong and built the temple between 1894 and 1896. The carved and painted rafters under the front eaves are especially attractive, as is the vividly painted carving of a sumptuous Chinese palace hung from the truss. Gilded bas-relief sculptures beneath three altars at the rear of the temple detail legendary scenes from Chinese history. In the niche to the right of red-faced Quan Kong is the god of earth, and to the left is the honor graduate Dong Vinh.

In town, at the intersection of Hoa Binh and Phan Dinh Phung, you'll find the magisterial **Can Tho Provincial Museum,** while farther south on Hoa Binh is the **Munirang Syaram Pagoda,** one of 400 Khmer pagodas on the delta. In 1948, this 19th-century pagoda was wholly made over in painted, molded cement. Its austerely appointed halls are less inspiring than the Khmer temples at Soc Trang and Tra Vinh (see p. 234).

A treat awaits in the Binh Thuy ward, where you'll find the 130-year-old **Duong home,** featured prominently in the 1992 French film *The Lover.* Two sweeping stairways meet on a terrace before a suite of five green-shuttered doors crested by arches and pediments. Inside, ironwood colonnades divide the open space into five bays, tastefully appointed with marble-topped tables, platform beds, massive mirrored hutches, chandeliers suspended from floral medallions, a time-worn porcelain sink, and an antique vase reputed to be 500 years old. The carved wooden screens between the columns are as elaborate as a pagoda's. The current owner, Duong Minh Hien, is the grandson of the home's builder, whose portrait hangs inside above the central door.

ON THE RIVER

After dawn, traffic along the river thickens with a potpourri of puttering long-tail boats, sampans oared by standing women, and barges sunk to the gunwales with cargo of dredged mud and gravel. Four miles (7 km) downstream from Can Tho, the **Cai Rang floating market** draws hundreds of waterborne buyers and sellers from nearby farms and villages. If you shove off from Can Tho before 7 a.m., this market won't disappoint. The anchored produce boats dangle fruits and vegetables from tall bamboo staffs lashed to the cabins as buyers glide up to purchase watermelons (five for a dollar), longans, pineapples, guavas, cabbages, bananas, pomelos, and other goodies that burst from the delta's rich alluvial soil. Six miles (10 km) farther down the channel, the **Phong Dien floating market** specializes in fruit and sees fewer tourists. Buyers at both markets are mainly seeking bulk sales, though the pineapple salespeople especially will cut and sell fresh fruit on a stick to tourists.

On the return trip to Can Tho, consider stopping at the riverside **Cao Dai temple** above My Khanh. You can't miss the well-maintained church, with its distinctive pair of tiered towers bracketing the facade and signature all-seeing eye. Its vaulted sky-blue ceiling is lofted by cement columns painted like turquoise candy canes. Ten more columns coiled in orange-scaled dragons cluster about a gilt-framed eye. If the church is closed, the on-site caretaker might be cajoled into unlocking the doors.

Nearby is **My Khanh Tourist Village,** a cluster of bungalows set amid a sapodilla orchard that caters to local tourists, hence the caged monkeys. The restored hundred-year-old house was moved to the property in 2002. ∎

Can Tho Provincial Museum

✉ 6 Phan Dinh Phung
☎ (071) 820-955
🕐 Closed Mon. & Fri.

Duong home

✉ 26/1A Bui Huu Nghia, Binh Thuy ward
☎ (071) 841-127

My Khanh Tourist Village

✉ 335 Lo Vong Cung
☎ (071) 846-260

Plight of the boat people

In the years after the fall of Saigon in 1975, an exodus of more than one million refugees took to the seas in tiny, overcrowded boats, sailing toward the promise of a better life outside Vietnam. They came to be known as "boat people," and for a time in the late 1970s, they gripped the world's attention.

Fearful of reprisals at the hands of the victorious North Vietnamese and National Liberation Front (Viet Cong), the first wave of 131,000 South Vietnamese refugees escaped as Saigon fell—some 6,500 by helicopter and plane, others by land, and many more by boat.

While the dreaded bloodbath did not happen, the communists were loathe to forgive or forget those who remained in Vietnam and who'd allied themselves with the South Vietnamese government during the Vietnam War. They imprisoned thousands of those who hadn't fled in "reeducation camps" while making a shambles of the country's economy with the miserable policies of command eco-

nomics. The Vietnamese look back on the decade that followed the war as the dark ages.

Meanwhile, the government in Hanoi shuttled for favors between its two wartime allies, the Soviet Union and China. Because the Soviets were more geographically removed and less of a threat to Vietnamese independence, and because antipathy toward China runs deep in the Vietnamese psyche, Hanoi favored the U.S.S.R.

The growing Soviet-Vietnamese relationship worried China. On Feb. 15, 1979, the Chinese government announced its intentions to invade Vietnam, giving two reasons: the mistreatment of Vietnam's ethnic Chinese minority, and the Vietnamese occupation of the Spratly Islands, claimed by China. Two days later, Chinese tanks rolled into North Vietnam. A brief incursion ensued, after which the Chinese troops withdrew, claiming their punitive mission had been achieved. Both sides, however, claimed victory.

The Vietnamese closed the businesses of ethnic Chinese, seized their gold, and began relocating 1.5 million into so-called new economic zones. Continual poverty and hopelessness precipitated an exodus. The plight of this second wave of refugees spawned an international crisis and worldwide appeals for the refugees.

Similar to their predecessors, the refugees embarked on deadly seas, subject to typhoons, hunger, starvation, and attacks by Thai pirates. Their reception in neighboring countries was hardly welcoming. Many Southeast Asian governments turned away the boat people who'd managed to cross the seas. In the first six months of 1979, Malaysia towed about 58,000 refugees out of its territorial waters. Some estimates say that as many as 500,000 to 600,000 people perished in the exodus.

The lucky ones who made landfall in Malaysia, Singapore, Thailand, Hong Kong, and the Philippines were herded into refugee camps, where they idled for months, sometimes years, awaiting resettlement in other countries. By the mid-1990s, the number of people fleeing Vietnam had dwindled. Many refugee camps were closed. Vietnam's market reform, the return of Hong Kong to China, and financial incentives for voluntarily returning home caused many boat people to move back to Vietnam, while the remaining asylees were forced to be repatriated. In 2005, the last few refugees in the Philippines were granted asylum in Canada and the U.S. At long last, the plight of the refugees had come to an end. ■

A vessel overloaded with boat people weighs anchor for the next port after Malaysian authorities refuse to grant them refuge in November 1978.

Chau Doc

Chau Doc
🗺 221 C4

Visitor information
✉ An Giang Tourist, 17 Nguyen Van Cung, Long Xuyen
☎ (076) 843-752

EN ROUTE FROM CAN THO TO CHAU DOC, THE EXUBERANTLY verdant Mekong Delta flaunts some of its fabled rice fields. From the 755-foot (230 m) summit of Nui Sam (Sam Mountain), views of the waterlogged region affirm the aptness of Vietnam's self-perception as a country of water and earth.

Seven miles (11 km) east of the Cambodian border, the town of Chau Doc is a commingling of Vietnamese, Khmer, Cham, and Chinese people. Driving the local economy are the many *ca ba sa* (catfish) farms that clog the river and waterways. A monumental statue to this local resource stands in the waterfront park. The region's bizarre mix of pagodas, temples, and mosques underscores its reputation as a seedbed of ardent religious devotion. That said, as a frontier town, Chau Doc was one of the last to be settled by the Vietnamese and still retains a bit of wild woolliness. Smugglers on motorbikes occasionally blaze through town, trafficking in cigarettes and CDs, and the incidence of AIDS among women who work the Cambodian sex trade is reportedly high.

Attractions are comparatively weak. On Tran Hung Dao near the market, **Dinh Chau Phu** is a 1926 communal hall where the local hero, Nguyen Huu Canh (1650–1700), drags on his beard at the main altar. Canh was the founding father of Saigon and a Horace Greeley of sorts—*Go southwest, young man?*—in this part of the country. On the other side of the market, a festively headdressed Quan Kong holds court in one of the least interesting temples to the Taoist deity and Buddhist bodhisattva, built in 1972.

SAM MOUNTAIN

Rising from the floodplain 3 miles (5 km) southwest of Chau Doc, Sam Mountain represents the region's most compelling attraction. The high road from Chau Doc—fittingly called Mountain Road—winds amid the granite outcrops to an unassuming military base at the summit, where you're free to poke around for views northwest into Cambodia and southeast over the delta.

At the foot of the mountain, eccentric **Tay An Pagoda** elaborates on traditional Buddhist architecture with Hindu and Islamic flourishes in a riot of tangerine, purple, aqua, and lime green. The pagoda dates from 1847, but its current look took shape during a 1958 restoration. A pumpkin crowns its central tower, and seven cobras in bas-relief flare off the Middle Eastern arch on the portico. Inside, more than 200 wood statues, glossed in vibrant colors, bedeck altars, shelves, and pedestals. You'll find the whole cast of characters—the jade emperor, the arhats, the four celestial kings, the dharma guardians, and many manifestations of Buddha. Look on the right side of the temple for a Grinch-like character with a yellow sword and inside the main door for a gang of statues done up in leafy garb like the Jolly Green Giant.

Farther up Mountain Road, the **Ba Chua Xu Temple** is a magnet for pilgrims who come to pray before a local goddess known as the Holy Lady, or Holy

Landlord. The clearly obese Holy Lady is a diva of a deity whose likeness was found on Sam Mountain by Khmer invaders in the early 19th century. The statue's weight foiled their plans to plunder the relic. Later, nine virgins managed to carry the Holy Lady as far as the mountain's base, where villagers promptly raised a temple. The current structure was last rebuilt in the early 1970s. Access to the temple is through a reception hall as big as a railway station, testifying to the swarms of devotees who flock here, especially during the festival in the fourth lunar month. Today, the diva reigns in robes of sequined silk before a disco-light halo. The neighboring three-story building was built as a repository for the robes and finery offered to the lady by devotees.

Just up the road is the 1930s **temple to Nguyen Van Thoai** (1761–1829), the mandarin-cum-engineer who first exploited the area's rich soil and spurred commerce on the delta with construction of its canals. He and his two wives are buried in the courtyard.

CON TIEN ISLAND

The ferry to **Con Tien Island** *($)* leaves from the end of Thuong Dang Le, past its intersection with Tran Hung Dao. The island and the village of **Chau Giang** are home to ten pretty mosques and a large percentage of the 15,000 Cham Muslims who live in the area. The Cham villages are bucolically charming, but offer little as tourist destinations. The best way to get around is by hired motorbike *($)*. As you ferry from island to island, take note of the pontoon houses, which float on empty barrels. Beneath each house, weighted netting contains each family's catfish farm. ■

The flanks of Sam Mountain provide fabulous views across the delta and into Cambodia.

Ha Tien

Ha Tien
221 B3

IN THE REMOTE SOUTHWEST, HA TIEN IS THE LAST STOP along the seaboard before Cambodia. Few push beyond Chau Doc to this quiet border town. Those who do will reap the rewards of isolation, peaceful pagodas and temples, and grandly beautiful landscapes.

The fierce hilt of a ceremonial weapon wards off adversaries at Ha Tien's Mac Cuu Temple.

With permission from the Khmer court, Cantonese merchant Mac Cuu settled Ha Tien in the 1670s and built a port visited by traders from as far away as the Netherlands. Envious Thai pirates repeatedly attacked the port, prompting Mac Cuu to strike an alliance with the Nguyen court. After the enterprising merchant died at age 81 in 1735, the deal he struck held fast for seven generations, whose members all enjoyed the privileges of titled nobility.

They're buried in terraces of hillside graves a half mile (800 m) northwest of town behind the **Mac Cuu Temple.** Cuu himself occupies the loftiest eternal perch, on Nui Lang, a short climb worth

Visitor information

✉ Kien Giang Tourist, 12 Ly Tu Trong, Rach Gia

☎ (077) 862-081

making for views of rice paddies and coastal hills. Ringed by a stone wall, the temple honors Cuu, his sons, and their wives at various altars. Original murals from 1846 honor locals who restored the place.

Closer to town on Mac Thien Tich, 300-year-old **Quan Thanh Temple** harbors the red-faced, beard-dragging Quan Kong and four colossal, armed attendants. Aggressively protuberant dragons coil up two of its columns. The murals above the doors to the side galleries and the granite threshold in the open-air courtyard all reputedly date from the original construction. Watch for tortoises, which have free run of the temple's heavenly well.

About 4 miles (6 km) west of Ha Tien along Mac Thien Tich, gulf waters lap the brown-sand strand at **Mui Nai,** the only beach of note in the area. A clutch of nicely situated hills lends the beach a feng shui feel, though that's likely to be compromised if the three-star hotel being built along its shores includes karaoke.

Two miles (3 km) farther along Mac Thien Tich, a monument of a clenched fist at the base of **Thach Hang cave** ($) memorializes the 130 people murdered nearby during a 1978 raid by Pol Pot's rampaging minions. You may choose to skip the humdrum pagoda within Thach Hang's vertical expanse, but do visit the overlooks on the far side of the cave. Views stretch down the rugged coast to Cambodia, just over a mile (2 km) away. ∎

Rach Gia

Coastal waters
here are placid
in comparison
to those of the
South China Sea.

RACH GIA'S FAME FLARED BRIEFLY IN 1868 WHEN THE FIRST
great Vietnamese nationalist, Nguyen Trung Truc, attacked the
French garrison here and briefly held the town. The coastal town
has quieted since then and mainly plays host to travelers bound by
ferry or plane to Phu Quoc (see p. 232). Rach Gia isn't much of a
magnet, though you could while away an afternoon traipsing from
the communal house to a Khmer temple and a pagoda.

The town sits on an islet in the Cai
Long River, centered on a statue of
Truc at Le Loi and Nguyen Hung
Son; the urban sprawl, however,
spills over to the river's north and
south banks. You'll find the market and hotels on the north bank.

On the north bank, too, is
Truc's **communal house,** at 18
Nguyen Cong Tru near the ferry
terminal. Inside the 1963 temple
are ceremonial weapons and altars
topped by portraits of Truc. Two
bas-relief murals depict him on
the deck of the *Espérance* (see
sidebar this page) and in the Rach
Gia garrison. A glass display case
holds timbers from the ship.

North of the market on Quang
Trung, the path to **Phat Lon
Pagoda** starts from an ornate
Khmer gate and skirts a *naga*
(divine serpent) balustrade supported by statues of the mythical
bird Garuda. Beneath the hornlike
finials and steep pitch of the roof,

a frieze of Sakyamuni's life story
wraps around the main hall above
a decent statue collection.

Across town on Su Thien An,
Tam Bao Pagoda centers on a
courtyard and a square lotus pond.
Outside is a statue of Muchalinda,
the seven-headed naga king who
used his hood to shelter the meditating Buddha from heavy rainfall. ■

Rach Gia
🅰 221 C3
**Visitor
information**
✉ Kien Giang Tourist,
12 Ly Tu Trong
☎ (077) 862-081

Resistance leader

From 1861 to 1868, Nguyen
Trung Truc led the first great
resistance movement against the
French. In December 1861, the
22-year-old swashbuckler boarded,
burned, and sank the French
warship *Espérance*. Six years later,
his forces overran the Rach Gia
garrison and held the town for six
days. The French later captured
Truc on Phu Quoc and executed
him in Rach Gia in 1868. ■

220 A3

The beaches of
Phu Quoc rival
the calm, dreamy
beaches of the
Indian Ocean.

Phu Quoc

OFF THE SOUTHERN COAST OF CAMBODIA, THE ISLAND OF
Phu Quoc is fast emerging as Vietnam's premier destination for sea
and sun. It's no wonder: The 237-square-mile (593 sq km) island
is lapped by the limpid waters of the Gulf of Thailand and fringed
with the country's finest white-sand beaches, while the mountainous
interior harbors a national park, thousands of monkeys, and nationally
famous pepper plantations.

Phu Quoc

220 A3

**Visitor
information**

✉ Kien Giang Tourist,
12 Ly Tu Trong,
Rach Gia

☎ (077) 862-081

Getting there

Boat ferries serve Phu
Quoc from Rach Gia
and Ba Hon, though most
travelers take one of
several daily flights from
Ho Chi Minh City to the
airport at Duong Dong.

In the early 19th century, the
future king Gia Long rallied here
before routing the short-lived Tay
Son dynasty to win back the coun-
try for the Nguyen. In the early
days of the French resistance,
Nguyen Trung Truc used Phu
Quoc as a base. More recently,
during the Vietnam War, South
Vietnam imprisoned 40,000 Viet
Cong guerrillas at Coconut Tree
Camp on the island's south tip.

A handful of facilities along
the river in Duong Dong distill
1.5 million gallons (6 million l)
of world-famous *nuoc mam* (fish
sauce) annually. But unless you're
a gourmand or can visit for more
than a few days, spend your time
in search of the perfect beach. *Phu
quoc* means "beautiful country,"
and these strands are Vietnam's
only serious rivals to the jewels of
Thailand and the Indian Ocean.

The island is best explored by
motorbike, available for rent at

the hotels. In the west and north
especially, roads are no more than
rutted laterite. North of An Thoi,
a paved road parallels the coast
and a naval base. The navy grants
sporadic access to undeveloped
Bai Khem. Always accessible is
Bai Sao ("star beach"), just north
of the base at the end of a 2-mile
(3 km) dirt track. Lightly developed and bracketed by promontories, it offers superb swimming.

Bai Truong ("long beach") is
a ruler-straight 12-mile (20 km)
stretch along the western shore.
The burgeoning resort scene is
encroaching from Duong Dong,
but its southern reaches remain
the province of fishermen, who
tie up at shoreline coconut trees.

Also on the west side, several
resorts cling to **Bai Ong Lang.**
Offshore rocks offer decent snorkeling here, though the fishscapes
are much better off smaller islands
to the north and south. ■

More places to visit around the Mekong Delta

BA CHUC

Between Chau Doc and Tri Ton, the countryside opens up on vast rice plains, hemmed by ranks of sugar palms *(thot not)*. Khmer pagodas abound, signaling a proximity to Cambodia that had devastating consequences for the people of Ba Chuc. Between April 18 and 30, 1978, the Khmer Rouge embarked on a series of killing sprees that claimed the lives of 3,157 villagers. At a **memorial** on the fringes of town, a glass-walled tomb holds the skulls of 1,159 victims, segregated by age. These bashed and fissured bones testify to the brutality of the massacre. A nearby gallery exhibits cudgels, daggers, and spears used in the attacks, as well as horrific photos of bludgeoned and impaled victims. The Khmer committed their atrocities at ten nearby sites, including the **Phi Lai Tu** communal house, a short stroll from the memorial. In the back hall of this house, two red painted lines low on the wall indicate where 150 people had been shackled

Ba Chuc's memorial to villagers killed by the Khmer Rouge in 1978 conveys the brutality of the attacks.

before execution. Another 40 people were crammed into the space beneath the altar and murdered.
🔼 221 B3

CON DAO ISLANDS

Since colonial days, the islands of Con Dao, 112 miles (180 km) southeast of the delta, earned notoriety as Poulo Condore, where the French and later the Saigon regime jailed 22,000 inmates in deplorable conditions. This environment would serve as a think tank for Vietnamese nationalists (including Pham Van Dong and Le Duc Tho) who buoyed each other's spirits with lessons in Marxism, literature, science, and language. Today, tourism centers on the main island of **Con Son,** where at **Phu Son** ("rich mountain") and **Phu Hai** ("rich sea") **prisons** the Saigon regime held captives in so-called tiger cages during the Vietnam War. The island also lures tourists with its beaches and the forest-sea ecosystem of **Con Dao National Park.** The park's waters boast 2,500 acres (1,000 ha) of coral reef. Dugongs—sea cows related to Florida's manatees—feed on nearshore sea grass, while thousands of hawksbill and green sea turtles nest here from June to September. Marco Polo anchored here following a storm in 1294, and the composer Camille Saint-Saëns finished his opera *Brünhilde* here in 1895. In 2006, a 150-seat hydrofoil service launched from Vung Tau, cutting travel time via boat from 12 to 5 hours. The islands are also accessible by helicopter or via daily plane service from Saigon. 🔼 221 E1 ✉ Ba Ria–Vung Tau Tourist, 19 Thu Khoa Huan, Vung Tau ☎ (064) 585-324

HON CHONG PENINSULA

Between Ha Tien and Rach Gia, Hon Chong is surrounded by clear, tranquil seas that wash gently onto sandy brown beaches. The turreted Green Hill guesthouse *(tel (077) 854-369),* which has a few immaculate rooms, lords over the premier beach at **Bai Duong.** Farther down the oceanfront road, the **Sea and Mountain Pagoda** crouches at the base of limestone outcrops. A grotto tunnels through to the beach, where the landmark Father and Son Islands rise just offshore. Beyond, the local tourist board compares the limestone **Ba Lua Islands** to Ha Long. Stop by any of the fishing villages to hire a boat for exploration.

 221 B3 Kien Giang Tourist, 5 Le Loi, Rach Gia ☎ (077) 862-081

LONG XUYEN

The district capital of An Giang Province, Long Xuyen lies midway between Can Tho and Chau Doc on the Hau River. If you've somehow missed the floating markets at Can Tho, there's one here. Otherwise, most sites line Nguyen Hue between the river and Highway 91. A statue of **Ton Duc Thang,** the Long Xuyen native who succeeded Ho Chi Minh as president of Vietnam in 1969, stands in one of the boulevard's rectangular parks. Beyond, two long arms clasp a cross atop the steeple of the **Catholic church.** On the same side of Nguyen Hue, Nguyen Huu Canh stands as the tutelary spirit in the **My Phuoc Communal House,** founded in the early 18th century.

221 C3 An Giang Tourist, 17 Nguyen Van Cung, Long Xuyen ☎ (076) 843-752

SOC TRANG

Soc Trang merits a secondary place on the tourist circuit for its handful of Khmer pagodas, including **Khleang, Dat Set** ("clay"), and especially **Doi** ("bat"), where thousands of fruit bats cling to the trees, sleeping by day and feeding by night—but never, rumor has it, from the pagoda's own fruit trees. Inside the 16th-century sanctuary, some of the Buddhist texts are incised on palm leaves.

221 D2 Soc Trang Tourist, 131 Nguyen Chi Thanh, Soc Trang ☎ (079) 822-024

TRA VINH TOWN

Most visitors to Tra Vinh are day-trippers out of Vinh Long, heading for **Ba Om Pool,** a clear blue pond surrounded by oddly rooted dipterocarps and tamarind trees. The same majestic trees shade nearby **Ang Pagoda,** one of the province's 140 or so Khmer pagodas. Another is **Hang Pagoda,** renowned for the storks that settle amid the trees at dusk. The colonial French developed a resort at **Ba Dong,** a 6-mile (10 km) strip of white sand that ranks as one of the delta's few beach destinations. Be forewarned, however, that the war-ravaged roads turn the 34-mile (55 km) jaunt from Tra Vinh town into an ordeal.

221 D3 Tra Vinh Tourist, 64–66 Le Loi, Tra Vinh ☎ (074) 862-559 ∎

An unpaved road fronts one of Vietnam's most beautiful beaches on the island of Phu Quoc.

Travelwise

A goldfish cyclo

TRAVELWISE INFORMATION

PLANNING YOUR TRIP

WHEN TO GO

While Vietnam lies in the tropics, that doesn't necessarily mean the weather is always tropical. With the exception of the extreme south (below Phan Thiet/Mui Ne), winter can bring long bouts of rain and temperatures in the 60s Fahrenheit (high teens Celsius) that can feel even colder due to the high humidity. By the end of January, you can usually start banking on the sun and warmer temps from north to south. (See more on climate on pp. 26–27.)

October through December is the high season in Hanoi and Ho Chi Minh City, and the weather is delightful. Rooms at luxury hotels may prove difficult to secure unless you book well in advance. Booking rooms at budget hotels is always easy.

Between mid-January and mid-February, the country's transportation network strains with travelers headed home for the Tet lunar new year. Unless you've booked a domestic flight long in advance, you'll likely be put on standby. The same holds true for the railways. The traveler cafés operate buses along the popular routes, and there's usually space there. However, that's changing as more affluent Vietnamese can now afford the more expensive tourist buses.

WHAT TO BRING

Men should wear trousers when visiting a pagoda, as shorts may offend the monks. Women should wear shirts that cover the shoulders. A handful of temples and pagodas will deny admission to anyone dressed inappropriately.

Locals often cringe at the sloppy appearance of foreign backpackers, whom they refer to pejoratively as tay ba lo (Westerners with bags). In contrast, the Vietnamese tend to dress up, however impractical it may be at the time.

Between November and February in the central and northern provinces, you'll need to bring a sweater or polar fleece. You could bring expensive rainwear, but the widely available cheap ponchos make more sense, especially if you're traveling by motorbike. Bring English-language reading materials, as bookstores offer little choice.

A wide-brimmed hat is a good idea. Even if you're trying to tan, the midday glare can be oppressive. Vendors throughout Vietnam hawk sunglasses, but the lenses are cheap and offer little protection. Bring your own.

Also bring your own sunscreen. Unless you buy sunscreen at a big chain hotel, you risk paying top dollar for some other cheap ointment with zero SPF.

Batteries and film remain widely available, though the digital revolution is in full swing here, and it's harder and harder to find film.

Outside of upscale hotels and restaurants, toilet paper can be scarce. Even the most popular museums often run out. Consider bringing spare tissues.

INSURANCE

Before leaving home, check with your insurance carrier regarding coverage limits. You may want additional coverage that includes an emergency evacuation.

Travelers do not actually drive rental cars in Vietnam. When you rent a car, you'll be hiring a driver as well, and he'll assume any responsibility for accidents. If you putter about on a rental motorbike, however, you'll be liable for damages. Driver's insurance is not readily available. If you do get into an accident, and it's your fault, the other driver will likely demand payment on the spot.

Hotels usually post a disclaimer that leaves you responsible for the security of

your own possessions, unless you check them with the front desk. Most mid-range and luxury hotels provide in-room safes for valuables. On-site theft is not an issue, as access to most hotels is very difficult for would-be thieves.

ENTRY FORMALITIES

VISA

Unless you're from Scandinavia, Japan, the Republic of Korea, or elsewhere in Southeast Asia, you'll need to obtain a visa for entry to Vietnam. It's possible to obtain a visa upon arrival, but don't chance it. It's too easy for something to go wrong.

Most tourists visit Vietnam on a 30-day, single-entry tourist visa, which costs $25. It can be extended twice, at a cost of $25 per extension, for an additional stay of up to 60 days.

If you overstay your visa, be prepared to explain why to the Department of Immigration of the Ministry of Public Security in Hanoi or Ho Chi Minh City.

You can obtain visas from consulates at the following overseas embassies:

United States
1233 20th St. NW, Ste. 400
Washington, DC 20036
Tel 202/861-0737
Fax 202/861-0917
www.vietnamembassy-usa.org

Australia
6 Timbarra Crescent
O'Malley, ACT 2606
Tel 02/6286-6059 or 6290-1549
Fax 02/6286-4534 or 6290-2908
www.vietnamembassy.org.au

Canada
470 Wilbrod St.
Ottawa, Ontario K1N 6M8
Tel 613/236-0772
Fax 613/236-2704
www.vietnamembassy-canada.ca

United Kingdom
12–14 Victoria Rd.
London W8 5RD
Tel 20/7937-1912
Fax 20/7937-6108
www.vietnamembassy.org.uk

CUSTOMS

Travelers age 19 and older may import up to 400 cigarettes, 100 cigars, 1.1 pounds (500 g) of tobacco, and 3 pints (1.5 l) of liquor duty free. For more information, see www.customs .gov.vn.

Vietnamese law prohibits the import of literature and materials that might provoke violence or debauchery or contradict Vietnam's customs and traditions. Restricted items include pornography, toxic chemicals, fireworks, and toys that might negatively impact education or social security.

Vietnam restricts the export of antiques; even artificially aged objects that look antique may pose a problem. If you buy that statue of a Cham *apsara*, be sure to carry a receipt with the name and phone number of the shop.

When leaving Vietnam, no outbound declaration is necessary if you leave with less than $7,000/11 ounces (300 g) of gold and 15 million dong (about $1,000).

In most cases, DVDs and CDs breeze through customs, although officials reserve the right to screen content for several days.

Drugs & narcotics

Vietnam bans all restricted drugs, so be sure to have a note from your doctor if you're carrying prescription substances that may be attractive to people who are not ill. You may notice people openly doing hits from bamboo bongs throughout Vietnam, but they're smoking a kind of tobacco, not the other stuff. The day of the opium den is long past in Saigon, though many tourist shops sell opium pipes and pillows as souvenirs.

HOW TO GET TO VIETNAM

AIRLINES

In December 2004, United Airlines became the first U.S. carrier to fly direct to Vietnam since 1975. The following year, Continental Airlines and American Airlines launched routes to Vietnam from the United States, via code-sharing deals with Vietnam Airlines and Japan Airlines, respectively.

About 18 international carriers fly into Ho Chi Minh City's Tan Son Nhat Airport, while 15 carriers fly into Hanoi's Noi Bai Airport.

It takes 15 to 16 hours to fly nonstop from New York to Hong Kong, then an additional 2 or 2.5 hours to fly from Hong Kong into Hanoi or Ho Chi Minh City, respectively. The flight time from Paris to Ho Chi Minh City is 13 hours, while from Sydney it's 8 hours.

The airports are served by the following carriers:

Air France
Hanoi: 04/825-3484
HCMC: 08/829-0981

British Airways
Hanoi: 04/934-7239
HCMC: 08/930-2933

Cathay Pacific
Hanoi: 04/826-7298
HCMC: 08/822-3203

China Airlines
Hanoi: 04/824-2688

Japan Airlines
Hanoi: 04/826-6693
HCMC: 08/821-9098

Korean Air
HCMC: 08/824-2878

Lufthansa
HCMC: 08/829-8529

Qantas
Hanoi: 04/933-3026
HCMC: 08/910-5373

Singapore Airlines
Hanoi: 04/826-8888
HCMC: 08/823-1588

Thai Airways
HCMC: 08/829-2809

United Airlines
HCMC: 08/823-4755

Vietnam Airlines
Hanoi: 04/832-0320
HCMC: 08/832-0320

NOI BAI AIRPORT, HANOI

Noi Bai Airport (tel 04/886-5029, www.hanoiairport.com) is 22 miles (35 km) from downtown Hanoi. A prominent information desk in the arrival hall provides basic tourist info. You can change money at a number of counters in the airport or make a withdrawal from one of several ATMs.

There are three ways to get into Hanoi: by taxi ($10/160,000 dong), by the Vietnam Airlines bus ($1.60/25,000 dong), or by public bus (35 cents/4,660 dong). Each leaves from just outside the main terminal, and the ride takes about 40 minutes.

TAN SON NHAT AIRPORT, HO CHI MINH CITY

Tan Son Nhat Airport (SGN) is 5 miles (8 km) from downtown Ho Chi Minh City. After passing through immigration and clearing customs, stop by the SASCO (Southern Airport Services Co.) desk for tourist information (tel 08/848-6711, www.saigon airport.com). SASCO provides free information and free maps, can change money or direct you to an airport ATM, and can book you a hotel room, limo, or tour.

A taxi to Saigon (District 1) costs about $5 (80,000 dong). Minivans are available to taxi larger groups for slightly higher rates. You can hire a motorbike taxi for about $2.50 (40,000 dong). You can also take public bus 152 to the Ben Thanh Market for about 15 cents (2,000 dong). Every 15 minutes between 6 a.m. and 6:40 p.m. these distinctive green buses stop outside the departure terminal. It takes about half an hour in light traffic to reach the city by bus.

GETTING AROUND

BY BICYCLE

Outside Saigon and Hanoi, a rental bicycle is a cheap, safe, interactive way to get around. Many hotels and traveler cafés rent bikes for as little as a dollar a day.

BY CAR

Traveling by car in Vietnam can be a hair-raising experience. Road rules devolve into a sort of vehicular Darwinism, as right of way often falls to the bigger vehicle. Many drivers flout basic safe driving practices, speeding to make up for lost time or perhaps passing in the face of opposing traffic. Police have been cracking down on such scofflaws and speed demons, and the experience is a lot tamer than it was, for example, in the 1990s, but road travel remains the least welcome part of a visit.

Tourists don't actually drive cars in Vietnam. Instead, they rely on the navigational skills and road savvy of hired native drivers. A car and driver costs about $40 (640,000 dong) per day. You can make arrangements at nearly any hotel, one of the established tour operators, or any of the traveler café-cum-agencies in Ho Chi Minh City's Pham Ngu Lao District. If you require a car for a multiday excursion, you'll be asked to pay about $7 (112,000 dong) per day for the driver's food and lodging.

BY CITY BUS

Public buses ply numerous routes through Saigon and Hanoi. Clean, air-conditioned, and incredibly cheap (about 15 cents/2,000 dong for a typical ride), they are proving a decent means by which to navigate the cities. The buses in Ho Chi Minh City (tel 08/822-4913) run from 4:30 a.m. until 7 p.m. or later, depending on the route. At rush hour, buses sweep through stops along the most popular routes every five to eight minutes.

BY CYCLO

The most charming means of transport is the cyclo, a three-wheeled pedicab that succeeded the rickshaw as the human-powered option. The rate is about the same as a motorbike (50 cents/mile or 5,000 dong/km). As with taxis, agree on the price before you climb aboard.

BY JITNEY

Small buses and vans—jitneys—go pretty much anywhere in this densely populated country. The jitneys are as cheap as the local bus, are never air-conditioned, and can be excruciatingly crowded. A jitney also vacillates between recklessly high speeds, when the driver is trying to make up time, and fits and starts, when the conductor is trolling for more passengers to cram aboard. These vehicles should be a last resort.

BY LOCAL BUS

Most Vietnamese travel by local bus. It's cheaper than the Sinh Café tour bus (see p. 239), but there are no assigned seats, and your leg room may be compromised by a couple of sacks of rice. While some are air-conditioned, most aren't. Most permit smoking.

The best place to pick up a local bus is at the city or town bus station (ben xe), usually found on the outskirts of smaller towns and up to several miles from the centers of larger cities. Be forewarned: As soon as you enter a bus station, you'll be mobbed by a half dozen facilitators. Ignore them and head to the ticket counter. Make sure your ticket includes an allowance for luggage, as the bus conductor might try to hit you up for more money if your luggage takes up a lot of room.

You can flag down a local bus on the highway, but you'll have to haggle with the conductor for the best price, which is likely to start at two to three times the local rate.

BY MOTORBIKE

You can rent your own motorbike (actually 125cc scooters) from the traveler cafés in most cities. These don't require a clutch to change gears; your foot simply clicks through the gears. Many new models provide automatic transmissions.

Usually the renter will ask to hold your passport as security. Rental motorbikes cost about $5 to $6 (80,000–96,000 dong) per day. There's no insurance, so you're liable for anything that goes wrong. Unless you're a very savvy driver, it's not advisable to rent your own bike in Saigon or Hanoi.

Motorbike taxis are ubiquitous in the big cities. The market rate for a motorbike taxi is about 50 cents per mile or 5,000 dong per kilometer.

Settle on a price before you hop on the bike. A driver will try to avoid this, as he'd rather tell you how much after the fact. Don't let this happen. The quoted rate is often exorbitant and can usually be halved or quartered to the regular price. Until you get a sense of the rates, counter at half the quoted price. He'll grimace, you'll walk away. If it's the right price, the driver will track you down.

BY PLANE

Vietnam Airlines' modern fleet offers the best way to get around the country. In the 1990s, the carrier dumped its rickety fleet of Tupolevs and Yakovlevs for ATRs, Fokkers, and Airbuses. The airline flies 22 domestic routes between 15 cities, with hubs in Ho Chi Minh City, Hanoi, and Danang. The flights are inexpensive (e.g., $53/848,000 dong between Ho Chi Minh City and Hue), and fares remain the same regardless of the time of purchase.

Fortunately for travelers, seat availability is rarely a problem, even up to the day of departure. (This does not hold true during the Tet lunar new year.) Don't be dismayed by reports that a flight is fully booked. You can be sixth on a waiting list for a flight that later leaves with 14 empty seats—a common scenario.

While the in-flight food lacks appeal, everything else about the airline is smart, efficient, and affordable.

Pacific Airlines is a second state-run airline with slightly lower fares than Vietnam Airlines. Pacific offers a half dozen daily flights between Ho Chi Minh City and Hanoi and at least one daily flight to Danang from either city.

Vietnam Airlines
Hanoi: 04/832-0320
Danang: 0511/821-130
HCMC: 08/832-0320

Pacific Airlines
Hanoi: 04/955-0550
HCMC: 08/955-0550

BY TAXI

Taxis are a cheap and convenient way to get around. In the major cities, any portion of the first half mile (1 km) costs between 50 and 90 cents (8,000–14,000 dong). Each subsequent half mile costs less than a dollar. In Ho Chi Minh City and Hanoi especially, this is the safest and most comfortable way to travel.

Be on your guard for scheming hacks who've rigged their meters to move at double the pace. If you notice the meter running out of synch with your distance, ask the driver to stop immediately and end the ride. If you choose to make a stand, tell the driver you're going to call the police (goi canh sat—pronounced goy kun saht). If he is scamming you, he'll back down at the threat.

BY TOUR BUS

Among tour bus operators, Sinh Café Open Tour (tel 04/912-2955) is the only way to go. Its clean, modern, air-conditioned buses make multiple daily trips up and down Highway 1, with stops in Hue, Hoi An, and Nha Trang. You can hop off at any of the designated stops, stay as long as you like, and resume your

journey all on the same ticket. The $25 (400,000 dong) ticket includes two side trips. One spur leads from Nha Trang up into the highlands for Dalat, while another trails south along the coast to Mui Ne.

BY TOUR COMPANY

Traveling to and learning more about any destinations beyond Vietnam's most popular tourist haunts can be frustrating. Fortunately, tour guides come relatively cheap, from just $5 to $10 (80,000–160,000 dong) for a walk around Hanoi's Old Quarter to hundreds of dollars per day for upscale tours that include food and lodging. Hundreds of licensed tour companies across the country vie for business. In Hanoi alone, Vietnam Tourism lists more than 200 operators. For more information, see the roll call of travel agents at www.vietnamtourism-info.com /english/cat_index_19.shtml. A select few boast established reputations among foreign travelers. Some of the more reputable agencies include: **Exotissimo**, Saigon Trade Center, 37 Ton Duc Thang, District 1, Ho Chi Minh City, tel 08/825-1723, fax 08/829-5800, www.exotissimo.com. Owned by the same company that built the Emeraude in Ha Long Bay and La Residence in Hue, Exotissimo caters to luxury and high-end adventure travelers. Its luxury tours stop at the country's finest hotels, while its adventure tours emphasize biking and trekking. **Handspan Adventure Travel,** 23 Phan Chu Trinh, Old Quarter, Hanoi, tel 04/933-2375, fax 04/933-2378, www.handspan.com. This popular company is owned by three Vietnamese who cut their teeth at the Green Bamboo, a onetime travel powerhouse here. They own their own junk on Ha Long Bay. With 32 guides, they do private and group tours, mainly in the north.
Indochina Ventures, 40 Truong Quyen, District 3, Ho Chi Minh City, tel 08/820-2563, fax 08/820-2565, www.indo

china-ventures.com. Another Vietnamese-owned venture that has dodged all the mistakes of its state-run brethren to match the polish of foreign-owned rivals. It runs several organized tours and visits many sites à la carte as well. In addition, its Ngon brand restaurants are among the best in Ho Chi Minh City.
Kangaroo Café, 18 Bao Khanh, Hanoi, tel 04/828-9931, www .kangaroocafe.com. This Aussie-run company near Hoan Kiem Lake is a good bet for trips to Ha Long Bay, Sa Pa, and Mai Chau. The staff meets you at the airport on arrival and sees you off at the train station when you leave. It's cheaper than some of the other tour companies.

BY TRAIN

Hanoi and Ho Chi Minh City are linked by the 1,072-mile (1,726 km) Reunification Express line, known during the colonial era as the Transindochinois line. The line parallels the coast and takes in some fantastic scenery, with the loveliest stretch lying between Hue and Danang. As romantic as that may sound, however, riding the rails can get tiresome. The trains are old, noisy, uncomfortable, and prone to long stalls. That said, the railway is always preferable to the highway.

In the north, southbound trains leave from the Hanoi railway station (120 Le Duan, tel 04/942-3697) for the 32-hour express or 40-hour regular train to Ho Chi Minh City. From Tran Quy Cap station (adjacent to the Hanoi railway station), trains run up several different spurs to Haiphong, Lang Son, and Lao Cai (Sa Pa).

In the south, northbound trains leave from the Saigon railway station (1 Nguyen Thong, tel 08/931-8952), headed for Hanoi and points in between, including Nha Trang, Danang, and Hue.

Several ticket classes are available on the 32-hour express. A soft bed in an air-conditioned, four-berth compartment costs

$60 (960,000 dong), while a hard bed in a six-berth compartment costs $53 (848,000 dong). A soft seat costs $36 (576,000 dong). Cheaper hard seats await on the slow train.

PRACTICAL ADVICE

COMMUNICATIONS

Post office

The post office (buu dien) is a fixture in every Vietnamese town, even in out-of-the-way tourist destinations like Bach Ma National Park. While it offers a cheap and efficient means of shipping, you'd be foolish to send anything of value through the system, which has a bad reputation for pilfering from packages and envelopes.

Ho Chi Minh City's main post office stands across from the Notre Dame Cathedral in Paris Square. Hanoi's main post office commands a whole block of Dinh Tien Hoang, on the eastern shore of Hoan Kiem Lake. Most clerks speak English.

You can also leave your letters and packages with hotel reception for delivery.

Telephone

Traditionally, the post office has served as the best place to make international calls. Unfortunately, many clerks decline to let foreigners place collect calls. It's not clear why; it simply may be that there's not much in it for them. However, you can call collect from a hotel or private residence.

In the big towns and many of the tourist towns, it's as cheap as a few pennies a minute to place international calls from Internet shops. Calls to the United States average about 6 cents per minute. For the best possible connection, go early or late when the ADSL lines are less crowded. It's even cheaper to buy your own calling card (many of the Internet shops sell them) or dial out on Skype or Yahoo Messenger.

In hotel rooms with a phone, the price of a local call can range from free to about 20 cents per minute. Domestic long-distance calls are more expensive, as are calls to mobile phones. If you plan to do a lot of calling or dialing into the Internet from your room, be sure to ask the rate in advance.

Mobile phone coverage is excellent. Though it may cost you $150 (2.4 million dong) to buy a phone, the per minute charges are cheap, and incoming calls are free.

For directory information, an English-speaking operator is available at 1080 for pennies per call. You'll reach an operator in the province from which you're calling. If you're after a number in another province, dial that area code, preceded by a 0.

To call Vietnam from abroad, dial the international access code (011 from the U.S., 00 from Europe) then 84 (Vietnam country code), then the area code minus the first 0 and number. To call abroad from Vietnam, dial either 171 00 or 00 followed by the country code (1 for Canada, 44 for the U.K., 1 for the U.S.) followed by the area code minus the first zero (if relevant) and the number.

Internet

Outside of the most remote rural villages, the Internet is available nearly everywhere. Internet shops are crowded with teenagers exchanging instant messages. The rates are ridiculously cheap, at about 12 cents per hour. If you've brought your own laptop, most shopkeepers will pull an Ethernet plug from one of their units so you can plug in.

Ethernet and Wi-Fi fees in the country's best hotels are as expensive as they in the United States, at about $15 per 24 hours. It's equally expensive in the hotel's business centers.

It's possible to dial into the Internet from virtually any phone line. The number is 1269, and the password is vn1269. Unlike in the United States, where you pay a monthly subscription to an ISP, there's only one dial-up ISP here, and it doesn't cost anything but the local call to dial in.

CONVERSIONS

Vietnam uses the metric system for weights and measures. An older Chinese system is also used, but unless you're buying and selling gold, you won't have much contact with it.

ELECTRICITY

Vietnam's current runs at 220V, which tends to work just fine with most modern electronics. If you need access to 110V, you'll have to bring your own converter or buy a unit here. Many electronic supply stores sell converter boxes, but most are big and heavy—fine if you're staying put for a while but otherwise a bear to travel with.

With rare exceptions, most hotel sockets can accommodate the two flat pins on plugs from the United States. The same slots also take the two standard round pins on most Vietnamese devices. You'll occasionally run across a socket that demands three pins.

The power grid is very reliable in the big cities and surprisingly good elsewhere.

HOLIDAYS

The Tet lunar new year dwarfs all other Vietnamese holidays, so much so that you wonder whether the country celebrates any others. In Saigon, streets are gridlocked at night during Tet as celebrants congregate for dance and music performances. In smaller cities and towns, the holiday is still boisterous though hardly on the same scale. For the first three days of Tet, many shops and restaurants remain closed. If you plan to be here for Tet, expect limited services over the holiday.

The Vietnamese also celebrate Saigon Liberation Day on April 30, International Labor Day on May 1, and the National Day of the Socialist Republic of

Vietnam on September 2.

See p. 264 for a rundown of popular festivals.

LIQUOR LAWS
You must be 18 to buy alcohol, although no one checks.

MEDIA
Magazines
Regional and international magazines such as *Newsweek*, *Time*, and *The Economist* are available at a few bookshops and hotels in the major cities.

The Guide is a popular English-language monthly, with up-to-date reviews, listings, and features about various travel destinations. *Time-Out* is another, albeit slimmer, compendium of tourist-related listings in magazine format. The *Saigon Times* also publishes a weekly magazine that provides news for business travelers and tourists.

Newspapers
You'll find day-old copies of *The International Herald Tribune* and *USA Today* in select bookshops and hotels, as well as from sidewalk vendors in Ho Chi Minh City and Hanoi.

The *Vietnam News* and the *Saigon Times* are the major English-language dailies. Both are state-run entities with restricted content, but the papers do a good job of keeping their fingers on the pulse of what's up and coming in the country.

Radio
You'll find some English-language programming on the state-run radio station at 105.5 FM. But you'll be far better connected to world events by tuning in a shortwave to the BBC, VOA, or Radio Canada.

Television
Most hotels, from high-end down to budget, offer satellite television with a wide range of channels, including CNN, BBC, HBO, National Geographic, and MTV Asia.

MONEY MATTERS
Dong
Vietnam's official unit of currency is the dong (pronounced dowm). The currency is fairly stable, with an exchange rate of about 16,000 dong to 1 U.S. dollar. The state issues 500, 1,000, 2,000, 5,000, 10,000, 20,000, 50,000, 100,000, and 500,000 dong notes. While the old currency was paper, newer 50,000, 100,000, and 500,000 notes are printed on a very durable plastic that lasts about four times as long. The downside is that it folds awkwardly, and you have to carry so much of it. The state also issues coins in 200, 500, 1,000, 2,000, and 5,000 increments, but locals aren't used to carrying them, and cyclo/motorbike drivers may balk at taking coins in payment.

U.S. dollars
Though Vietnamese merchants will always accept their own currency, there's an ingrained preference for U.S. dollars that goes back to the 1970s and '80s when the government devalued the currency on several different occasions. The newer the bills, the better. Merchants will often reject notes with slight blemishes.

Exchange
Most banks in cities and towns are set up to exchange Western currency for Vietnamese dong. There's no surcharge for the exchange of currency notes, but you'll lose 1–2 percent when exchanging traveler's checks for Vietnamese cash. Remember that most banks close between 11:30 a.m. and 1:30 p.m. Many hotels will also exchange currency at favorable rates. Beware of touts in Ho Chi Minh City and Hanoi who promise better exchange rates; those black market days are over.

Credit cards
Many Vietnamese hotels, restaurants, and shops accept credit cards, but in most cases, you'll have to pay a 3 percent surcharge for the privilege.

ATMs
ATM withdrawals are the best way to handle money in Vietnam. Traveler's checks are increasingly less attractive, as you have to pay surcharges to cash them. But ATMs are proliferating in the major tourist hubs, as well as secondary cities and towns.

Tipping
Vietnam is not a tipping culture. They don't tip each other. But there is an expectation that foreigners will tip, especially if the foreigner is American. Cab drivers don't expect tips, though they do expect that you won't ask for change if it's a matter of a few thousand dong. There's a higher expectation among waitstaff and a still higher expectation from bellhops, who'll be pleased with 5,000 or 10,000 dong (30 to 60 cents) for toting your luggage. Tour guides do work for tips. Some will ask for the tip, especially boat paddlers at places like Tam Coc and the Perfume Pagoda.

OPENING TIMES
Businesses tend to open early, by 8 a.m., and close by 4:30 p.m. But there's a long siesta every day, from 11:30 a.m. to 1:30 p.m. Restaurants and bistros, obviously, stay open through lunch.

Many museums also plow through the siesta, catering to Western tastes. But just as many close. Since Sunday is the busiest museum-going day, many close on Monday to rest and recuperate. Be sure to check schedules ahead of time.

PASSPORTS
Be prepared to surrender your passport to hotel clerks. In larger cities more dependent on tourism, they're less likely to insist on holding your passport overnight. But in places like Chau Doc and the highland towns, where paranoia is still prevalent, the police insist on knowing who's in town. Thus, hotel clerks are obliged to bring everyone's passport to the cops at 10 p.m. It's a crummy practice, because if

you change hotels often, you're bound to forget it, and the clerks are bound to forget to tell you.

RELIGION

Although nominally communist, the Vietnamese are largely free to worship as they please. There have been reports of persecution against Christians in the central highlands. The government's motivation in those situations seems to be more politically oriented than religious.

The vast majority of Vietnamese are enmeshed in a culture strongly influenced by Buddhism, Confucianism, Taoism, and ancestor worship. That said, about 8 percent of the population is Catholic, and churches are widespread, visible, and active.

Many of the Cham people, especially in the Mekong Delta, are Muslim.

REST ROOMS

Public bathrooms in Vietnam are often less welcoming than their Western counterparts. While the days of squat treads and basin holes are largely over, many bathrooms still forgo paper wipes for water nozzles. Be sure to carry spare tissues, even when visiting the best museums.

In the countryside, a query about the location of a bathroom is sometimes dismissed with a wave of the hand, which may be interpreted as "among the bushes." In an emergency, most Vietnamese will open their facilities to you. Ask for the *ve sinh* (pronounced vay sin), and they'll help you on your way.

TIME

The time difference from Greenwich Mean Time is + 7 hours. From New York, it is +12 hours (one hour less during daylight saving time).

TOURISM OFFICES

Despite their resemblance to visitor bureaus, Vietnam's provincial tourism offices function as state-run rivals to private tour companies. Like

Saigon Tourist, these offices often own and manage several hotels. They maintain staffs of tour guides and vehicles for hire. Except for offices in the larger cities, their services are largely geared to domestic tourists, not international travelers.

As information sources, these folks can be rather useless. They often don't speak English, and even basic information is hard to come by. Vietnam Tourism's website (www .vietnamtourism.com) is a decent source for general travel information.

The best firsthand sources are local travel agents. In Hanoi and Ho Chi Minh City, local agents keep longer hours than state-run agents, their English is usually better, and they're often far more savvy than state-run operators. If you're desperate for additional information in a remote region, call the biggest hotel; its reception staff will likely speak passable English.

TRAFFIC

Crossing the street in Vietnam's urban centers remains a dodgy prospect for the uninitiated. Instead of waiting, drivers will swerve wildly around you, while scofflaws run rampant through red lights and intersections. Follow this procedure: Step from curb to street during a relative lull in traffic, then maintain a steady pace across the street. Don't do anything unpredictable. Drivers will anticipate your path.

TRAVELERS WITH DISABILITIES

As a country that still ranks among the poorest in the world, Vietnam's accommodations for travelers with disabilities are predictably scarce. Even the pavement is often uneven, and crossing the street via wheelchair can be a nightmarish proposition. Domestic flights do not use jetways but require a walk across the tarmac and up a flight of mobile stairs.

EMERGENCIES

EMERGENCY PHONE NUMBERS

Emergency: 115
Fire: 114
Police: 113
Directory assistance: 1080
International operator: 110
Time: 117

HEALTH

The overriding health concern of late among travelers to Vietnam has been Asian bird flu. Several dozen Vietnamese died during a 2003–04 outbreak.

Unlike the 2003 outbreak of severe acute respiratory syndrome (SARS), the reports of bird flu hardly disrupted travel to the region in 2005. The Vietnamese press wrote at length about efforts to curb bird flu at home and abroad. The government ordered mass slaughters of suspect poultry and inoculation of other birds. It also ordered restaurants to remove chicken from their menus. By early 2006, poultry was back on the serving plate.

Vietnam does not require any vaccinations of travelers. For travel to Southeast Asia, the Centers for Disease Control recommends vaccinations for hepatitis A and B, Japanese encephalitis, rabies, and typhoid, as well as a course of antimalarial drugs.

Inoculation against hepatitis A and B is especially important, as the disease is prevalent. Typhoid is another advisable inoculation. This disease is often spread through fecal contamination of water, a risk when eating street food in Vietnam.

Few expats bother with antimalarial drugs or inoculation against Japanese encephalitis. If you're planning a highland trek or think you might come into contact with dogs, consider an inoculation against rabies.

In bistros, soup stalls, and rice shops, utensils (chopsticks, forks) are typically kept in holders at the table. Vietnamese diners often just wipe down such utensils with a napkin before dining. Better yet, bring your own chopsticks, as well as antibacterial fluid for cleanup.

Always drink bottled water. The Vietnamese boil water for their own consumption and presumably use this water to make ice. Since you can't always be sure, it's better to avoid ice unless you're eating at a high-end place.

MEDICAL SERVICES

Vietnam's hospitals are generally good, especially for outpatient care, though less comfortable than Western hospitals if you must stay overnight. Doctors are not paid well and, unfortunately, tend to respond better when patients pay them an incentive. The same is true of nurses. Most expats make do with the international clinics, which are widespread in Ho Chi Minh City and Hanoi.

REPRESENTATIVE OFFICES

Foreign embassies and consulates in Vietnam provide a range of traveler services, including voter registration, passport renewal, provision of federal income tax forms, and limited emergency services. What they won't do is help find your luggage, issue driving permits, intercede in disputes with local hotels, or let you stay at the office if stranded. They can offer advice in such circumstances, however.

United States
U.S. Embassy
7 Lang Ha
Hanoi
Tel 04/772-1500
Fax 04/772-1510
http://hanoi.usembassy.gov/
Walk-in: Mon.–Fri. 8–11:30 a.m.;
closed on local/U.S. holidays
Tel 04/831-4590, ext.133

U.S. Consulate
American Citizen Services
4 Le Duan
District 1
Ho Chi Minh City
Tel 08/822-9433, ext. 2159
http://hochiminh.usconsulate.gov
Walk-in: Mon.–Thurs. 8:30–

11:30 a.m., 1:30–3:30 p.m.; closed Fri. and local/U.S. holidays

Australia
Australian Embassy
8 Dao Tan
Ba Dinh District
Hanoi
Tel 04/831-7755
Fax 04/831-7711
www.vietnam.embassy.gov.au
/index.html
Hours: Mon.–Fri. 8:30 a.m.–noon,
1–5 p.m.
Australian Consulate General
Landmark Building
5th Floor
5B Ton Duc Thang
Ho Chi Minh City
Tel 08/829-6035
Fax 08/829-6031
Hours: Mon.–Fri. 8:30 a.m.–noon,
1–5 p.m.

Canada
Canadian Embassy
31 Hung Vuong
Hanoi
Tel 04/734-5000
Fax 04/734-5049
www.dfaitmaeci.gc.ca/asia
/vietnam/menu-en.asp

Canadian Consulate General
The Metropolitan
10th Floor
235 Dong Khoi
District 1
Ho Chi Minh City
Tel 08/827 9899
Fax 08/827 9935
Hours: Mon.–Thurs. 8–11 a.m.,
1:30–4 p.m., Fri. 8:30–11 a.m.

United Kingdom
British Embassy
Central Building
4th Floor
31 Hai Ba Trung
Hanoi
Tel 04/936-0500
www.britishembassy.gov.uk
Hours: Mon.–Fri. 8:30 a.m.–
12:30 p.m., 1:30–4:30 p.m.

British Consulate General
25 Le Duan
District 1
Ho Chi Minh City
Tel 08/829-8433
Fax 08/829-5257

Hours: Mon.–Fri. 8:30 a.m.–noon,
1–4:30 p.m.

SAFETY

Vietnam is an exceptionally safe place to travel. In 2005, a major insurance carrier singled out the country as one of the half dozen safest destinations for travel worldwide. Violent crime is not an issue.

The greatest health hazard posed to travelers is the traffic. Only in the last decade has the country begun to install traffic lights, and old, bad driving habits die hard. For example, motorbike drivers often violate one-way restrictions. Truckers and bus drivers also routinely flout safe driving habits. The situation is improving, but use extreme caution when crossing the street.

Robbery can be a problem, especially in downtown Saigon. Women should not wear gold hoop earrings or anything else conspicuous that might tempt a drive-by thief on a motorbike. Leave your purse in the hotel room. Don't carry cameras by straps; keep them in a bag.

In March 2006, Ho Chi Minh City rolled out a force of 108 tourist police officers to patrol the main streets and the top tourist attractions in Districts 1 and 3 from 8 a.m. to 11 p.m. The English-speaking officers serve as both a resource for travelers and a hedge against harassment and scams. The provisional police office is at 13 Dien Bien Phu. The emergency hot line is 08/510-6573.

FURTHER READING

Biography
A Bright Shining Lie: John Paul Vann and America in Vietnam, by Neil Sheehan (Vintage, 1989). This Pulitzer Prize–winning biography serves as a monumental history of the U.S. war in Vietnam.
Ho Chi Minh, by William J. Duiker (Theia, 2001). Compelling portrait of a Vietnamese leader admired and respected by Americans who

knew him intimately between the end of World War II and the partition of Vietnam in 1954.

Culture

Fire in the Lake, by Frances Fitzgerald (Vintage, 1973). A remarkably insightful look at Vietnamese culture.

Wandering through Vietnamese Culture, by Huu Ngoc (Gioi Publishers, 2004). Available only in Vietnam, this thousand-plus-page tome of a cultural historian's musings on Vietnam's villages, landscapes, traditions, food, and family is beautifully written, unimpeachably authoritative, and indispensable for any traveler who wants to plumb the depths of this culture.

Fiction

A Good Scent from a Strange Mountain, by Robert Olen Butler (Grove Press, 2001). Pulitzer Prize–winning collection of short stories written with a Vietnamese sensibility.

Paradise of the Blind, by Duong Thu Huong (HarperPerennial, 2002). A grim novel about a young woman's relationship with her family in postwar Hanoi of the 1980s.

The Quiet American, by Graham Greene (Penguin, 2002). First published in 1955, this novel remains vital reading. The story charts the love triangle between a detached journalist, his Vietnamese mistress, and an idealistic American.

The Sorrow of War, by Bao Ninh (Riverhead, 1996). Tells the story of the war's impact on a North Vietnamese soldier, without any nationalistic trumpeting.

The Things They Carried, by Tim O'Brien (Houghton Mifflin/ Seymour Lawrence, 1979). A collection of transcendent short stories about U.S. infantry soldiers during the war.

General history

Birth of Vietnam, by Keith Taylor (University of California Press, 1983). This academic work is peerless in its appreciation of Vietnam's roots.

The Smaller Dragon, by Joseph Buttinger (Praeger, 1958). A hard-to-find but eminently readable account of Vietnam's history through 1900.

Literature

The Tale of Kieu, by Nguyen Du, translation by Huynh Sanh Thong (Vintage, 1973). This nationally renowned epic poem details the tragic story of a girl who sells herself as a concubine to save her family.

Understanding Vietnam, by Neil L. Jamieson (University of California Press, 1993). Spotlights Vietnamese prose from the 1930s to sort out what U.S. policy makers failed to see or understand during the war.

Nonfiction

A Dragon Apparent, by Norman Lewis (Trans-Atlantic Publications, 1995). A travel-writing tour de force by a master of the genre who explored Vietnam in the waning days of French colonialism.

The Girl in the Picture, by Denise Chong (Penguin, 1999). Intimate life story of the napalmed girl who appeared on the front pages of the world's newspapers one day in 1972.

Sacred Willow, by Duong Van Mai Elliott (Oxford University Press, 1999). This multigenerational saga relates how a scholarly family coped with the upheavals of Vietnamese society over four generations.

Where the Ashes Are, by Nguyen Qui Duc (Addison-Wesley, 1994). A poignant memoir by a man whose indomitable family suffered imprisonment, death, and exile, yet endured it all with courage and grace.

Postwar

Over the Moat, by James Sullivan (Picador, 2004). The story of a young American's romance with a woman from Hue during the last days of the U.S. trade embargo.

Shadows and Wind, by Robert Templer (Penguin, 1999). Tough, well-written look at the harsh state of the nation in postwar

Vietnam, written by a former AFP correspondent who worked in Hanoi in the mid-1990s.

War

Dispatches, by Michael Herr (Vintage, 1991). Reflects the grit, passion, and insanity of the war.

Reporting Vietnam (Library of Vietnam, 1998). A two-volume, 1,500-page anthology of American journalism and nonfiction about the war.

A Rumor of War, by Philip Caputo (Owl Books, 1996). Searing memoir by a U.S. Marine who marched into the rice paddies with the convictions of a 1960s idealist and marched out with his world turned upside-down.

The Tunnels of Cu Chi, by Tom Mangold and John Penycate (Berkeley, 1985). Explores the wartime stories from this 125-mile (200 km) network of Viet Cong tunnels west of Saigon.

Vietnam: A History, by Stanley Karnow (Penguin, 1983). Centers on the Vietnam War, with background on Vietnam's early history and French colonialism.

HOTELS & RESTAURANTS

In the early 1990s, Vietnam lacked even a single hotel as smart, clean, or efficient as a typical Holiday Inn in the U.S. But those days are past. Now, first-rate accommodations are available in all the major tourist hubs—Hanoi, Ho Chi Minh City, Hue, Hoi An, Nha Trang, Dalat, and Phan Thiet. While the restaurant scene is not as expansive, the dining in Hanoi and Ho Chi Minh City is superb.

HOTELS

Vietnam Tourism rates its hotels on a five-star system to distinguish between grades of hotel. Unfortunately, too many of the hotels that won, say, three stars from Vietnam Tourism ten years ago have not reinvested in the property or kept pace with contemporary standards.

The best hotels in Hanoi and Ho Chi Minh City rival the best hotels anywhere. The rooms can be posh, the staff elegant, the service a joy, and the character both deep and resonant. With the exception of the Metropole in Hanoi and the Palace in Dalat, however, most of Vietnam's historic hotels—the Continental, Grand, Majestic, Morin, and Rex—remain in the grip of state-run enterprises that don't have the expertise to provide a world-class hotel experience. Among the more impressive state-owned entities are the Ana Mandara and the Evason Hideaway, each run by professional hoteliers.

Beyond Ho Chi Minh City and Hanoi, the ranks of high-caliber hotels thin rapidly, though that's changing. Hue, for example, lacked a decent hotel as recently as early 2005. Now it boasts one of the best hotels in the country, and three more high-end hotels will be up and running by the summer of 2007.

The resort hotel scene along the coast is a mixed bag. At places like the Life Resort, Novotel, and Furama, there's a high degree of sophistication, but too many other resorts have been built by amateur hoteliers who failed to seek professional advice.

With rare exceptions, hotels off the beaten path are almost always state-run, which usually means bland decor prevails, the restaurant often closes for weddings, and the karaoke lounge is still blaring at 11 p.m. In the hinterlands, refrain from booking a room in the biggest hotel. Instead, go in search of the newest hotels. They're usually owned by Vietnamese entrepreneurs who are hard working, friendly, accommodating, and anxious to make a dollar.

In terms of rates, most of the high-end hotels in Ho Chi Minh City and Hanoi start at about $200 per night, with only a handful of accommodations ranging higher.

A wide variety of charming hotels lie in the budget range, often charging less than $25 per night, though it may take some browsing to find one that meets your expectations. Again, a newer hotel usually signals an entrepreneur at work. Start there.

There seems to be less variety in the $25 to $75 bracket. In other words, you could end up paying $75 for a room in a hotel only as good as a high-end budget place. With few exceptions, you'll need to pay more than $75 to be catapulted into the next category of luxury.

Most hotels include a buffet breakfast in the standard rate. At high-end places, these breakfasts are worth getting up for. At budget places in the cities, expect something continental, while in the outskirts, they'll serve Vietnamese fare.

Hotels across all budget ranges provide some measure of in-room amenities—from high-end sponge wash pads to little plastic shampoo bottles in the budget rooms. Most rooms include small refrigerators and a selection of snacks.

RESTAURANTS

Dining out has become quite popular in Vietnam, especially at high-end restaurants. For $12, a meal out in Hanoi will get you ambience, sumptuous cuisine, and friendly service. It's like Paris of the 1920s—cheap, exquisite, and guaranteed not to remain this good much longer.

Both Ho Chi Minh City and Hanoi boast an ample selection of restaurants and cuisines beyond the hotel lobbies, from high-end Vietnamese to Italian, French, Indian, and American. They fly in lamb from Colorado these days, and most of the beef comes from Australia.

Beyond Ho Chi Minh City and Hanoi, quality restaurants are harder to find than quality hotels. Places like Hue, Dalat, Danang, and Nha Trang remain bereft of options beyond the high-end hotels. You can still find wonderful food, but the ambience is often subpar.

Except at high-end restaurants, don't expect courses to arrive in traditional succession: appetizer, soup, salad, and entrée. It's more likely to come either all at once or as it's prepared. If you'd prefer the kitchen to stagger the dishes, go ahead and ask, but then cross your fingers (a gesture best done beneath the table, however, as it's an obscenity in Vietnam).

Except at high-end places, diners often choose their own chopsticks from a tabletop bin. Consider bringing your own utensils, as washing with piping hot water is not customary in Vietnam. Don't be surprised if you're charged for the wet napkin provided for cleanup. Better yet, bring your own chopsticks, as well as antibacterial fluid for cleanup.

If you're forced to wing it for a restaurant choice, follow the universal rule of thumb and eat where the locals eat. Avoid places thronged with tourists. As the Vietnamese say, such places "cut your head off" with the price and serve subpar fare.

HOTELS & RESTAURANTS

ORGANIZATION & ABBREVIATIONS

Hotels and restaurants for each city or town are listed by price, then in alphabetical order.

Hotel restaurants are noted only if they are stand-out destinations; all luxury hotels will have in-house restaurants.

Many hotels and restaurants accept all major cards. Smaller ones may accept only some. Abbreviations used are: AE (American Express), DC (Diners Club), MC (MasterCard), and V (Visa).

 HANOI

HOTELS

🏨 HILTON HANOI OPERA
$$$$$
I LE THANH TONG
TEL 04/933-0500
FAX 04/933-0530
www.hanoi.hilton.com
Adjacent to the Opera House in Hanoi's most elegant neighborhood, this Hilton is challenging the Metropole as the city's leading high-end hotel. With spacious rooms, Wi-Fi connectivity in the lobby, and marble appointments in the bathrooms, the Opera may be the city's most comfortable perch.
ⓘ 269 ⬜ ⬛ ⬛ 🌊 🍸 ⬛ All major cards

🏨 MELIA HOTEL
$$$$$
44B LY THUONG KIET
TEL 04/934-3343
FAX 04/934-3344
www.meliahanoi.com
This high-rise business hotel is sandwiched between Hoan Kiem Lake and the French Quarter. You may not need the rooftop heliport, but the third-floor outdoor swimming pool offers a great escape from the inner city. In-room amenities include pillowed bathtubs. A band plays in the lobby every night.
ⓘ 306 Ⓟ ⬜ ⬛ ⬛ 🌊 🍸 ⬛ All major cards

🏨 SHERATON HANOI
$$$$$
K5 NGHI TAM
II XUAN DIEU
TAY HO DISTRICT
TEL 04/719-9000
FAX 04/719-9001
www.sheraton.com/hanoi
Ten minutes from the city center, the Sheraton sprawls across its own peninsula on West Lake and abuts the city's most fashionable expat neighborhood. The rooms are spacious, and the upper floors feature long water views. Though the main body of the hotel is a world-class high-rise, a collection of terra-cotta-tiled Asian pavilions with flying eaves cluster about the hotel's ground floor, the swimming pool, and lush landscaped gardens.
ⓘ 299 Ⓟ ⬜ ⬛ ⬛ 🌊 🍸 ⬛ All major cards

🏨 SOFITEL METROPOLE 🍽 HANOI
$$$–$$$$$
15 NGO QUYEN
TEL 04/826-6919
FAX 04/826-6920
www.accorhotels.com/asia
If you want to enter a living fantasy of indolence à la *Indochine*, look no further. The Metropole is a perfectly preserved outpost of colonial French elegance. The decor is period perfect, and the hotel's two restaurants—Spices Garden (see p. 248) and Le Beaulieu—are among the best in Hanoi. With the reserve of a grande dame, the Metropole lives up to its legendary status.
ⓘ 232 Ⓟ ⬜ ⬛ ⬛ 🌊 🍸 ⬛ All major cards

🏨 ZEPHYR HOTEL
$$$
4 BA TRIEU
HOAN KIEM DISTRICT
TEL 844/934-1256
FAX 844/934-1262
www.zephyrhotel.com.vn
Location, location, location. A smart, 40-room boutique hotel a short walk from the south end of Hoan Kiem

---

HOTELS
An indication of the maximum high-season cost of a double room with breakfast is given by $ signs.

$$$$$	Over $175
$$$$	$125–$175
$$$	$75–$125
$$	$25–$75
$	Under $25

RESTAURANTS
An indication of the cost of a three-course dinner, without drinks, is given by $ signs.

$$$$$	Over $20
$$$$	$15–$20
$$$	$9–$15
$$	$3–$9
$	Under $3

Lake, the Zephyr is central to everything in Hanoi. You won't get the luxurious touch that you'd find at a five-star hotel, but this makes for a comfortable central base from which to explore.
ⓘ 40 Ⓟ ⬜ ⬛ ⬛ All major cards

🏨 CHURCH HOTEL
$$
9 NHA THO
HOAN KIEM DISTRICT
TEL 04/928-8118
FAX 04/828-5793
This newer accommodation is well aware of Western tastes. While small, the rooms are clean and nicely appointed, with wood floors, comfortable furniture, and nice lighting. The location is also superb, on fashionable Nha Tho.
ⓘ 20 ⬛ ⬛ ⬛ None

🏨 LUCKY HOTEL & LUCKY 2 HOTEL
$$
12 HANG TRONG
& 46 HANG HOM
HOAN KIEM DISTRICT
TEL 04/825-1029
FAX 04/825-1731
http://luckyhotel.com.vn
The Lucky and its annex, Lucky 2, are can't-miss mid-range options with one

---

KEY 🏨 Hotel 🍽 Restaurant ⓘ No. of guest rooms ⬛ No. of seats Ⓟ Parking ⊕ Closed

foot in the Old Quarter and another on the west side of Hoan Kiem Lake. Amenities include free in-room ADSL Internet access and a wide-ranging breakfast menu.

📋 40 🛗 ❄ 💳 All major cards

🏨 CLASSIC I HOTEL
$–$$

22A TA HIEN
HOAN KIEM DISTRICT
TEL 04/826-6224
FAX 04/828-1727
www.hanoiclassichotel.com

In Hanoi's Old Quarter, the Classic is a clean, comfortable, seven-story budget hotel with the usual amenities, including an elevator. Free Internet access is available in a first-floor computer room, and the small restaurant serves good breakfasts.

📋 37 ❄ 💳 MC, V

🏨 PRINCE II HOTEL
$

42B HANG GIAY
TEL 04/926-1203
FAX 04/828-0156
www.hanoiprincehotel.com

In the Old Quarter, the Prince II is a slightly nicer upgrade to the Prince I, a 15-room option just a short stroll away at 51 Luong Ngoc Quyen. For budget accommodation among backpacker travelers, either offers fine digs. The beds are firm, the bathrooms clean, and the air-conditioning powerful.

📋 10 ❄ 💳 All major cards

🏨 SUNSHINE HOTEL
$

42 MA MAY
HOAN KIEM DISTRICT
TEL 04/926-2239
FAX 04/926-1558
www.hanoisunshinehotel.com

You may not get a room with a view, and the air-conditioning might be a little cranky, but in a city where the real estate is absurdly expensive, you can't beat the price. The friendly staff will point you toward the free Internet station in the lobby and a tour company

desk on the ground floor.

📋 12 ❄ 💳 MC, V

RESTAURANTS

🍽 BOBBY CHINN
$$$$$

I BA TRIEU
HOAN KIEM DISTRICT
TEL 04/934-8577
FAX 04/716-4120

The waitstaff scatters rose petals on the tablecloth as you take your seat in Hanoi's hippest restaurant, on the south end (and with views) of Hoan Kiem Lake. Crab in a seaweed nest, pan-fried salmon, plump seared scallops —each is a connoisseur's delight. The inventive menu is complemented by one of the best wine lists in Vietnam.

🪑 60 ❄ 💳 All major cards

🍽 VINE WINE BOUTIQUE BAR & CAFÉ
$$$$$

XUAN DIEU
TEL 04/719-8000
FAX 04/719-8001

Don't be surprised if you find yourself ordering a bottle of wine at this intimate restaurant in Hanoi's West Lake District: 1,200 bottles grace the wall-mounted racks, imbuing the dining nooks with a deliciously lit ambience. The menu dabbles in Vietnamese, pushes Thai with more gusto, is especially strong with Italian, and is anchored by international fare. Want Colorado lamb? This is the place. Montreal-born executive chef Donald Berger is one of Hanoi's finest.

🪑 80 ❄ 💳 AE, MC, V

🍽 GREEN TANGERINE
$$$$–$$$$$

48 HANG BE
TEL 04/825-1286
FAX 04/926-1797

The Green Tangerine fuses French and Eastern fare in a shop that is itself a fusion of French colonial and Old Quarter "tube house" architecture. Both of the owner's

French grandfathers married Vietnamese women during the colonial era, and the chef is French, too. Look for the ironwood stairway, framed 1928 blueprints of this onetime silk shop, and the poems in the Heavenly Well Courtyard—an exquisite setting for a menu that is refreshed every six months. The lamb and beef are flown in from New Zealand, the salmon from Norway. Try the crab remoulade as an appetizer and the scallops marinated in a tangy, orangey base.

🪑 80 ❄ 💳 All major cards

🍽 LY CLUB
$$$$–$$$$$

51 LY THAI TO
TEL 04/936-3069
FAX 04/936-3079

In a one-of-a-kind brick villa, onetime home to the colonial French director of the Bank of Indochina, the Ly Club indulges privacy in a clubby upstairs dining area that pays homage to the Nguyen dynasty. The menu includes generous selections in both Asian and Western cuisine. Downstairs, another dining area is laid out as a sophisticated nightclub, staging traditional Vietnamese opera and court music once a week, with plans to do more.

🪑 44 ❄ 💳 All major cards

🍽 SPICES GARDEN
$$$$–$$$$$

SOFITEL METROPOLE HANOI
15 NGO QUYEN
TEL 04/826-6919, ext. 8208

At the landmark Metropole (see p. 246), the Spices Garden dishes out some of the country's finest cuisine, whether your appetite calls for traditional Vietnamese or a nouvelle fusion. With a singular passion for Vietnamese soul food, master chef Didier Corlou is blazing new ground.

🪑 70 ❄ 💳 All major cards

HOTELS & RESTAURANTS

🍴 EMPEROR RESTAURANT
$$$$
18B LE THANH TONG
TEL 04/826-8801
Set in an elegant compound amid a historic French villa, a brick courtyard, and a two-story traditional Vietnamese home, the Emperor fulfills all your dreams of a colonial dining experience. The cuisine is traditional but high-end and flawlessly prepared. The fresh spring rolls, crab with sautéed onions, and grouper steamed in banana leaf are favorites.
🔲 250 🅢 🅢 🅢 All major cards

🍴 PRESS CLUB
$$$$
59A LY THAI TO
TEL 04/934-0888
FAX 04/934-0899
You'll feel like a businessman at the end of a long day in old Indochina when you sit down to dinner at the Press Club, on the top floor of a six-story downtown building. The menu is continental, the chef is renowned, the outdoor terrace is a grand place for a cocktail, the bar is deep, and the atmosphere lives up to its billing as a club. The Norwegian salmon is marinated and cured in a house recipe, then smoked with green tea. Austrian rack of lamb is drizzled with a lamb-balsamic reduction sauce. Be sure to leave room for the exquisite melted chocolate pudding with vanilla ice cream and raspberry sauce.
🔲 70 🅢 🅢 🅢 All major cards

🍴 WILD RICE
$$$–$$$$
6 NGO THI NHAM
TEL 04/943-8896
FAX 04/943-6299
The fledgling restaurant barons who opened Wild Rice a few years ago really stir up the creativity at Wild Lotus (see below), which they also own. Here, they've checked their nouvelle impulses at the door

to deliver classic renditions of traditional Vietnamese favorites. The prawns in tamarind sauce are exceptional, as are the shrimp and banana spring rolls. Garbed in traditional *ao dai* dresses, waitresses make their rounds through the salon-style dining rooms of an old French villa.
🔲 100–120 🅢 🅢 🅢 All major cards

🍴 AU LAC HOUSE
$$$
13 TRAN HUNG DAO
TEL 04/933-3533
FAX 04/933-3522
Dine on the second-floor terrace of this monumental colonial French villa, which boasts a menu as Vietnamese as Au Lac, the legendary mother of Vietnam, herself. Tamarind and chili sauces are delightful on the crab and shrimp, while the crab spring rolls are generously stuffed. During the colonial era, the home belonged to a Vietnamese doctor whose wife still lives in a first-floor apartment.
🔲 150 🅢 🅢 🅢 All major cards

🍴 INDOCHINE
$$$
16 NAM NGU
TEL 04/942-4097
FAX 04/942-4104
In four separate dining areas of an old French bungalow, a cozy, sapodilla-shaded courtyard, and two floors of a simple French villa, Indochine has been dishing out Vietnamese standards since 1994, which makes the restaurant a pioneer of fine dining in Hanoi. The menu may be the city's broadest, covering more than a hundred of the estimated 500 dishes in the Vietnamese repertoire. Traditional musicians serenade diners between 7:30 and 9:30 p.m. on Tuesdays and Thursdays.
🔲 85 🅢 🅢 🅢 All major cards

🍴 MEDITERRANEO
$$$
23 NHA THO
TEL 04/826-6288
FAX 04/928-7690
Strategically located between St. Joseph's Cathedral and Hoan Kiem Lake, the dining area of this Italian trattoria spills onto a chic street of popular cafés and boutiques. The homemade mozzarella is delicious. Also try the roast beef, sliced thick and sandwiched between grilled eggplant, zucchini, and tomatoes. Don't leave without tasting the homemade chocolate ice cream, which holds its own with any ice cream anywhere.
🔲 60 🅢 🅢 🅢 All major cards

🍴 WILD LOTUS
$$$
55A NGUYEN DU
TEL 04/943-9342
FAX 04/943-9341
Housed in a creatively restored, three-story art deco building, Wild Lotus is a feast of architecture, design, and Vietnamese cuisine. The decor and menu are the brainchildren of three Vietnamese owners, one of whom attended Harvard. The executive chef studied and cultivated his craft in Hanoi, but the cuisine makes no concessions to more cosmopolitan rivals. Try the crab and leek soup and the white fish tikkas bound in pandanus leaves.
🔲 170–200 🅢 🅢 🅢 All major cards

🍴 HOA SUA
$$–$$$
28A HA HOI
TEL 04/942-4448
FAX 04/822-3499
Housed in a renovated French villa, this nonprofit restaurant feeds the soul as well as the stomach. It serves as a proving ground for orphans being trained for service in the country's hospitality industry. Try the tuna in wild mushroom sauce or the beef tenderloin in a blue cheese and black pepper sauce and finish with the

signature chocolate mousse.
🏨 128 🚭 🛗 🅰️ All major cards

SOMETHING SPECIAL

🍴 CHA CA LA VONG

They'll bring you the menu at Cha Ca, but you won't have any choice about the order. There's only one dish—grilled fish. And, oh, what fish. With a tableside charcoal-stoked brazier and a helping hand from the waitstaff, you simmer your own chunks of fresh saltwater fish in a small pan of oil and herbs. The fish goes down easily, and fast, with bun noodles and basil.

$$
14 CHA CA
OLD QUARTER
🏨 50 🛗 🚫 None

🍴 PHO 24

$$
26 BA TRIEU
HOAN KIEM DISTRICT
Though traditionalists might balk at this restaurant's prettified version of a classic Vietnamese dish, the pho ingredients here are fresh and unimpeachable. This is a great place for street food without the associated risks.
🏨 60 🛗

🍴 BUN BO NAM BO

$
67 HANG DIEU
TEL 04/923-0701
If you visit only one noodle shop, make it this classic spot in Hanoi's Old Quarter. By the end of lunch, the floor here is a tangle of banana leaves, napkins, and other detritus, but first and foremost all that trash is a testament to the popularity of this place. *Bun bo* is the specialty. The bowls are deep, and the shaved beef is lean and palatable. Each bowl of dry bun noodles is frosted with chopped peanuts, garlic, and fresh herbs.
🏨 120 🚫 None

THE NORTH
CAT BA ISLAND

🏨 HOLIDAY VIEW

$$
ROAD 1/4
CAT HAI DISTRICT
TEL 031/887-200
FAX 031/887-208
Occupying a high-rise at the east end of Cat Ba town, the Holiday View is a clean and functional if somewhat unsophisticated mid-range option.
🏨 120 🅿️ 🛗 MC, V

HA LONG

SOMETHING SPECIAL

🏨 *EMERAUDE* CLASSIC
🍴 CRUISES

The *Emeraude*, a modified replica of a French paddle wheeler that cruised Ha Long Bay in the 1920s, is the best venue for enjoying the scenic wonders of Vietnam's most dazzling seascape. The 38 air-conditioned cabins are classically appointed. Decked with potted ferns and banana plants, the planked and canopied rooftop terrace inspires indolence. If you've dreamed of a nostalgic journey through colonial Indochina, this is it.

$$$$$
59A LY THAI TO, STE. 214
HANOI
TEL 04/934-0888, ext. 3001
FAX 04/934-0899
www.emeraudecruises.com
🏨 38 🚭 🛗 🛗 🖥️ 🅰️ All major cards

🏨 HUONG HAI JUNK

$$$
1 VUON DAO
BAI CHAY
TEL 033/845-042
FAX 033/846-263
www.halongtravels.com
A fleet of nine Huong Hai junks launches from the Ha Long wharf every afternoon at 12:45 and overnights in a vast arena of limestone karsts. Meals are served on board. Rooms are

air-conditioned, and each comes with stunning water views.
ℹ️ 59 on 9 boats 🅿️ 🛗 🅰️ All major cards

HAIPHONG

🏨 HARBOUR VIEW

$$$
4 TRAN PHU
TEL 031/827-827
FAX 031/827-828
www.harbourviewvietnam.com
A faithful re-creation of a grand colonial hotel, the Harbour View is as good as it gets in the busy port city of Haiphong. The hotel caters to business travelers, with in-room DSL ports and comfortable common areas. Rooms exude a warm, colonial glow with rich teak furnishings. An experienced English hotelier holds the staff to high standards.
ℹ️ 120 🅿️ 🛗 🛗 🖥️ 🅰️ All major cards

🍴 GREEN MANGO

$$$
GROUP 19, BLOCK 4
ROAD 1/4
TEL 031/887-151
That fusion cuisine this good is available in Cat Ba is simply astonishing. The fresh seafood is artfully prepared by a chef who opened one of Hanoi's finest restaurants and is now on his own in an otherwise culinary backwater. With indirect lighting and a musically imaginative atmosphere, the ambience is city hip.
🏨 70 🅰️ All major cards

SA PA

SOMETHING SPECIAL

🏨 TOPAS ECOLODGE
🍴

Perched atop a 3,000-foot (900 m) mountain, the Topas Ecolodge is a frill of white-granite bungalows far removed from downtown Sa Pa. Each bungalow offers a breathtaking view of the Muong Hoa Valley and the Ta Van River, whose rapids and waterfalls are audible from each room's pri-

HOTELS & RESTAURANTS

vate veranda. Meals are served in a renovated Tay communal house with similarly spectacular views. The lodge dispatches guests to the valley's farthest reaches in the company of smart, friendly guides.
$$$
24 MUONG HOA
CAU MAY
TEL 020/871-331
FAX 020/871-596
www.topas-adventure-vietnam.com
① 25 🅾 DC, MC, V

🏨 ROYAL VIEW HOTEL
$$
CAU MAY
TEL 020/872-989
FAX 020/872-992
www.royalsapa.com
Offering valley views from nearly every room, this is a relative newcomer to Sa Pa's overaccommodating hotel scene. The spacious rooms feature working fireplaces and hardwood floors.
① 42 ☎ 🅾 All major cards

🍴 BON APPETIT
$$–$$$
25 XUAN VIEN
TEL 020/872-927
This is the place for hearty breakfasts, hamburgers, and other Western options, as well as Vietnamese fare. The bar is cozy, the decor lovely, and the service reliable.
🪑 40 🅾 None

🍴 BAGUETTE AU CHOCOLAT
$–$$
THAC BAC
TEL 020/871-766
www.hoasuaschool.com
Graduates of the Hoa Sua school/restaurant (see p. 248) staff this restaurant and bakery. The cuisine is both Western and Vietnamese, and the restaurant's ovens turn out bread, cakes, and pastries daily. A large open hearth can take the chill off after a long trek.
🪑 35 🅾 🅾 All major cards

🍴 MIMOSA
$
OPPOSITE 21–22 CAU MAY
TEL 020/871-377
A cheap and cheerful perch after a long climb, this long-time Sa Pa restaurant serves many Vietnamese and some Western dishes.
🪑 30 🅾 None

NORTH CENTRAL
DONG HOI

🏨 SUN SPA RESORT
🍴 **$$–$$$**
MY CANH, BAO NINH
QUANG BINH
TEL 052/842-999
FAX 052/842-555
www.sunsparesortvietnam.com
In the 370 miles (600 km) between Hue and Hanoi, there's no more pleasant accommodation than the Sun Spa Resort. The rooms are surprisingly sophisticated, with laptop portals, tasteful decor, and banks of windows. While new to the hospitality industry, the staff is well trained, and their earnest friendliness more than compensates for their lack of English.
① 234 🅿 🅾 🅾 🅾 🅾 🅾 All major cards

🏨 HIEU GIANG
$–$$
138 LE DUAN
TEL 053/856-856
FAX 053/856-859
Built in 2000, Dong Hoi's most expensive hotel is a decent option for travelers seeking proximity to the DMZ. The rooms are plain but functional, with air-conditioning, satellite TV, and minibars.
① 27 🅿 🅾 🅾 🅾 None

NAM DINH

🏨 VI HOANG
🍴 **$–$$**
153 NGUYEN DU
TEL 0350/849-290
FAX 0350/646-704
Run by Nam Dinh Tourism,

this is the best hotel in town, in a spot that overlooks the town's central park and lake. While you wouldn't write home about the accommodations, the hotel crams all the basics into small, comfortable rooms.
① 90 🅿 🅾 🅾 🅾 None

NINH BINH

🏨 THUY ANH HOTEL
$
55A TRUONG HAN SIEU
TEL 030/871-602
FAX 030/876-934
www.thuyanhhotel.com
To keep his hotel spotless and the staff attentive, the owner, Mr. De, holds monthly meetings and maintains rigorous quality control. The hotel deserves high praise for such cleanliness and attentiveness at budget rates. Rooms in the back wing are newer, more comfortable, and less noisy than streetside rooms. A rooftop bar catches the breeze at night.
① 37 🅾 🅾 🅾 🅾 All major cards

VINH

🏨 SAIGON KIM LIEN
$$–$$$
25 QUANG TRUNG

TEL 038/838-899
This state-run hotel is about as good as it gets in Vinh, though the decor is outdated. The hotel faces an East German–designed apartment complex.
ⓘ 77 🅿 ⓢ 🈂 🏋 🅂 All major cards

HUE & CENTRAL VIETNAM

DANANG

🏨 FURAMA RESORT DANANG
$$$$$
68 HO XUAN HUONG
TEL 0511/847-333
FAX 0511/847-220
www.furamavietnam.com
Vietnam's first and finest beach resort, Furama is a five-minute drive from downtown Danang, but a posh world away. The architecture is both Scandinavian simple and highly elegant. Balconies encourage lounging, and the hotel stakes a claim to its own stretch of China Beach. Guests can also relax in the hotel's lagoon pool.
ⓘ 198 🅿 ⓢ ⊟ ⓢ 🈂
🏋 🅂 All major cards

🏨 ROYAL HOTEL
$$
17 QUANG TRUNG
TEL 0511/823-295
FAX 0511/827-279
www.royaldananghotel.com
Danang's best budget option. Amenities are part Vietnamese (heavy drapes, clumsy signage, kitschy flourishes) and part Western, with decent lighting, comfortable furniture, wood floors, and free in-room Wi-Fi and ADSL access. There are also on-site massage facilities and a nightclub.
ⓘ 40 🅿 ⓢ ⓢ 🈂 🅂 All major cards

🍴 APSARA
$$$
222 TRAN PHU
TEL 0511/561-409
FAX 0511/562-001
www.apsara-danang.com
Apsara's decor was inspired

by the nearby Cham Museum. Outdoor gardens include a faithful copy of Phan Rang's Cham towers, and mealtime performances feature Cham dancing. But the food is all Vietnamese, highlighted by Danang's best seafood dishes.
🍴 300 ⓢ 🅂 All major cards

🍴 MY HANH
$$$
265 NGUYEN VAN THOAI
SON TRA DISTRICT
TEL 0511/831-494
This packed restaurant serves a mostly local clientele. Its menus don't detail prices or dishes in English, but the seafood is fresh and well prepared. Try the cuttlefish, the steamed grouper, the rocket shrimp, or the crab in tamarind sauce. You can't miss. The restaurant sits one street back from China Beach.
🍴 200 🅂 None

🍴 CHRISTIE'S RESTAURANT & THE COOL SPOT
$$
112 TRAN PHU
TEL 0511/824-040
Christie's menu draws from Vietnam, Italy, Japan, and Thailand, and they grill a remarkably good hamburger. The spot downstairs is little more than a pub and hosts meetings of Danang's Hash House Harriers running club.
🍴 25 ⓢ 🅂 None

HOI AN

🏨 HOI AN RIVERSIDE RESORT
$$$–$$$$$
175 CUA DAI
TEL 0510/864-800
FAX 0510/864-900
www.hoianriverresort.com
The Do River winds past this cluster of French-Vietnamese villas, set in a tropical garden several miles from Old Town and a half mile (1 km) from the beach. One of Hoi An's oldest resorts, it's a bit frayed around the edges, but the views are

lovely. From river-view rooms and the restaurant, you can watch farmers working sweet potato fields on the far bank.
ⓘ 62 🅿 🈂 🏋 🅂 All major cards

🏨 LIFE RESORT HOI AN
$$$–$$$$$
1 PHAM HONG THAI
TEL 0510/914-555
FAX 0510/914-515
www.life-resorts.com
A five-minute walk from Old Town, this riverside resort is the poshest place in Hoi An. The rooms are terraced, with an upper-level bedroom and lower-level seating area, fronted by a plushly furnished balcony. The large, inviting pool beside the river is complemented by a bar and a massage hut.
ⓘ 94 ⓢ 🅿 🈂 🅂 All major cards

🏨 LOTUS HOTEL
$$
330 CUA DAI
TEL 0510/923-357
FAX 0510/923-359
www.hoianlotushotel.com
This lower- to mid-range compound of modern villas lies a taxi ride from Old Town, with scheduled shuttles throughout the day. The smallish rooms are air-conditioned and provide good beds. The buffet breakfast is wanting, and the decor lacks polish, but at this price point, it's more or less what you might expect.
ⓘ 45 🅿 ⓢ 🈂 🅂 None

🍴 MANGO ROOMS
$$$
111 NGUYEN THAI HOC
TEL 0510/910-839
This eclectic Old Town hot spot is an incubator for some of the most fun, creative, and delicious fusion dishes around. The fusion here, however, is not with the traditional Europe but with Latin America. Go for the melt-in-your-mouth scallops, the tuna medallions, or the jumbo shrimp wrapped in beef. The

ambience is as irrepressibly hip and cheerful as Duc, the young owner-chef, who emigrated to the U.S. as a boy and returned to Vietnam in 2003.

🛏 105 💳 MC, V

🍴 GOOD MORNING, VIETNAM
$$
34 LE LOI
TEL 0510/910-227
This Italian-run chain restaurant makes for a fine detour through Italian fare when you need a break from rice and noodles. The pizza is superb, and the dining area is cozy. Look for other locations in Saigon, Vung Tau, Mui Ne, and Nha Trang.

🪑 30 💳 None

🍴 HAI SCOUT CAFÉ & RED BRIDGE COOKING SCHOOL
$$
98 NGUYEN THAI HOC
TEL 0510/863-210
www.visithoian.com
Old Town's Hai Scout serves traditional Vietnamese fare, and its charismatic chefs will show you how to create some of the dishes—squid salad, spring rolls, grilled fish in banana leaves—in an hour-long class before dining. Hai's sister outfit is the Red Bridge Cooking School, which offers a half-day class and lunch but not dinner.

🪑 67 💳 All major cards

HUE

🏨 CENTURY RIVERSIDE
🍴 $$$-$$$$$
49 LE LOI
TEL 054/823-390
FAX 054/823-394
www.centuryriversidehue.com
Once Hue's best hotel, this Soviet-inspired riverside hotel still touts its four-star rating from Vietnam Tourism, though that's simply the benefit of grandfathering. That said, all rooms are balconied, and the river views are grand, especially if you bunk in the right wing.

🛏 138 🅿 💿 ⬆ 💺 ⬇ 📺 💳 All major cards

🏨 SAIGON MORIN
$$$-$$$$$
30 LE LOI
TEL 054/823-526
FAX 054/825-155
www.morinhotel.com.vn
Opened in 1901 and spruced up during a 1995–97 renovation, the Morin is Hue's grande dame of hospitality, perched along the south side of the river at one end of the city's old French trestle.

🛏 180 🅿 ⬆ 💿 ⬇ 📺 💳 All major cards

SOMETHING SPECIAL

🏨 LA RESIDENCE
🍴 This is not just Hue's best hotel, but one of the top three in all Vietnam. Anchored by a 1930 guesthouse built for the colonial administration and restored for a 2005 grand opening, the hotel flaunts art deco lines, fixtures, and decor. The pool overlooks a lush, wild garden on the Perfume River's south bank, as well as the flag tower bastion of the citadel. Furnishings are comfortable, thematically consistent, and visually enticing. The business center is equipped with free Internet access, and the lobby is wired for Wi-Fi. Its Le Parfum restaurant (see below) is Hue's only fine-dining venue.
$$$$
5 LE LOI
TEL 054/837-475
FAX 054/837-476
www.la-residence-hue.com
🛏 122 🅿 💿 ⬆ ⬇ 💺 📺 💳 All major cards

🍴 LE PARFUM
$$$$
LA RESIDENCE, 5 LE LOI
TEL 054/837-475
FAX 054/837-476
www.la-residence-hue.com
At La Residence (see above), Le Parfum is Hue's only elegant fine-dining venue. Trimmed in art deco fixtures, the dining room's big windows take in river views. In the able hands of a German chef, the Western cuisine is as delicious as the decor.

Try the tuna steaks, breaded pork cutlets, and any salad with roasted eggplant and goat cheese.

🪑 146 💿 💺 💳 All major cards

🍴 AN DINH VIEN
$$-$$$
7 PHAM HONG THAI
TEL 054/824-076
FAX 054/833-019
If you come with a group—and make an advance request—you can deck yourself in the silk robes and headdresses of a king, queen, and attendant mandarins for dinner. Court musicians will lead your procession through the corridors to royal banquet rooms for a feast of royal fare. In a city widely celebrated for its cuisine, this is sumptuous dining. The presentations are fancifully arranged (e.g., radishes cut into peacocks, tomatoes sliced like lanterns), and the dishes excellent. Though it lacks the polish of a world-class venue, it's long on honesty and earnestness.

🪑 300 💺 💳 None

🍴 ONG TAO
$$-$$$
134 NGO DUC KE
TEL 054/822-057
Mr. Minh used to run Ong Tao out of a garden in the Imperial City, but his crab and asparagus soup and the bo la lot taste just as fine at this less charming venue in Hue's hotel hub.

🪑 80 💳 None

🍴 TROPICAL GARDEN
$$-$$$
5 CHU VAN AN
TEL 054/828-074
A troupe of traditional musicians plays for patrons every evening in this restaurant's indoor dining hall. Outside, diners sit under a thatched cabana and amid an intimate tropical garden. The food passes muster, with well-prepared beef, fish, and shrimp dishes, while the service is just adequate.

🪑 100 💳 MC, V

🍴 MANDARIN CAFÉ
$$

12 HUNG VUONG

TEL 054/821-281

For 15 years the Mandarin has been dishing out hearty fare to a mostly backpacker clientele. The affable owner, Mr. Cuu, is an excellent resource for travel info regarding central Vietnam.

🔲 60 🚫 None

■ SOUTH-CENTRAL COAST

DAI LANH BEACH

🍴 THUY TA
$

HIGHWAY 1

TEL 058/842-530

FAX 058/842-101

A thatched cabana shades a dozen tables at this seaside spot in a day-trippers' compound off the main drag. Dai Lanh supports a small fishing fleet, so the seafood here is fresh. The dishes are simple, but hearty and nicely prepared.

🔲 40 🚫 None

LONG HAI

🏨 ANOASIS BEACH RESORT
$$$

DOMAIN KY VAN

TEL 064/868-228

FAX 064/868-229

www.anoasisresort.com.vn

Cottage and family bungalows and villas drape the hillside of this 32-acre (13 ha) tropical getaway that overlooks a long stretch of beach. Decor in the bright, high-ceilinged bungalows features terra-cotta tiles and furnishings styled from green-painted wrought-iron. The resort's general manager used to run a number of posh Sofitel properties in Vietnam, and this is his "retirement project."

🛏 46 🅿 🚭 🏊 🏋
🚫 All major cards

NHA TRANG

🏨 ANA MANDARA RESORT & SPA
$$$$$

TRAN PHU

TEL 058/522-522

FAX 058/525-828

www.sixsenses.com

Fronting Nha Trang's municipal beach, the Ana Mandara is renowned for exquisite service, its Six Senses Spa, beautifully appointed bungalows, and tropical gardens nourished with water from bamboo pipes. The resort's two pools and two restaurants overlook the sea and offshore islands.

🛏 74 🅿 🚭 🚭 🏊 🏋
🚫 All major cards

🏨 SUNRISE BEACH RESORT NHA TRANG
$$$$–$$$$$

12 TRAN PHU

TEL 058/820-999

FAX 058/822-866

www.sunrisenhatrang.com.vn

The Sunrise towers over the beachside boulevard in an elegant, neo–French colonial high-rise. Highlights include marble floors, spacious rooms with balconies and sea views, a tenth-floor lounge, and an ornate, round pool that resembles a Roman bath.

🛏 121 🅿 🚭 🚭 🚭 🏊
🏋 🚫 All major cards

🏨 YASAKA SAIGON NHATRANG
$$$–$$$$$

18 TRAN PHU

TEL 058/820-090

FAX 058/820-000

www.yasanhatrang.com

At this Vietnamese-Japanese venture, the narrow end fronts the ocean, but jutting alcoves in every room provide sea views. You'll find free Wi-Fi and a tour desk in the lobby, an on-site disco, and no less than seven rooms devoted to karaoke.

🛏 201 🅿 🚭 🚭 🏊 🏋
🚫 All major cards

🏨 NHA TRANG LODGE
$$–$$$$

42 TRAN PHU

TEL 058/810-900

FAX 058/828-800

www.nt-lodge.com

This solid mid-range option on beachfront Tran Phu boasts balconies and ocean vistas in every room. The blonde-wood furnishings are tasteful and comfortable. Guests are granted a half hour of free Internet access in the ground-floor business office. The adjacent hotel casino stays open through early morning.

🛏 121 🅿 🚭 🏊 🚫 All major cards

🏨 BAO DAI VILLAS
$$–$$$

CAU DA

VINH NGUYEN

TEL 058/590-147

FAX 058/590-146

www.vngold.com/nt/baodai/

The setting and views here are spectacular. But these five villas offer rather drab guest rooms, while the hotel lacks polish and suffers from its proximity to a working port.

🛏 48 🅿 🚭 🚫 All major cards

🏨 DONG PHUONG 2
$

96 A6/1 TRAN PHU

TEL 058/814-580

FAX 058/825-986

This nine-story budget hotel sits amid a bank of like hotels across from a water park on the municipal beach. The tiled rooms are spotless, and sea-view rooms include private balconies. The English-speaking staff is helpful and charming.

🛏 91 🅿 🚭 🚭 🚫 All major cards

🍴 TRUC LINH
$$–$$$

21 BIET THU

TEL 058/825-742

FAX 058/895-290

Seafood is the specialty at this corner spot, one block in from beachside Tran Phu. The best tables sit amid potted plants on

HOTELS & RESTAURANTS

terraces overlooking the sidewalks. A chef fires up some dishes on an outdoor grill. In addition to seafood and Vietnamese dishes, the menu offers American T-bones and Australian beef.

🛏 200 🚫 None

SOMETHING SPECIAL

🍴 LAC CANH

A Nha Trang institution since before 1975, Lac Canh is a griller's delight. Here diners cook their own marinated slabs of tuna, chunks of spicy beef, and other meats on small, tableside, charcoal-stoked braziers. The menu otherwise roams the Vietnamese repertoire and packs a punch with its rocket shrimp spring rolls. Lac Canh is especially popular with the locals and is always crowded, both inside and outside in a shaded dining area.

$$
44 NGUYEN BINH KIEM
TEL 058/821-391
🛏 100 🚫 None

🍴 NHA TRANG SEAFOODS

$$
46 NGUYEN THI MINH KHAI
TEL 058/822-664
FAX 058/524-729
This place has a tremendous reputation among locals, who throng to its fluorescent-lit dining areas for great seafood. Diners can sit inside, as well as on an upstairs terrace or outdoor courtyard. Try the mackerel, tuna, or squid.

🛏 150 🚫 None

🍴 HAO VAN LAI

$–$$
1D BIET THU
TEL 058/827-292
This sidewalk eatery in the budget hotel district serves everything from burgers and fish and chips to Vietnamese noodle dishes and Japanese and Chinese stir-fry. Hong Kong–style barbecues are the specialty.

🛏 42 🚫 None

NINH HOA

🏨 EVASON HIDEAWAY & SPA

$$$$$
NINH VAN BAY
TEL 058/728-222
FAX 058/728-223
www.sixsenses.com
You get your own butler at the Evason Hideaway, as well as your own pool and wine cellar—among the reasons this is the most expensive night's stay in the country. While the resort is state owned, the management is foreign, and the service is sophisticated. Inaccessible by land, the bungalows cling to the end of a rocky peninsula on land once managed by the military.

ⓘ 58 🚫 🅿 🚭 🛌
🚫 All major cards

PHAN THIET/MUI NE

🏨 PRINCESS D'ANNAM RESORT & SPA

$$$$$
KE GA BAY
TEL 08/840-9646
FAX 08/840-9647
www.princessannam.com
Spread over 45 acres (18 ha) on the booming coast south of Phan Thiet, the Princess d'Annam rivals Danang's Furama (see p. 251) for sheer luxury and commitment to a stylistic ethic. Designed by a renowned Singaporean architect, the villas and their furnishings evoke a cool, modernist sensibility. Nine pools inspire indolence, as does the 20,000-square-foot (1,850 sq m) spa. The private beach looks out on a hundred-year-old landmark lighthouse.

ⓘ 58 🅿 🚫 🚭 🚭 🛌
🚫 All major cards

🏨 COCO BEACH

$$$
58 NGUYEN DINH CHIEU
MUI NE BEACH
TEL 062/847-111
FAX 062/847-115
www.cocobeach.net
You'd be hard-pressed to find a

HOTELS

An indication of the maximum high-season cost of a double room with breakfast is given by $ signs.

$$$$$	Over $175
$$$$	$125–$175
$$$	$75–$125
$$	$25–$75
$	Under $25

RESTAURANTS

An indication of the cost of a three-course dinner, without drinks, is given by $ signs.

$$$$$	Over $20
$$$$	$15–$20
$$$	$9–$15
$$	$3–$9
$	Under $3

---

more exquisitely manicured garden than the one at Coco Beach, and there's plenty more to keep you within the confines of this high-walled compound. The varnished wood bungalows are cozy, nicely situated, and angled so everyone has a view of the sea from their verandas. One restaurant teeters over the strand, while the other spills tables and chairs onto a veranda with ocean views. There's also a fine on-site pub.

ⓘ 31 🚫 🅿 🚭 🚭
🚫 All major cards

🏨 NOVOTEL OCEAN DUNES & GOLF RESORT

$$$
1 TON DUC THANG
TEL 062/822-393
FAX 062/825-682
www.accorhotels.com/asia
Embraced by a Nick Faldo–designed golf course on three sides and by beachfront to the east, the Novotel is the dean of the local resort scene. Every room boasts a private balcony and views of the ocean or golf course. Minutes from downtown Phan Thiet, the resort feels far removed. *Golf* voted the ninth hole here one of the 500 best holes worldwide.

ⓘ 123 🅿 🚫 🚭 🚫 🚭
🛌 🚫 All major cards

SOMETHING SPECIAL

🍴 RUNG (FOREST)

The same cultural eccentricities that inspired the Crazy House in Dalat and the Cao Dai Great Temple in Tay Ninh also spawned this quirky restaurant-in-a-forest on the Mui Ne strip. The food is beside the point here, where tree slices serve as tabletops, cement columns are wrapped in bark, and mechanized bamboo chimes serenade diners on a terrace garden. Kids are thrilled by the decor. The strains of a *dan bau* fiddle accompany surprisingly good Vietnamese and Western cuisine.

$$$
67 NGUYEN DINH CHIEU
MUI NE BEACH
TEL 062/847-589
FAX 062/847-590
🚪 150 🔇 All major cards

QUY NHON

🏨 LIFE RESORT QUY NHON

$$$-$$$$$
GHENH RANG
BAI DAI BEACH
TEL 056/840-132
FAX 056/840-138
www.life-resorts.com
This resort lies well off the blazed tourist trail on Bai Dai Beach, 10 miles (16 km) south of Quy Nhon. Offering stunning views, the rooms are big (a minimum 450 sq ft/42 sq m) and soulfully imagined, bearing architectural echoes of the Cham culture.
ⓘ 63 🅿 🔇 🔇 🏊 🏋
🔇 All major cards

SON TINH

🏨 MY KHE RESORT

🍴 **$**
TINH KHE
TEL 055/686-111
FAX 055/686-064
My Khe fronts a beautiful and largely deserted 4-mile (7 km) strand along the South China Sea that's great for swimming. The spacious rooms are tiled and clean, and the decor is

nicer than at most hotels this price. If you're overnighting in the My Lai area, choose this cheerful spot—after touring the memorial, you'll want it.
ⓘ 20 🅿 🔇 🔇 None

WHALE ISLAND

SOMETHING SPECIAL

🏨 WHALE ISLAND
🍴 RESORT

Twenty-eight bamboo-and-thatch bungalows hug a short strand that overlooks a blue-water bay on otherwise deserted Hon Ong (Whale Island). These quaint bungalows are purposely rustic, in keeping with the principles of responsible ecotourism. That said, electricity powers the lights, and there is hot water in the winter months. Diving and snorkeling are favorite pastimes, as are catamaran sailing, canoeing, birding, swimming, and hiking on a 2.5-mile (4 km) loop trail.

$$$$
2 ME LINH
NHA TRANG
TEL 058/513-871
FAX 058/513-873
www.whaleislandresort.com
ⓘ 28 🔇 MC, V

SOUTHERN & CENTRAL HIGHLANDS

BUON MA THUOT

🏨 THANG LOI

$$
1 PHAN CHU TRINH
TEL 050/857-615
FAX 050/857-622
Thang Loi is the best downtown lodging. Spacious tiled rooms feature attractive, lacquered wood furnishings and big bathrooms with tubs.
ⓘ 40 🔇 🔇 None

🍴 THANH VAN

$
20 LY THUONG KIET
TEL 050/859-561
Thanh Van only serves *nem*

nuong, a spring roll of pork strips, lettuce, herbs, dried banana slices, and cucumbers that you pack and roll yourself. The dipping sauce is peanut based. Locals crowd this and neighboring nem joints nightly.
🚪 80 🔇 None

DALAT

SOMETHING SPECIAL

🏨 SOFITEL DALAT
🍴 PALACE

With chandeliers in the lobby, in the chambers, and in the bathrooms, the Dalat Palace is the most sumptuous hotel in Vietnam. In contrast to the hotel's art deco facade, the interior is opulent Victorian. The rooms' heavy draperies, brass bathroom fixtures, old-style floor fans, 1920s-era telephone handsets, and oriental rugs on polished wood floors, complemented by the notes of a pianist drifting up from the salon, are the elements of a working time machine. Its Le Rabelais restaurant offers gourmet French cuisine in one of the city's most elegant venues.

$$$$-$$$$$
12 TRAN PHU
TEL 063/825-444
FAX 063/825-457
www.sofitel.com
ⓘ 43 🅿 🔇 🔇 🔇
🔇 All major cards

🏨 NOVOTEL DALAT

$$-$$$
7 TRAN PHU
TEL 063/825-777
FAX 063/825-888
www.accorhotels.com/asia
Opened in 1932 as L'Hôtel du Parc, the Novotel is a polished mid-range hotel and the best option in town after the opulent Dalat Palace. Daylight streams through the antique casement windows, showing off the polished wood floors. The stairway wraps around a classic open elevator shaft that houses an antique cabin of iron filigree.
ⓘ 144 🅿 🔇 🔇 🔇
🔇 All major cards

HOTELS & RESTAURANTS

🍴 CAFÉ DE LA POSTE
$$$
12 TRAN PHU
TEL 063/825-444
Once a French colonial department store, this café now offers bistro dining downstairs, with massive burgers and other Western dishes, and fine Vietnamese dining upstairs at the **Y Nhu Y.** Aside from Le Rabelais at the Dalat Palace, these two restaurants deliver the city's finest mealtime ambience.
🪑 90 🚭 💳 💳 All major cards

🍴 NAM SON
$$
54 KHU HOA BINH
TEL 063/821-147
Centrally located Nam Son serves a broad menu of Vietnamese dishes anchored by shrimp, pork, chicken, beef, and fish served with locally grown vegetables. The plate-glass facade frames views of downtown and the central market.
🪑 60 🚭 None

🍴 V CAFÉ
$$
1/1 BUI THI XUAN
TEL 063/837-576
Burritos, quesadillas, nachos, and Tabasco—it's all here. While the neutral decor won't kid you into thinking you're in Oaxaca, the dishes are cheap and tasty. Save room for the lemon meringue and chocolate pies, and say hola to Michael, the proprietor, who first visited Dalat in 1970 and now may never leave.
🪑 40 💳 All major cards

🍴 LONG HOA
$
6 3 THANH 2
TEL 063/822-934
This menu cuts to the marrow of Vietnamese cuisine, with one slight diversion for spaghetti. Specialties include hot pots, barbecued shrimp, and venison. Try the excellent homemade yogurt for dessert.
🪑 42 🚭 None

🍴 NHAT LY
$
88 PHAN DINH PHUNG
TEL 063/821-651
In Dalat's backpacker district, Nhat Ly offers fine dining at budget prices. Try the shrimp in tamarind sauce, or any of the pork or beef dishes in tomato sauce. Vegetarian fare is a hit.
🪑 38 🚭 None

KON TUM

🏨 DAKBLA HOTEL
$-$$
2 PHAN DINH PHUNG
TEL 060/863-333
FAX 060/863-336
The Dakbla's best attributes are its architecture, which mirrors the blade-shaped roofs of the local Bahnar people, and its location, on the banks of its namesake river. The rooms are decent, with hot water and air-conditioning, and a helpful tourist bureau staffs a ground-floor office.
🛏 42 💳 None

◼ HO CHI MINH CITY

HOTELS

🏨 CARAVELLE HOTEL
$$$$$
19 LAM SON SQUARE
DISTRICT 1
TEL 08/823-4999
FAX 08/824-3999
www.caravellehotel.com
Opened on Lam Son Square in 1959, the Caravelle is a Saigon classic and landmark unto itself (see p. 196). The ten original stories were refurbished in 1998 and complemented by a neighboring 24-story tower. The tenth-floor Saigon Saigon Bar in the old wing remains the city's best perch for a drink.
🛏 335 🅿 💳 💳 💳 💳 All major cards

🏨 LEGEND HOTEL SAIGON
$$$$$
2A–4A TON DUC THANG
DISTRICT 1
TEL 08/823-3333
FAX 08/823-2333
www.legendsaigon.com
Opened in 2001, the Legend caters to international guests with four on-site restaurants, serving Japanese, Chinese, Italian, and international cuisine. Some rooms overlook the river, and the hotel boasts three pools. The vaulted stained-glass ceiling in the lobby recalls an Edwardian-era railway station.
🛏 282 🅿 💳 💳 💳 💳 All major cards

🏨 PARK HYATT SAIGON
$$$$$
2 LAM SON SQUARE
DISTRICT 1
TEL 08/824-1234
FAX 08/823-7569
www.saigon.park.hyatt.com
Boasting great views from its upper stories, this Hyatt does everything you'd expect of a high-end New York hotel, only better, with an earnest, highly trained staff. The finest in-room touch? A shower head that rains onto the bathroom's marbled floor. Were he still living, this is where Graham Greene would hang his hat.
🛏 252 🅿 💳 💳 💳 💳 All major cards

🏨 SHERATON SAIGON
$$$$$
88 DONG KHOI
DISTRICT 1
TEL 08/827-2828
FAX 08/827-2929
www.sheraton.com/saigon
The Sheraton is its own world within a world. Inside are eight bars and restaurants, a spa, pool, tennis courts, and boutiques. The plush, business-ready rooms overlook the river and the city's top attractions.
🛏 382 💳 💳 💳 💳 All major cards

🏨 SOFITEL PLAZA
🍴 SAIGON
$$$$–$$$$$
17 LE DUAN
DISTRICT 1
TEL 08/824-1555
FAX 08/824-1666
www.accorhotels.com/asia

Among the world's best business hotels, the Sofitel sits on Le Duan, 150 yards (135 m) from the U.S. Consulate. Rooms boast all the five-star amenities, while the poolside bar specializes in gin and vermouth. Its L'Olivier restaurant (see below) offers fabled French cuisine.

ⓘ 290 🅿 🚭 ⬆ 🄰 ⚊
🎽 🄲 All major cards

🏨 RENAISSANCE RIVERSIDE HOTEL SAIGON
$$$–$$$$$
8–15 TON DUC THANG
DISTRICT 1
TEL 08/822-0033
FAX 08/822-5666
www.renaissancehotels.com/sgnbr
Marriott's only hotel in Vietnam, the Renaissance rises 21 floors above the river, with sweeping views. A classic, glass-vaulted atrium lightens the main corridors, and the spacious rooms feature colonial decor.

ⓘ 349 🅿 ⬆ 🄰 ⚊ 🎽
🄲 All major cards

🏨 REX HOTEL
$$$–$$$$$
141 NGUYEN HUE
DISTRICT 1
TEL 08/829-2185
FAX 08/829-6536
www.rexhotelvietnam.com
During the war, this building served as the U.S. Bachelor Officers' Quarters, while the ground floor hosted the legendary Five O'Clock Follies press briefings for a spell. Today, the hotel is a relic, though better days may be in store. In 2006, a renovation and five-star upgrade was put into motion. Thankfully intact is the rooftop terrace, which plays second fiddle to the Caravelle as a downtown perch for a drink but is well worth the elevator ride up.

ⓘ 217 ⬆ 🄰 ⚊ 🎽
🄲 All major cards

🏨 MAJESTIC SAIGON
$$$–$$$$$
1 DONG KHOI
DISTRICT 1

TEL 08/829-5517
FAX 08/829-5510
www.majesticsaigon.com.vn
Owned by Saigon Tourist, the recently restored Majestic is one of the city's colonial grande dames. At the base of Dong Khoi, its art deco facade curves around the corner, while balconies jut from its river-view rooms. Look for the original stained-glass dome in the lobby. The rooms are comfortable but lack the elegant touch of a refined eye this gem deserves.

ⓘ 176 🄰 ⬆ 🄰 ⚊ 🎽
🄲 All major cards

🏨 METROPOLE
$$$–$$$$
148 TRAN HUNG DAO
DISTRICT 1
TEL 08/920-1939
FAX 08/920-1960
www.libertyhotels.com.vn
The Metropole sits on the edge of District 1, near the budget backpacker zone. During the Vietnam War, it quartered U.S. officers and thus was bombed several times. Today, the privately owned hotel includes a restaurant, an ecotourism facility, a third-floor pool, in-room satellite TV, and air-conditioning.

ⓘ 76 🅿 ⬆ 🄰 ⚊ 🎽
🄲 All major cards

🏨 CONTINENTAL
$$–$$$
132–134 DONG KHOI
DISTRICT 1
TEL 08/829-9201
FAX 08/829-0936
www.continentalvietnam.com
Like Tennessee Williams' Blanche DuBois, the Continental has seen better days and is sustained by them. Still, it's a solid mid-range option, with spacious rooms. The famed Continental Shelf terrace bar is today a forgettable, walled-in annex to the hotel's Italian restaurant.

ⓘ 83 ⬆ 🄰 🎽 🄲 All major cards

🏨 EQUATORIAL
$$–$$$
242 TRAN BINH TRONG
DISTRICT 5

TEL 08/839-7777
FAX 08/839-0011
www.equatorial.com
The Equatorial occupies a ten-story tower between downtown and Cholon. Unless you plan to explore the latter, the location is a bit far-flung. But the well-appointed, modern rooms represent the city's cheapest five-star option.

ⓘ 333 🅿 ⬆ 🄰 ⚊ 🎽
🄲 All major cards

🏨 SPRING HOTEL
$$
44–46 LE THANH TON
DISTRICT 1
TEL 08/829-7362
FAX 08/822-1383
When you factor in its price and central location, the Spring may be the best deal in town. Rooms come with satellite TV and comfortable beds with clean linens. Breakfast in the lobby features a set menu.

ⓘ 45 ⬆ 🄰 🄲 MC, V

RESTAURANTS

🍽 L'OLIVIER
$$$$$
SOFITEL PLAZA SAIGON
17 LE DUAN
DISTRICT 1
TEL 08/824-1555
Every seven weeks, a marquee chef parachutes in from somewhere like France or Spain for a weeklong tour de force in the kitchen of the Sofitel Plaza's French restaurant (see above). Between tours, the regular Cambodia-born, French-reared chef explores French cuisine in this airy space overlooking South Vietnam's old embassy row. Each month, the chef offers a half-day cooking class in French cuisine, while the sous chef does the same for Vietnamese cuisine.

🍴 80 🄰 🄰 🄲 All major cards

🍽 SQUARE ONE
$$$$$
2 LAM SON SQUARE
DISTRICT 1

🄰 Nonsmoking ⬆ Elevator 🄰 Air-conditioning 🄰 Indoor/⚊ Outdoor pool 🎽 Gym 🄲 Credit cards   **KEY**

TEL 08/824-1234
FAX 08/823-7569
Teams of chefs man five open kitchens scattered about this Saigon steak-and-seafood place, with terraced and private dining areas that overlook the storied Opera House. The lobsters and jumbo shrimp are plucked from on-site aquariums, while steaks are flown in from the U.S., Australia, and New Zealand.
🔧 80 🚭 🔳 None

🍴 MAXIM'S NAM AN
$$$–$$$$
13/15/17 DONG KHOI
DISTRICT I
TEL 08/829-6676
FAX 08/823-0644
Maxim's is a storied 1950s–60s nightclub, with a stage, dance floor, booths, and raised seating. But it's all dining now. The chic restaurant serves Vietnamese classics. Try the grilled red snapper and shrimp paste appetizer, cooked around a sugarcane core. A three-piece orchestra plays jazz and pop nightly.
🔧 200 🚭 🔳 🔳 MC, V

🍴 THE TEMPLE CLUB
$$$–$$$$
29–31 TON THAT THIEP
DISTRICT I
TEL 08/829-9244
FAX 08/914-4271
www.templevn.com
During the colonial era, this spot served as a guesthouse for pilgrims to the still-active Hindu temple across the street. The brick walls, colonial fixtures, separate bar, and club room out back portend a great Saigon evening. The largely Vietnamese menu specializes in regional street foods.
🔧 80 🚭 🔳 🔳 All major cards

🍴 COM NGON
$$$
88 NGUYEN DU
DISTRICT I
TEL 08/827-7896
FAX 08/827-7895
Traditional musicians play nightly on the ground floor of this renovated three-story French

villa. The upper two stories are balconied, and the music carries up through the building's open core. As its name ("rice delicious") suggests, the ubiquitous grain provides the foundation of these meals. The third-floor open kitchen grills seafood and meats, while downstairs kitchens add their own aromas.
🔧 170 🔳 🔳 All major cards

🍴 MANDARINE
$$$
IIA NGO VAN NAM
DISTRICT I
TEL 08/822 9783
FAX 08/825-6185
Dine on one of six levels in this refurbished home on a calm side street in the midst of downtown. The specialty here is duck, though the menu strays as far as bird's nest soup, shark fin soup, and sliced abalone. Musicians play Vietnamese tunes on Tuesdays and Thursdays and European classics other nights.
ℹ️ 160 🔳 All major cards

🍴 SKEWERS
$$$
9A THAI VAN LUNG
DISTRICT I
TEL & FAX 08/822-4798
Skewers' menu roams the Mediterranean, from sea bass basted in Moroccan sauces to Greek gyros and Turkish baklava. The house specialty is anything skewered. Lamb chops imported from New Zealand are as plump and round as small steaks. Also try the goat cheese appetizer, nestled in a crumbly homemade pastry cup. Finish with the cinnamon-spiced apples and ice cream.
🔧 80 🔳 🔳 All major cards

🍴 BUNTA
$$–$$$
136 NAM KY KHOI NGHIA
DISTRICT I
TEL 08/822-9913
FAX 08/822-9915
Another upscale place for street food, Bunta specializes in dishes built atop a bed of thin rice noodles. Bowls of

HOTELS
An indication of the maximum high-season cost of a double room with breakfast is given by $ signs.

$$$$$	Over $175
$$$$	$125–$175
$$$	$75–$125
$$	$25–$75
$	Under $25

RESTAURANTS
An indication of the cost of a three-course dinner, without drinks, is given by $ signs.

$$$$$	Over $20
$$$$	$15–$20
$$$	$9–$15
$$	$3–$9
$	Under $3

dry or wet soups are filling and carefully arranged.
🔧 150 🔳 🔳 MC, V

🍴 GIVRAL CAFÉ & RESTAURANT
$$–$$$
169 DONG KHOI
DISTRICT I
TEL 08/824-2750
From Vietnamese noodles to curries to Australian sirloin, the Givral covers a variety of international bases. But it works better as a café than a restaurant. The historic spot on Lam Son Square served as the model for Graham Greene's milk bar in The Quiet American, and it remains one of the best places to watch passersby.
🔧 54 🔳 🔳 All major cards

🍴 SANTA LUCIA
$$–$$$
14 NGUYEN HUE
DISTRICT I
TEL 08/822-6562
All the Italian basics, including great lasagna, are served here on a busy boulevard between the colonial French Hôtel de Ville and the Saigon River.
🔧 50 🔳 🔳 All major cards

🍴 TU CHON NGON
$$–$$$
25 LE THANH TON

DISTRICT I
TEL 08/824-3790
FAX 08/824-3931
It's a Vietnamese smorgasbord at this Saigon restaurant. The buffet is fresh, extensive, and delicious, featuring grilled skewers of pork, shrimp, squid, and oysters, cooked to order. Save room for a bowl of che dau van (bean pudding) with a dollop of creamy coconut sauce.
⊞ 120 ⊗ ⊗ All major cards

🍴 ALIBABA
$$
60 LE THANH TON
DISTRICT I
TEL 08/823-3594
Generous portions, a quiet setting, and understated decor are the hallmarks of this Indian restaurant, where the spices don't come too spicy. Try the vegetable samosa.
🚻 50 ⊗ ⊗ ⊗ MC, V

🍴 LITTLE SAIGON
$$
185/16 PHAM NGU LAO
DISTRICT I
TEL 08/836-0678
FAX 08/836-7947
On a well-trodden alley in the backpacker district, Little Saigon is a nicely lit indoor-outdoor place that delivers all of the Vietnamese basics, as well as burgers, pizza, Hue cuisine, Japanese cuisine, vegetarian fare, clay pots, and hot pots.
⊞ 46 ⊗ All major cards

🍴 MY HUONG
$
131 NGUYEN TRI PHUONG
DISTRICT 5
TEL 08/856-3586
After exploring Cholon, stop here for delicious (and deliciously cheap) wonton and dry pork noodle soups. Stainless-steel tables double as rolling and wonton prep surfaces, while 14 wall and ceiling fans keep patrons cool.
⊞ 80 ⊗ None

SOMETHING SPECIAL

🍴 QUAN AN NGON
It's standing room only for lunch and dinner at this modern Saigon classic, where street food is king and the ambience is perfect. Here you'll find the best *bun bo Hue, bun thit nuong, banh xeo, che,* and *pho,* but you don't have to sit on tiny stools or suck in bus exhaust to indulge this fare. The dining areas spill from a gutted French villa into courtyards and up stairways to balconied perches in adjoining annexes. The prices are ridiculously low, the clientele mostly expats and overseas Vietnamese.
$
138 NAM KY KHOI NGHIA
DISTRICT I
TEL 08/825-7179
FAX 08/825-7178
⊞ 500 ⊗ None

▦ MEKONG DELTA

CAN THO

🏨 GOLF HOTEL
$$–$$$$$
2 HAI BA TRUNG
TEL 071/812-210
FAX 071/812-282
http://golfhotel.vnn.vn/g_cantho.htm
There's not a golf course within 50 miles (80 km) of this grass green tower, but it still rates as the best digs on Can Tho's main drag. The carpeted rooms are also painted grass green. Bathrooms are especially nice. The second and eighth floors host dining rooms.
🚻 101 🅿 ⊗ ⊟ ⊗ ⊠
🎙 ⊗ All major cards

🏨 QUOC TE (INTERNATIONAL) HOTEL
$–$$
12 HAI BA TRUNG
TEL 071/822-080
FAX 071/821-039
A somewhat tired, lower- to mid-range hotel with musty industrial carpets and polyester spreads. It is set right on the riverfront, though. The air-

conditioning works fine, but you have to hold up the shower nozzles while bathing. Management claims an upgrade is in the works.
🚻 50 ⊟ ⊗ ⊗ None

🍴 DU THUYEN CAN THO
$$$
NINH KIEU WHARF
TEL 071/810-841
This boat-based eatery shoves off from the wharf at 8 p.m. for a 90-minute river cruise. While under way, you can indulge a menu of traditional Vietnamese cuisine that includes such regional specialties as grilled mouse and weasel meat.
⊞ 550 ⊗ None

🍴 SAO HOM (EVENING STAR)
$$–$$$
HAI BA TRUNG
TEL 071/815-616
Perched along the river in a restored French colonial market, Sao Hom boasts the best real estate of any restaurant in town. Its menu runs from East to West, including Mekong specialties and good pizza.
⊞ 60 ⊗ MC, V

🍴 NAM BO
$$
50 HAI BA TRUNG
TEL 071/823-908
A balcony spot with views of the esplanade, the Ho Chi Minh statue, and the river, Nam Bo is the second best perch in town after Sao Hom. This tried-and-true place is popular with foreign diners, thanks largely to the setting and lovely ambience of its old French building. The menu spans Vietnamese, Western, pizza, and vegetarian, while the varied beer list includes Guinness.
⊞ 80 ⊗ All major cards

🍴 MEKONG
$–$$
38 HAI BA TRUNG
TEL 071/821-646
Open since 1965, but for a five-year hiccup after 1975, the Mekong fronts the river

HOTELS & RESTAURANTS

on Hai Ba Trung. The friendly owners speak English, and their ample, affordable menu is almost wholly Vietnamese.
🎫 28 🚫 None

CHAU DOC

🏨 VICTORIA CHAU DOC
$$$–$$$$$
32 LE LOI
TEL 076/865-010
FAX 076/865-020
www.victoriahotels-asia.com
One of five Victoria hotels in Vietnam, the Chau Doc looms large on the river. The floors are wood planked, and river-view rooms have balconies.
🛏 92 🅿 ⇄ 🏊 🏖 📺
🚫 All major cards

🏨 TRUNG NGUYEN
$–$$
86 BACH DANG
TEL 076/866-158
FAX 076/868-674
Unlike other budget hotels in Chau Doc, Trung Nguyen powers up its generator for air-conditioning during the city's frequent power outages. While small, the tiled rooms are scrupulously clean, the beds are great, and the hotel will loan you a DVD player.
🛏 15 🏊 🚫 All major cards

HA TIEN

🏨 DU HUNG
$
17A TRAN HAU
TEL 077/951-555
FAX 077/852-267
The staff doesn't speak English, but the manager is learning, and their friendly demeanor more than compensates. Rooms are tiled. Amenities include air-conditioning, refrigerators, and hot showers.
🛏 24 🅿 ⇄ 🏊 🚫 None

🍴 HUONG BIEN
$
44 TO CHAU
TEL 077/852-072
A simple rice place with a truly great kitchen, just off the waterfront with views

of an old French hotel. The seafood is fresh, the portions are generous, and the beverages are refrigerated. It's all Vietnamese food and all good.
🎫 90 🚫 None

MY THO

🏨 CHUONG DUONG
$–$$
10 30 THANG 4
TEL 073/870-875
FAX 073/874-250
www.chuongduonghotel.com
This cheerfully bright place on the river is plagued by director's choice decor and musty rooms—but as good as it gets in My Tho. The rooms do boast river views, with balconies on the second floor.
🛏 27 🅿 🏊 🚫 None

PHU QUOC

🏨 MANGO BAY
$$
ONG LANG BEACH
090/338-2207
www.mangobayphuquoc.com
This collection of tastefully appointed, thatched-roofed bungalows on the island's west side boasts great sunset views. Far from the developing strip on Long Beach, this isolated getaway is perfect for reading, lounging, or simply enjoying the peaceful surroundings. The wonderful on-site restaurant is perched on a terrace along the water, and decent snorkeling lies just offshore.
🛏 16 🅿 🚫 None

RACH GIA

🏨 HONG NAM
$–$$
BLOCK B1 LY THAI TO
TEL 077/873-090
FAX 077/873-424
Beside the town market and near plenty of decent places to eat, Hong Nam is new, its rooms equipped with air-conditioning, refrigerators, desks, and phones. Some of the rooms have several beds.
🛏 28 🅿 🏊 🚫 None

🍴 HAI AU
$$
2 NGUYEN TRUNG TRUC
TEL 077/863-740
While this restaurant was obviously built as a reception hall for weddings and other functions, the terrace along the canal makes for pleasant, canopied dining. The menu is all Vietnamese and well executed. Try the grilled pork.
🎫 500 🚫 None

🍴 NGOC HANH
$
12–16 NGUYEN TRI PHUONG
TEL 077/877-737
Behind the town market, this street bistro dishes up plain but delicious fare in a kitchen that abuts the sidewalk to entice passersby. Diners sit inside under a high ceiling or in a courtyard where street performers sometimes entertain.
🎫 120 🚫 None

VINH LONG

🏨 CUU LONG B HOTEL
$–$$
1 1 THANG 5
TEL 070/823-656
FAX 070/823-848
Vinh Long's best hotel falls short with polyester drapes and bedspreads, thin foam mattresses, and steel-framed doors of opaque glass, but its riverside setting is grand. The balconied rooms are equipped with air-conditioning, small refrigerators, and local TV.
🛏 34 ⇄ 🏊 🚫 MC, V

🍴 PHUONG THUY
$$
1 1 THANG 5
TEL 070/824-786
Perched along the Mekong, this place offers great upriver views to the My Thuan Bridge. The food's only so-so, but you can eat your fill of shrimp, fish, squid, frog, and other Vietnamese favorites.
🎫 80 🚫 None

SHOPPING

The low cost of labor has turned Vietnam into a deliriously attractive shopping experience for buyers with First World spending power. Silks, tailored suits, and such handicrafts as ceramics, lacquerware, baskets, and wood carvings remain popular items throughout the country.

Most Vietnamese cities and towns orbit a market that caters to local needs, where merchants sell such staples as food, clothing, and household goods. Westerners generally visit these markets out of curiosity, though you're apt to find far better buys here than in shops geared to tourists.

Traditionally, most items for sale lack price tags, though that trend is changing, especially in upscale shops. On Saigon's Dong Khoi, the most popular shopping strip in the country, vendors commonly hold out three prices—one to locals, another to foreigners, and still a third to Japanese, who are less likely to haggle.

While such name-brand companies as Nike and Ikea operate factories in Vietnam, most branded items you'll find for sale—Gucci, Coach, North Face—are knockoffs. Piracy remains a huge problem. In the Pham Ngu Lao District, pirated CDs sell for about 60 cents and DVDs for about a dollar, despite official prohibition.

Vietnamese artists and craftspeople also have a flair for mimicry. Painters copy the old masters with such exceptional skill that one of the country's leading hotels has seen fit to drape its walls with homegrown copies of European masterpieces. Tailors will try their hands at pictures of clothes torn from magazines, often with better results than if you're measured for clothing.

Don't look for bargains on electronics in Vietnam. And don't expect to return anything. Vietnamese merchants hew to the old-school rule of "you buy it, you own it," case closed.

AMERICANA

It's still possible to buy war-related Americana in Saigon's downtown shops. On Dong Khoi especially, look for U.S. government clocks made by Boston's Chelsea Clock Company, old cameras, watches, pipes (as well as medals from the Army of South Vietnam, French piastres, and coins from the imperial dynasty). You'll find lots of Zippo lighters for sale here, bearing trench art purportedly commissioned by GIs. The Zippos are real, but nearly all of them have been artificially aged and inscribed by Vietnamese craftsmen, just as they were during the war when some 200,000 lighters were in circulation here. The dog tags for sale are of questionable origin. Most people figured they were fakes until one American bought several and contacted soldiers, some of whom indeed lost them during the war. Buyer beware.

ANTIQUES & ARTIFACTS

Be careful not to buy anything so old that you'll have trouble getting it out of the country. Vietnamese law prohibits travelers from exporting antiques. Even if you purchased a knockoff Cham sculpture or an intentionally distressed wood carving, be sure to carry a receipt. More than one hapless traveler has surrendered that old-looking opium pipe to airport customs officials.
Asia Culture, 25A Le Duan, Hanoi, tel 04/942-3841.
Le Cong Kieu, District 1, Ho Chi Minh City. This Saigon street is an antique hunter's dream. Look for a lot of old colonial decor—lamps, cameras, fans, picture frames, phones, tables, and trunks. If it's fake, it's a well-done fake. Also shop here for parallel sentences, imperial coins, and abacuses.
Lost Art, 18 Nguyen Hue, District 1, Ho Chi Minh City, tel 08/827-4649.

ARCADES & MALLS

Saigon Center, 65 Le Loi, District 1, Ho Chi Minh City, tel 08/823-2505. Appliances, menswear, bedding, cafés, a supermarket, and a toy store.
Saigon Square, 39 Le Duan, District 1, Ho Chi Minh City. Expats shop at this arcade, which is a step up from the municipal market but a step down from the trendy, modern mall. Lots of name-brand stuff here, sold in shops that strive to look Western. Want to see a Vietnamese version of a Western supermarket? Stop in.
Trang Tien Plaza, intersection of Trang Tien and Dinh Tien Hoang, Hoan Kiem District, Hanoi. If boisterous open-air markets and garage bay–size stalls leave you homesick for more upscale shopping venues, head to Trang Tien Plaza, where you'll find jewelry and cosmetics, high-end luggage, digital cameras and supplies, men's and women's fashions, a Sony electronics outlet, and bona fide wines and liquor. Two glass-walled elevators ferry shoppers and their finds.

BOOKS

Vietnam's English-language book selection is slim. Be sure to bring your own, or browse the used-book shops in the backpacker districts for the best selection of contemporary titles. Otherwise, try your luck at:
Book Worm, 15A Ngo Van So, Hanoi, tel 04/943-7226. Australian-owned shop on a short street one block south of Tran Hung Dao. Sells new and used books. Will buy back any book it sells for one-third the original purchase price.
Fahasa Bookstore, 40 Nguyen Hue, District 1, Ho Chi Minh City, tel 08/822-5796.
Infostones Bookshop, 41 Trang Tien, Hanoi, tel 04/826-2993. Centrally located near Hoan Kiem Lake. Several

SHOPPING

neighboring booksellers also offer English-language titles. **Xuan Thu Bookstore,** 185 Dong Khoi, District 1, Ho Chi Minh City, tel 08/822-4670. The best place for English-language titles in the city.

CLOTHING

Vietnam's tailors are today what Hong Kong's tailors were in years past—fast, cheap, and talented. Men can have suits made for less than $100, though you'll have to pay up to $200 or more for high-quality material. Women can have silk *ao dai* dresses made for much less. You can also buy interesting, off-the-rack designs at many places in Ho Chi Minh City and Hanoi, including the following: **Khai Silk,** 96 Hang Gai, Hanoi, tel 04/825-4237. Khai was catering to Westerners as far back as 1992, long before the current rash of silk shops realized there was money to be made from foreign tourists. **Song,** 76D Le Thanh Ton, District 1, Ho Chi Minh City, tel 08/824-3652, www.asiasong design.com. Embroidered evening wear, sarongs, resort wear, and dresses by French designer Valerie Gregori McKenzie. Also bedding and crockery.

DEPARTMENT STORE

Diamond Department Store, 34 Le Duan, District 1, Ho Chi Minh City, tel 08/822-5500. The prices at Vietnam's first modern department store are fixed, and you can trust the brand names.

FOOD & DRINK

Annam Gourmet Shop An Phu, 41A Thao Dien, District 2, Ho Chi Minh City, tel 08/744-2630. Sells such imported and specialty foods as flavored olive oils and vinegars, *nuoc mam* (fish sauce), pasta, teas, bitters, and lagers. **The Warehouse,** 178 Pasteur St., District 1, Ho Chi Minh City, tel 08/825 8826, and 59 Hang Trong, Hanoi, tel 04/928-7666; www.warehouse-asia.com. In a country where you can't always trust the authenticity of a bottle

of wine, you can trust the merchandise here. Also sells wine-related accessories, books, and glassware.

MARKETS

Ben Thanh Market, Quach Thi Trang Square, District 6, Ho Chi Minh City, tel 08/855-1439. Vietnam's most famous market, as popular with locals as tourists. A good place for off-the-rack clothes, luggage, and street food. **Binh Tay Market,** Thap Muoi, District 5, Ho Chi Minh City. This market in the heart of Cholon offers better buys than the more touristy Ben Thanh Market. Short of actually buying rice bowls from the person who made them, this is the place to go for staples. **Dong Xuan Market,** Old Quarter, Hanoi. Dating from the 1880s, the city's best known market is a lively place where it's as much fun to people-watch as browse.

SHOPPING AREAS

Hanoi

Nha Tho. Home furnishings, clothing, coffee, and restaurants that cater to foreign travelers all line this little row between St. Joseph's Cathedral and Hoan Kiem Lake. Also check out **Au Trieu** (a short walk north on Ly Quoc Su and then left) for fashions that court Western tastes. **Old Quarter.** This section of town comprises Vietnam's most fascinating market, a unique fusion of commercial and residential space. Streets are named after the products historically sold here, though the lines are somewhat blurred today. For example, you'll find silk on Hang Gai (hemp).

Ho Chi Minh City

Cholon, District 5. This is China-town. *Cho lon* means "big market," and you'll find two of the city's three best known markets here. One is Binh Tay (see Markets) and the other is **An Duong,** on An Duong Vuong, which is very popular with Taiwanese.

Dong Khoi, District 1. Vietnam's version of Fifth Avenue features upscale shops selling silk, jewelry, handicrafts, antiques, and home decor. Definitely worth the stroll, but expect to pay top dollar. **Le Thanh Ton,** District 1. Embroidered fabrics, handbags, and furnishings in boutiques with the kind of flair you find in Western malls.

Hue

Tran Hung Dao. You'll find Hue's storied **Dong Ba Market** along this street, as well as most of the city's boutiques.

SPECIALIZED SHOPPING

Vietnam's craft villages are major tourist attractions in their own right, especially those outside Hanoi, including Bat Trang, which turns out the country's best ceramics, and Van Phuc, a thousand-year-old silk village. Others include:

Danang. In nearby Lang Da ("stone village") at the base of the Marble Mountains, villagers churn out sculptures carved mostly in stone imported from Thanh Hoa, not local limestone and marble.

Hoi An. In the past ten years, Hoi An's tailors have carved out a reputation for being fast, deft, and reliable. Buy your silk, get measured, and walk away with a custom suit or dress for incredibly little money.

Hue. Hue is renowned for its traditional conical hats, with embroidered motifs fashioned around the underside. You'll find the best selection on the ground floor of the central Dong Ba Market.

Phu Quoc. If you've acquired a taste for *nuoc mam*, Phu Quoc Island and Phan Thiet are the well-springs of this pungent condiment.

Sa Pa. The embroidery and brocade of ethnic minority craftspeople are on display at a tourist market beside Sa Pa's central market, while hill-tribe minorities peddle handmade blankets and garments along the street and in their villages.

ENTERTAINMENT

With the exception of water puppetry and court music (nha nhac), it's difficult to find venues for Vietnam's traditional performing arts, such as cheo (folk opera), cai luong (classical theater), ca tru (chamber music), and quan ho (folk singing). In Hanoi and Ho Chi Minh City, be on the alert for sporadic performances at the opera houses and theaters. Those drawn to nightlife will find a range of hot spots in Hanoi and Saigon.

THEATER

Cinema

English-language cinema is in its infancy in Vietnam. Unless you succumb to the lure of curbside pirates selling illegally copied DVDs, your choices are slim. These two movie houses are your best bets:
Cinebox 212, 212 Ly Chinh Thang, District 3, Ho Chi Minh City, tel 08/846-8883.
Hanoi Cinematheque, 22A Hai Ba Trung, Hanoi, tel 04/936-2648.

Court music

Royal Theater, Imperial City, Hue. This is Vietnam's best venue for this music, which UNESCO recognizes as a masterpiece of the oral and intangible heritage of humanity. Access to the historic theater itself is worth the price of admission. Sadly, the musicians and dancers often outnumber the audience members. Another sporadic venue for this music is the **Minh Khiem Royal Theater** at King Tu Duc's tomb.

Opera houses

The French built three opulent opera houses in Vietnam in the early 20th century. They've all been restored, but there are no set performance schedules. Call or, better yet, stop by to check on upcoming shows.
Haiphong Opera House, Hoang Van Thu, Hong Bang District, Haiphong. **Hanoi Opera House,** 1 Trang Tien, Hanoi, tel 04/825-4312.
Municipal Theater, 7 Lam Son Square, District 1, Ho Chi Minh City, tel 08/829-9976.

Water puppetry

Saigon Water Puppet Theater, 2 Nguyen Binh Khiem, Ho Chi Minh City, District 1, tel 08/829-8146, www.hcmc-museum.edu.vn. This troupe conducts a 20-minute show at regular intervals throughout the day. You'll have to pay admission to both the Saigon Botanical Gardens ($) and the Museum of Vietnamese History ($) to access the ticket counter for the water puppet theater ($).
Thang Long Theatre, 57 Dinh Tien Hoang, Hanoi, tel 04/825-5450, www.thanglongwaterpuppet.org. This thousand-year-old art form finds its ideal venue at Thang Long, just off the northeast shore of Hoan Kiem Lake. The music is great, and the theater is plush and air-conditioned. Buy tickets at least a day in advance for the best seats. The troupe also travels widely to perform the staple skits of water puppetry.

NIGHTLIFE

Hanoi

Ho Guom Xanh, 32 Le Thai To, tel 04/828-8806. One of the better nightspots in downtown Hanoi, this bar overlooks Hoan Kiem Lake. Draws mostly locals and some foreigners with nightly live music.
Jazz Club, 31 Luong Van Can, tel 04/828-7890. The place for jazz in Hanoi. Club owner and saxophonist Quyen Van Minh is a legend on the rise.
New Century, 10 Trang Thi, Hanoi, tel 04/928-5285. Monday through Sunday, foreigners and locals dance a-go-go to techno beats in the city's most hopping venue. Three stories of nightlife with a VIP lounge on the top floor.

Nutz, Sheraton Hanoi Hotel, K5 Nghi Tam, 11 Xuan Dieu, Tay Ho District, tel 04/719-9000. This hip hotel bar is especially popular with expats. Occasional live music, otherwise a DJ spins tunes. Jam-packed on weekends.
Seventeen Saloon, 98B Tran Hung Dao, tel 04/942-6822. A cover band from the Philippines rocks the stage nightly at this raucous Wild West–theme bar close to the train station.

Ho Chi Minh City

Allez Boo, 187 Pham Ngu Lao, District 1, tel 08/837-2505. In the heart of the budget district, Allez Boo jams in backpackers for drinks, music, and cheap eats. Great spot for in-country tips.
Apocalypse Now, 2B-2C Thi Sach, District 1, tel 08/825-6124. For nearly 15 years, expats and hip locals have gathered nightly at Saigon's Apocalypse Now to drink, dance, play pool, and otherwise cavort. The later it is, the better it gets.
Q Bar, Opera House, 7 Lam Son Square, District 1, tel 08/823-3479. As hip as Saigon gets, with lots of cozy nooks and dim lighting. Don't come early—nothing gets going until after 10 p.m.
Qing, 31 Dong Du, District 1, tel 08/823-2414. This restaurant and wine bar boasts a great list. Under same ownership as the Temple Club (see p. 258), one of the city's finest restaurants.
Saigon Saigon, Caravelle Hotel, 10th Floor, 19 Lam Son Square, District 1, tel 08/823-4999. The best perch in the city for a drink, with views of historic Lam Son Square and the nearby Continental on up Le Loi toward the Ben Thanh Market. Also overlooks the rooftop elevator shaft made famous by a photo snapped during the fall of Saigon in 1975.

ACTIVITIES & FESTIVALS

The active set can choose from cycling, mountain biking, diving and snorkeling, trekking, kayaking, golf, and tennis, while more than 200 major festivals are held in Vietnam throughout the year.

ACTIVE SPORTS

Cycling & mountain biking

Scenic Highway 1 is a perfect cycling venue, with few climbs outside of passes over spurs of the Truong Son mountains. Many tour companies offer cycling packages that include support vehicles. Or you could just head south with a bike and packed supplies. You'll find lodgings within a day's ride all along the highway. Off-road biking is a bit risky, given the amount of unexploded ordnance in the countryside, although the following company has blazed several safe routes: **Phat Tire Ventures,** 73 Truong Cong Dinh, Dalat, tel 063/829-422, cell 091/843-8781, fax 063/820-331, www.phattireventures.com.

Diving & snorkeling

Diving and snorkeling operators have discovered sites all along Vietnam's 2,135-mile (3,444 km) seaboard, especially off the south-central coast near Nha Trang and around Con Dao Island. Check out the reefs off Hon Mun Island near Nha Trang via an inexpensive tour boat or on a trip with the following operator: **Rainbow Divers,** 90A Hung Vuong, Nha Trang, tel 058/524-351, www.divevietnam.com.

Golf

Golf remains a fledgling enterprise in Vietnam, with only about a dozen active courses. That said, the existing courses are world-class. Most cluster about Ho Chi Minh City, while others lie near Hanoi and in the resort towns of Dalat and Phan Thiet. All allow walk-ins. Typical greens fees range from $40 to $70 on weekdays and $60 to $100 on weekends. **Vietnam Golf Resorts,** 76 Le Lai, Ste. 328, Ho Chi Minh City, District 1, tel 08/827-4270, fax 08/824-3641, www.vietnamgolfresorts.com.

Kayaking

Paddlers should venture north to Ha Long Bay, where a kayak will grant you entry to caves that bore through karst islets into stunning interior lagoons. **Vietnam Adventures Travel,** 33B Pham Ngu Lao, Hanoi, tel 04/933-1362.

Rock climbing

Ha Long Bay is also a climber's dreamscape. Some independent climbers have tested routes, but commercial support remains on the horizon. A rock-climbing gym called Viet Climb was under construction in Ho Chi Minh City in 2006.

Swimming

Vietnam's best beaches fringe Phu Quoc Island in the clear waters of the Gulf of Thailand. Other fabulous strands line the Mekong Delta, the Con Dao Islands, and the south-central coast. Ha Long Bay is notable both for its scenery and buoyant salt water. Coastal waterfalls also offer great swimming holes.

Tennis

Top hotels maintain courts, as do many state-run organizations. And if you show up at a court with racket in hand, chances are players will rise to the challenge of some foreign competition.

Trekking

The top trekking destinations are Sa Pa, Dalat, Kon Tum, and Dak Lak, roughly in that order. Many tour companies (see p. 239) lead treks in these regions, and it's possible to do some limited trekking on one's own, especially around Sa Pa; the most challenging climb is up nearby 10,312-foot (3,143 m) Fan Si Pan, Vietnam's tallest peak.

FESTIVALS

January/February

Keo Pagoda Festival. Duck catching, rice cooking, and hurling contests are among the attractions at this Buddhist celebration, held twice yearly (Jan./Feb. and Sept./Oct.) at this beautiful pagoda in north-central Vietnam, just east of Nam Dinh.

Perfume Pagoda Festival. From late January through the end of spring, thousands of Buddhist pilgrims worship at this scenic cluster of temples, shrines, and pagodas southwest of Hanoi.

Tet Nguyen Dan. Tet, which begins on the first day of the first lunar month (Jan. or Feb.), is the granddaddy of all holidays in Vietnam. See p. 240.

March/April

Thay Pagoda Festival. This Buddhist festival on the seventh day of the third lunar month (March or April) commemorates Tu Dao Hanh, a monk considered by many to be the father of water puppetry. The pagoda grounds just west of Hanoi host puppetry performances and the ceremonial bathing of Hanh's statue.

August/September

Kate Festival. The Cham celebrate their New Year in late September (or early October) by commemorating their ancestors, heroes, and deities. The festival is especially vibrant at the Po Klong Garai temple, west of Phan Rang along the south-central coast.

Keo Pagoda Festival (see January/February).

Mid-Autumn Festival. Also known as the Moon Festival, or Children's Tet. Celebrations are marked by colorful lanterns, dragon dances, and lots of candy.

Ongoing

Hoi An Full Moon Festival. On the 14th day of each lunar month, residents of this central Vietnam port turn off the regular streetlights, illuminate Old Town with colorful lanterns, and stroll the avenues free of vehicles.

ILLUSTRATIONS CREDITS

Cover: (Left) Daryl Benson/Getty Images, (Center) Angelo Cavalli/Getty Images, (Right) Jeffrey Sylvester/Getty Images.

Interior: All photographs by Kris LeBoutillier except the following: 29, Barbara A. Noe; 34, Van Nguyen; 35, Nguyen Thi Kim; 39, © Dinh Dang Dinh/Another Vietnam; 40, AP/Wide World Photos/Fairchild Corp.; 43, Patrick Christain/Getty Images; 45, Bettmann/CORBIS; 51, Courtesy European Art Gallery; 120, AP/Wide World Photos/David Longstreath; 121, AP/Wide World Photos/Vietnam Pictorial/Trong Thanh; 126, Courtesy The Zoological Society for the Conservation of Species and Populations (ZGAP), Germany; 167, Medford Taylor/NG Image Collection; 172, Glen Allison/Stone/Getty Images; 186-187, William Manning/ CORBIS; 211, Barbara A. Noe; 226-227, Alain DeJean/Sygma/CORBIS.

Published by the National Geographic Society
John M. Fahey, Jr., *President and Chief Executive Officer*
Gilbert M. Grosvenor, *Chairman of the Board*
Nina D. Hoffman, *Executive Vice President,
    President, Books and School Publishing*
Kevin Mulroy, *Senior Vice President and Publisher*
Marianne Koszorus, *Design Director*
Kristin Hanneman, *Illustrations Director*
Elizabeth L. Newhouse, *Director of Travel Publishing*
Cinda Rose, *Art Director*
Carl Mehler, *Director of Maps*

Staff for this book:
Barbara A. Noe, *Series Editor and Project Editor*
Kay Kobor Hankins, *Illustrations Editor and Designer*
Dave Lauterborn, *Text Editor*
Dr. Andrew Forbes, David Henley, *Researchers*
Lise Sajewski, *Editorial Consultant*
XNR Productions, *Map Research and Production*

R. Gary Colbert, *Production Director*
Mike Horenstein, *Production Manager*
Rebecca Hinds, *Managing Editor*

Abby Lepold, *Illustrations Assistant*
Margie Towery, *Indexer*
Jack Brostrom, Steve D. Gardner, Jane Sunderland *Contributors*

Artwork by Maltings Partnership, Derby, England (pp. 74–75 & 140–141)

ISBN-10: 0-7922-6203-4
ISBN-13: 978-0-7922-6203-9

Printed and bound by Cayfosa Quebecor, Barcelona, Spain.
Color separations by Digital Image Services, National Geographic Society.

The information in this book has been carefully checked and to the best of our knowledge is accurate. However, details are subject to change, and the National Geographic Society cannot be responsible for such changes, or for errors or omissions. Assessments of sites, hotels, and restaurants are based on the author's subjective opinions, which do not necessarily reflect the publisher's opinion. The publisher cannot be responsible for any consequences arising from the use of this book.

NATIONAL GEOGRAPHIC
TRAVELER

A Century of Travel Expertise in Every Guide

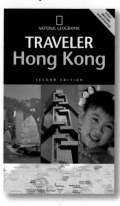